Ivan Franko:
Moses and Other Poems

IVAN FRANKO:

M O S E S
and Other Poems

Translated from the Ukrainian
by
Adam Hnidj

VANTAGE PRESS
New York / Atlanta / Los Angeles / Chicago

Published by Vantage Press, Inc.
516 West 34th Street, New York, New York 10001

Manufactured in the United States of America
ISBN: 0-533-07262-X

Library of Congress Catalog Card No.: 86-90341

To my "angels":
Roman, Chris, and Samantha Hnidj;
L. Nick and Sigrid Hnidj;
Pam and Mark Hnidj;
Myron and Sophia Dupelych

Contents

Acknowledgments

My thanks to Oleksander Dombrovsky, Ph.D., for his permission to print his article "Yahweh and Yahwism in the poem *Moysey* by Ivan Franko."

I am indebted to Bohdan Romanenchuk, Ph.D., for his permission to reprint Dr. Dombrovsky's article, which first appeared in Ukrainian, in the cultural magazine KYIW, Nos. 2 and 3, 1962. Dr. Romanenchuk was editor and publisher of KYIW.

Professor Louis J. Shein, Professor Emeritus of McMaster University, Hamilton, Ontario, was kind enough to permit inclusion of his article "Ivan Franko's Religious *Weltanschauung*." *The Ukrainian Quarterly*, vol. XXXV, No. 4, Winter 1979, first published Professor Shein's article, and I am grateful to Professor N. G. Bohatiuk, Le Moyne College, Syracuse University, editor of *The Ukrainian Quarterly*, for permission to reprint it in the present volume.

Professor J. B. Rudnyckyj, Professor Emeritus, University of Manitoba, Professor George Luckyj, University of Toronto, Professor, W. Zyla, of Lubbock, Texas, and Professor L. J. Shein read and criticized parts of the manuscript, and I am greatly indebted to them, but I alone am responsible for any deficiencies in it.

The first version of *Ivan Vyshensky* appeared in *Studia Ucrainica,* a literary magazine of the University of Ottawa, Canada. The present "second" version has been extensively revised.

Adam Hnidj

TEXT AND PHOTOGRAPHS

The original text of *Moysey* and *Ivan Vyshensky* came from *Ivan Franko: Selected Works*. Academy of Sciences, Ukrainian SSR. Kiev, 1956.

Ivan Franko, *Works* (New York: Knyhospilka Publishing Company, 1958) supplied the Ukrainian text to *Fox Mykyta* and *Lordly Jests*.

INTRODUCTION

I. IVAN FRANKO: A Titan of Thought and Work

Had Ivan Franko been born an Englishman or a Frenchman or a German, today his fame would ring around the world. But Franko was born into a poor family, a son of a village blacksmith, in one of the poorest regions of Eastern Europe, the Carpathian foothills. As he was growing up, he discovered that he was a member of a subjugated ethnic group, the Ukrainians. The fact of his national origin affects his standing in European literature even today.

When Ivan Franko was born, the Ukrainians were not even a nation, although their numbers and the territory they inhabited were equal to that of territorial France. They were divided among Russia, Austria-Hungary, and Romania, their neighbors. Most of them were peasants because only in 1848 in Austria-Hungary and in 1861 in Russia had feudal servitude been abolished by decree. Only a small class of clergymen, lawyers, and teachers had risen from the peasant masses.

Culturally, the Ukrainians were repressed. The Ukrainian language was illegal in Russia. Polish was the official language of West Ukraine because the Poles, themselves divided among Russia, Prussia, and Austria in the 1790s, but possessing economic power, were given cultural control of West Ukraine after the revolution of 1848, to keep them on the side of the tottering Austro-Hungarian monarchy.

How did this situation come about? West Ukraine was controlled until the middle of the fourteenth century by the Kievan State, which existed for four hundred years. But Kiev was destroyed by the Mongols in 1241, the center of power moved to the more defensible wooded areas of the north (Moscow and Novgorod), and the Ukraine existed, predominating culturally, as part of the Lithuanian confederation, which colonized the practically empty, post-Mongolian Ukrainian steppes. West Ukraine became part of Poland around 1340 through feudal marriages and extinction of the male line on the Ukrainian side. The Cossacks of the sixteenth and seventeenth centuries, who formed a fortified area on the Lower Dnieper, defended the land from repeated Tartar attacks often in alliance with Poland or Russia.

A new era began in 1648 when Bohdan Khmelnitsky led the Cossacks in a national uprising against the Poles, who occupied the Ukraine up to the Dnieper. The national uprising took the Ukrainian Cossacks into Poland, but in the end, in 1656, Khmelnitsky had to look for allies. He signed a treaty of friendship with Russia, which after his death turned into Russian subjugation of the Ukraine. Ivan Mazepa, the Russian-approved leader of the Ukraine, tried to throw off the Russian yoke in 1707–1709, when he allied himself with Charles XII of Sweden, but in the battle of Poltava, in July 1709, Charles and Mazepa were defeated by Russia's Peter I. In 1775 Catherine II leveled the Cossack fortress *Sich* and cancelled all vestiges of Ukrainian autonomy.

Ukrainian intellectuals did not despair. Artistic expression arose in many forms. Rich Ukrainian nobles maintained academies and libraries. The Ukrainian Orthodox Church, far away intellectually and spatially from the reactionary influences of the clergy in Moscow, escaped reactionary trends and splintering into obscure sects, oriented itself on the West. One of its leaders, the Kievan Metropolitan Petro Mohyla, supported by Ukrainian nobility, founded the Mohyla Kievan Academy, which graduated over twenty thousand young men in the seventeenth and eighteenth centuries. They became leaders of Ukrainian intellectual life in every sector. Persecutions of expressions of Ukrainian life and discrimination against all things Ukrainian were a double-edged sword: rejected by others, Ukrainians drew together and cultivated and preserved their culture, language, and traditions. Each new onslaught by Moscow was met by the emergence of charismatic leaders, so that Ukrainian accomplishments grew, the body of their literature increased, the people's ethnic distinctiveness fostered national unity. "Like the Nile inundations," as Franko describes Jewish accomplishments in Egypt and swelling of their national power in his *Moysey* in spite of persecutions, the Ukrainian cause continued to gain momentum.

Ukrainian intellectuals displayed a tenacity of purpose and of the will to survive under the most terrible handicaps. Ivan Franko's father, an ordinary illiterate blacksmith, Yats (Jake), and his wife, much younger than her husband, Maria Kulchytsky, had no children for a long time, but finally Ivan was born on August 27, 1856, and then three brothers followed and one sister, who soon died. The Carpathian village where Franko was born, Nahuyevychi, is considered remote and poverty-stricken even today. There was no school in his native village, so Ivan went to elementary school in nearby Yasenytsia, where he lived in the house of his mother's brother, Pavlo Kulchytsky. He started school in 1862. He remained there for two years, and then was transferred to the school run by the Order of St. Basil (Basilians) in Drohobych, the chief town of the district. Everywhere he was a brilliant student.

In 1867 Ivan's father died and his mother married an ordinary young man from the village, Hryn Havryluk, but she was also to die five years later. Franko's stepfather, however, did not hesitate to send his "unusual," rather small, red-headed stepson to the *gymnasium,* a classical high school, in Drohobych, in 1868. Upon entering the *gymnasium,* Ivan already knew three languages: German, Polish, and his own. The initial jeering at the village hayseed, dressed in village clothes, changed to admiration and respect because Franko was usually first or second throughout his high school years in scholastic standing.

Throughout high school he studied Latin and Greek. He taught himself Russian. He read constantly: Shakespeare, Klopfstock, Schiller, Krasinski, Krasicki, Goethe, Mickewicz, Slowacki, Eugene Sue, Dickens, Heine, Hugo, Dostoyevsky, Tolstoy, and Ukrainian authors. He began to write. The year his mother died, 1873, he wrote a drama, *Iuhurta,* for the school magazine. His first poetry and a drama *Three Kings for One Throne* were published there in 1874. The same year Franko was on the editorial board of the school magazine. The year he graduated from high school, he published *Petrii i Dovbushchuky,* a novel.

His first influences, to which Franko admitted in 1910, were Romantic in nature—"contrasts between the beauty of nature and human misery"—especially E.T.A. Hoffmann, but at the same time collected sketches from real life and read realist and naturalist writers, especially Emile Zola, who wrote "literature collects and describes facts of daily life, minding only about the truth, not esthetic rules." He also read Karl Marx, J. S. Mill, and other socialists because, for a time, he saw socialism as a salvation for the Ukrainian peasant.

In 1875 Franko registered at the philosophical faculty of Lvov University. Apart from lectures and other university routine, even before his twentieth birthday, Franko set out his life's work on four different tracks, on which he remained until his devastating illness in 1908, and in some areas until his death in 1916.

He was always a journalist, writing in Ukrainian, Polish, and German on a range of subjects—from ethnology to poetry and philosophy of art to labor problems and religion. From 1887 to 1897 he was on the staff of the Polish daily *Kurjer Lwowski.* For many years he contributed to the Viennese weekly *Die Zeit* on cultural topics. He edited the Ukrainian daily *Dilo* from 1883 to 1885. With M. Pavlyk he published the journal *Narod,* from 1890 to 1895. From 1897 to 1907 he edited the prestigious *Annals* of the Shevchenko Scientific Society in Lvov. There were many other publications.

During the same time Franko founded the Ukrainian Radical Party, he was intensively studying political science and economics, searching for ways to alleviate the appalling poverty of his countrymen. At first he was excited by Marx, Engels, and Chernyshevsky, but later decided that Marxism was not suitable for the underdeveloped rural economy of West Ukraine. Eventually he agreed mostly with John Stuart Mill and leaned toward Fabianism. Because of his interest in the working classes, Franko was arrested three times on suspicion of fomenting resistance against the ruling classes of the creaking Austro-Hungarian Empire; the first arrest came at the age of twenty-one, when he served nine months. Thrice Franko ran for the Vienna Parliament on the Radical Party ticket, but his Polish opponent, as well as Ukrainian conservatives, made certain that Franko did not win. Historians speak of bribery and election fraud, but in reality few West Ukrainian voters understood or sympathized with Franko's ideas.

Despite his lack of success in practical politics, Franko continued to write on political and economic subjects. The titles of his articles reveal Franko's interests: "Scholarship and Its Attitude to the Working Class" (1878); "Factory Workers" (1881); "About Labor" (1881); "The Servitude of Women in Ukrainian Folk Songs" (1883); "Land Ownership in the Land of Halich (West Ukraine)" (1887); "Emigration of Galician Farmers" (1892); "Feudal Servitude and Its Abolition in the Land of Halich" (1898). These are but a handful of examples from Franko's output of forty years.

As a scholar and researcher, Franko contributed studies on Ukrainian ethnology, linguistics, prosody, and even theology. In 1882 he published a study of folklore in the Boryslav region; a collection of research materials on folk proverbs, which filled three volumes, was published in 1907. "How Folk Songs Originate" was published in 1887, and in 1894 his *Etymology and Phonetics in Ukrainian Literature* came out. "Literary Language and Dialects" was published in 1907, to name just a few titles.

However, Franko lived most intensively in his novels, poems, and short stories. This titan of work filled every moment of his waking life, for almost forty years, with creative activities which defy our normal human faculties of belief. The present "full" edition of his writings begun in Kiev in 1956 is planned for fifty volumes, but even so only "selected works" will be included in it. One of the editors, O. Bilynsky, writes that another fifty volumes would be required to print everything Franko ever wrote. A Russian translation of his *major* works, in 1956, comprised ten volumes. We can offer a few titles from his gigantic output.

At the age of twenty-two, Franko published his famous poem *The Stone Cutters,* the novel *Boa Constrictor,* about the activities of an oil town (Boryslav) entrepreneur, and a programmatic article on labor and scholarship.

At the age of thirty-one, Franko published a major collection of poetry, about three hundred pages, *From the Heights and the Depths,* a major narrative poem, *Lordly Jests,* and two major studies on economics.

In 1895 and 1896, when Franko was thirty-nine and forty, he published four dramas, a major collection of poems, one novel, and one long poem for children, *Abu Kassim's Slippers*—all that in addition to making speeches, editing magazines, doing scientific research, writing articles in three languages, translating Homer, Goethe, and other great writers, raising three children, and taking care of a difficult wife. He did this year after year after year, in the end with paralyzed hands, according to his prescription, as written in one of his works: " . . . to work, to work, and to labor,/In harness to die . . ." for his people, for his great ideal, bearing his cross of being a Ukrainian, attached to the destiny of his people like an ox to a cart.

Translators of Franko's work must chuckle occasionally at Franko's protestations that he was a mere laborer, a stone cutter paving a road to the future, filling in holes in the Ukrainian cultural structure, with no time to polish and refine his work. For Franko displays a mastery of styles, techniques, and composition which stand up to any standards.

II. FOUR GREAT POEMS

The four great poems included in this selection offer a great variety of moods, styles, rhyming techniques, and a luxuriance of interests.

Franko wrote *Pans'ki Zharty (Lordly Jests)* at the age of thirty-one, when his creative powers were at their peak: his mastery of technique was fuelled by yet untarnished intensity of emotion, especially of love for his native land and of outrage at the injuries inflicted on his people. Varied rhyming techniques allow him to manipulate artistic emphasis with great success. But the poem's greatest value and attraction lie in the richness of idiomatic Ukrainian (which again belies Franko's assertion that he had to struggle with an undeveloped language), picturesqueness of the story, and high reader interest throughout.

As already mentioned, feudal servitude was finally abolished in Austria by decree in 1848. It was high time because revolutionary disorders in various areas had reached a point that the troops had to be called out, and Lvov, the capital of West Ukraine, was shelled by artillery to bring the unrest to heel. The story is told through the medium of a peasant who gradually unfolds the scene of suffering, turmoil, and popular enlightenment in the last years before the emancipation of 1848. Here, as in *Jedermann* and other medieval morality plays, actors of the drama have no names (except in two cases, where the names are incomplete) but descriptions of their social or official positions: the Priest, the Elder, the Commissioner, the *Starosta*, et cetera.

Lordly Jests is as rich as life, and I had much pleasure (sweetening the labor over the giant poem) translating it. The Polish verse, the German words, and French cultural items (reflecting Polish admiration for everything French) have been left untranslated, except in the footnotes, for their exotic value in the poem. Although the Jew in the poem is a thoroughly negative character, Franko was not anti-Semitic. His poems and short stories about the poor Jews in West Ukraine are heart-rending; he deeply sympathized with the Jewish people. But there were Jews who acted as helpers to the Polish landowners, and Franko simply called a spade a spade.

Franko wrote *Ivan Vyshensky* in 1900. Here he poses the problems of personal salvation versus national obligations. A special historical background has been added to the poem in this selection.

Although he mentioned Moses in other works, Franko wrote *Moysey* only in 1905, at the age of fifty-one. It is an important work of a mature poet almost at the end of his most creative period. There is some evidence that Franko, who spent his life in a feverish struggle for the Ukrainian nation, identified himself with Moses, who led his people out of Egyptian captivity, and in the end suffered at the hands of his people for his immutable resolve. Moses is analyzed in his hour of defeat and death.

As Professor Shein points out in his essay, Franko studied the Bible from childhood and needed no stimulation from other writers. Perhaps a twist of misfortune in his personal life supplied an immediate nudge to use the analogy of his own life and begin writing. There is evidence that he wrote the Prologue to *Moysey* at the behest of a publisher—in one evening. There is also a curious parallel from Alfred de Vigny's *Moise,* a mere fragment of a never realized poem, which contains the same images as Franko's songs XV and XX of *Moysey.* Here are a few lines for those who care for such matters and understand French:

> Le soleil prolongeat sur la cime des tentes
> Ces oblique rayons, ces flammes éclatantes . . .
> Le pourpre et l'or semblaient revêtir la
> > campagne.
>
> Bientôt le haut du Mont reparut sans
> > Moise . . .

There is an English translation of *Moysey* by the Canadian scholar Percival Cundy, exact but unrhymed, following the tendency of many scholars to treat the work as a philosophical treatise, and not a poem or a work of fiction. I have treated the poem as a work of art, trying to preserve all its poetical resources, including the rhyme and meter.

Fox Mykyta is a different type of poem. In between his "serious" literary works, Franko wrote half a dozen shorter and longer poems for children, or ostensibly for children. Some of them are rambunctious and whimsical, with a quasi-Oriental background, such as *Abu Kassim's Slippers* or *Blacksmith Bassim,* meant to awaken fantasy and provide entertainment. The series *When Animals Could Talk* is indirectly morally instructive.

In a short foreword to Fox Mykyta, Franko claims, tongue in cheek, that his poem is a translation from the German, but in the end he admits that there is nothing German in it. The clever Fox has been on the European scene since the Middle Ages, be he *Reynard, Reineke,* or *Mykyta.*

Franko sets up a royal court, presided over by King Leo and his Lady, peopled with courtiers jockeying for royal favor, plotting and counterplotting—like real human beings. On the outskirts of this "establishment," contemptuous of it, operates Fox Mykyta, who lives in a fortress we have translated as "Foxkeep," from Franko's *Lysynychi*. Mykyta operates according to his lights, but preserves a tenuous connection with the Royal Court.

In conversations with other animals, Mykyta justifies his *modus vivendi et operandi*. One cannot expect justice from the Establishment, which is irrational and corrupt; one has to look out for oneself, making good use of one's wits, if one is to remain a hunter, not a prey. Social and political criticism permeates not only the Fox's discourse, but also different social circumstances of animal interaction.

Yet the tone of the poem remains light and entertaining. West Ukrainian ethos and its lore form the background of the poem. The Fox and his family observe the social amenities of better Ukrainian homes in the nineteenth century; their capital city of Lvov; the family of chickens returning from court sing "The Gnat," a humorous Ukrainian song, somewhat modified to suit Franko's versifying needs. Everywhere Franko teaches and entertains.

III. THE TRANSLATOR'S APOLOGIA

When one translates poetry, the inspirational stimuli one receives and any subconscious solutions one arrives at form merely a very tentative draft for a structure that can rise and remain standing only after much hard work. Cultural and linguistic values of the original must be assessed and transposed into English equivalents and approximations. It is a deeply synthetic exercise, which includes elements of grammar, clarification of authors' intentions and meaning, historical backgrounds of words and the things they stand for, onomastics, and other things too numerous to be comprehensively accounted for.

What is *cinnabar*? The translator must do research into making of ancient dyes. Is Franko using the names of monasteries on Mount Athos in the nominative or possessive case? Should we use the letter *f* or *ph* when transcribing Greek names? What is the name of the diacritical marks often used in the Middle Ages to abbreviate frequently used names: *Dño* for *Domino* or *Ic̄ Xp̄* for Jesus Christ? Is the word *megrim* still usable in English? Why do the animals going to the animal convention "bear the banners of their churches"? (We will answer this last one: a West Ukrainian congregation going as a body to an official function often carried church banners, and Franko transfers the human behavior to the animals, perhaps to make them more human right from the beginning.) There are several such problems on every page. And what about major issues? Who was Ivan Vyshensky? For that matter, who was Franko? The unfamiliar must be made clearer to the English reader. Special articles, by me and Professor Shein, have been added in appropriate places.

Then there are the fundamental characteristics of the two languages. The English language is very rich in available lexical alternatives. A translator must judge nuances and suitability of the available alternatives, using his linguistic and esthetic judgements. In my selections I have used a good many of the language resources of the Anglo-American world. Although the majority of idiomatic expressions are American, I did not hesitate when a suitable expression more common in England fitted the bill. Most of them are understandable to American readers anyway because of wide distribution of British television shows.

All of the translator's choices must be fitted into a frame set up by the author, constructed of meter, rhyme, and rhythm. These are the musical paraphernalia which appeal to our emotions, in addition to any rational appeal. Without the "music" of rhythm and rhyme, translations of poetry simply do not work. In Ukrainian there are a great abundance and variety of rhymes. In English, however, true rhymes are rare. Over the centuries, English prosody has freed itself from the oppression of rhymes, coming to the conclusion that inventiveness in rhyming may actually distort poetic intentions. In English much free verse is written today, and rhyming is seldom used, except for specific purposes. Facing this situation of the scarcity of rhymes, one must often rely on near-rhymes, alliterations, and assonance when translating rhymed poetry from other languages.

We translate ideas, not words or sentences. The ideas contained in Ukrainian lines must be restated in English without leaving out anything substantial. While doing this, the translator discovers the truth of the linguists that the linguistic and cultural elements in English and in Ukrainian stem from the same European phyllum. I have not come across ideas, idiomatic expressions, or rationales that cannot be rendered from one language into the other. Monolingual poets like to say that poetry cannot be translated because poetry is so ethereal and language-bound, apart from the mysterious spirit of each poem. This is nonsense. If this were true, Homer's *Illiad* and *Odyssey* would still be closed books; there are excellent translations of the Greek epics in every language of Europe! Goethe's *Faust* remained untranslated for almost 150 years, until Professor Kaufmann of Princeton University produced a brilliant and true translation, including *Faust II.*

Translators have fun, and they like to add their touches. In *Lordly Jests,* I took into account Polish admiration for all things French, since the sixteenth century, and used a few French lines. They and some German and Polish lines left in the original languages give the poems some exotic coloration.

The names of the animals in *Fox Mykyta* have been changed to make them more palatable to the English reader. *Mykyta* is more snappy than the other alternative (Nicetas) as long as you remember to pronounce it Me*K*eta. *Unsated* is a compromise from "Insatiable," which is too unwieldy. *Borsuk,* Ukrainian for *badger,* has been made into a first name, and the full name Borsuk F. Babbai seemed just right for his personality. *Leo* comes from the same Latin source as the Ukrainian *Lev. Bruin* has been found to be more usable than *Burmillo,* the Ukrainian nickname for bears, which connotes growling and grumbling. *Frusya* seemed just right. The names of the fox kits (or cubs) have been slightly modified to Mick and Minah. *Billy* is the English nickname for the male goat (*Basil* in Ukrainian); *Jack* is accepted for the Rabbit.

In some quasilegalistic talk, I have made the Fox use Latin terms (he also slips into Latin under the stress of the final battle) of which he seems to be clearly capable, although he admits to the Wolf (perhaps less than truthfully) ignorance of the equine alphabet (which may be a phyllum of a different color).

When the translator is "inspired," many *mots justes* and ready rhymes come to mind in a flash as he reads the original text: the word order and line order are hardly touched in the translation. At other times the translator may spend two hours on one line or one verse, searching for suitable rearrangements, digging for rhymes, trying to find suitable analogies, restore the original humor, or a meaningful alliteration. At other times still, two or even three versions of the same verse appear at the same time. Then comes the agony of selecting the best or the better one. Even more mysteriously, solutions to knotty problems left behind days or weeks ago come to mind, crisp and incontrovertible, one morning at breakfast. The subconscious seems to be at work.

Otherwise, the subconscious and occasional inspiration are not enough. Excellent knowledge of two languages, patience, a variety of sources, various dictionaries and other sources are indispensable to good results. And, of course, the conviction of the translator that the work he tries to make available in another language is worth the labor.

Ivan Vyshensky in the Context of History

At the end of the sixteenth century, Pope Clement VIII became aware of the religious situation in Poland: perhaps one-third of the population was not Catholic. They were Orthodox Ukrainians within the Polish state, who did not recognize the pope as the head of their church. They had received their Christianity, and the bishops their office, from Constantinople, whose clergy had broken with the Roman Church in the twelfth century. The pope ordered that these "schismatics" should be returned to the Roman Church.

The Polish clergy went immediately into action. The most famous revivalist of the day, Father Piotr Skarga, arranged revivalist meetings all over Poland, to create a sense of urgency of the mission of "conversion." In 1590 a group of Ukrainian Orthodox bishops began negotiations with Zygmunt III, King of Poland. As a result of these negotiations, Kyrylo Terletsky, Bishop of Lutsk, and Ipaty Potiy, Bishop of Volodymyr, went to Rome in 1595 and recognized the pope as head of the Ukrainian Church. In October, 1596, Mykhaylo Rohoza, Archbishop of Kiev, was empowered by the pope to call a synod of Ukrainian Orthodox bishops, and to formalize a union with the Roman Church. The synod met at Berest.

The assembly split hopelessly into two camps almost at once, but the Union of Berest was declared a fact. The most powerful bishops accepted the basic dogmata of the Roman church, but retained its ancient rites and the Church Slavonic as the liturgical language. There are some indications that the bishops who accepted the union did so as an inevitable development hoped to be admitted to the Polish senate, and thus be able to influence the destinies of their flock more directly. They hoped in vain, for the Polish bishops barred their admission.

A period of strife and bloodshed followed the imposed union, and it was short-lived in most areas of the Ukraine. Bohdan Khmelnytsky, the leader of the Ukrainian uprising in 1648–53, swept out everything connected with Polish domination, including Catholicism. Ukrainian parishes reverted to Orthodoxy and were later swallowed up by the Patriarchate of Moscow, which acted as just another agent of Russian imperialism, as the Russians annexed Ukrainian lands.

Ukrainians remained Catholic only in the Polish-dominated West Ukraine, which was taken over by Austria after Poland's demise at the end of the eighteenth century. In 1946, Stalin, having killed or imprisoned many of the legally instituted clergy of the Ukrainian Catholic Church, appointed new men to take their places, and these appointees of the Soviet regime renounced the Union of Berest and attached themselves to the Soviet Orthodox Church.

Although the Union of Berest of 1596 was doubtlessly engineered by the Roman Church and the king of Poland, over the centuries the Ukrainian Catholic Church developed into a positive force in Ukrainian life. From its ranks came many national leaders; economically better situated, Ukrainian clergy—who married and usually had large families—bred generations of Ukrainian professional men and provided national and cultural leadership in the most remote villages.

The hero of Ivan Franko's poem *Ivan Vyshensky* is a historical figure. We know him as Ivan from Sudova Vyshnya, a small town in West Ukraine; Vyshensky is an adjective meaning "from Vyshnya." He was born between 1545 and 1550 and was well-educated, especially in theology; he belonged to the Ukrainian cultural society in Lvov. At the end of the sixteenth century he moved to Mount Athos, the ancient monastic community in Greece. It is known that he was in Lvov in 1604, but returned to Athos and died there after 1620, having spent the end of his life as an anchorite, in a cave.

Ivan Vyshensky's name has survived through the centuries because of his polemical writings, of which we have seventeen titles. They all deal with the theological and moral problems, seen in a larger social context, and their tone is incisive and abrasive. Vyshensky attacks Catholicism and the bishops who "have run away from the Orthodox faith," ridicules Latin theologians, bitterly reproaches Poland. Vyshensky continued to send his epistles from Mount Athos, as the Orthodox battled the Catholics.

Ivan Franko's presentation of Ivan Vyshensky is almost wholly consonant with known historical facts. The climax of the poem is Ivan's dilemma: personal salvation, so important to this profoundly religious man, or social and national responsibility, which up to the time of his exile had formed the woof of his life. Franko has the hermit ask himself:

> By what right may you aspire,
> you half-broken earthen vessel,
> to seek personal salvation,
> when a million could die?

But it is too late, and the outcome must be tragic.

The author, who had begun his work on Ivan Vyshensky in the form of a learned treatise before he wrote the poem, investigated the conditions of the times, which are brilliantly presented in the letter to Ivan Vyshensky from the Orthodox Ukrainians assembled at Lutsk. Vyshensky's life in the cave, his self-induced hypnotic intoxication, and other episodes betray Franko's knowledge—in 1900—of psychic states now commonly known as hallucinogenic experiences. Franko's rationalist outlook on life causes him to put materialist interpretations of phenomena experienced in the cave into Vyshensky's mouth: Could it be that the ordinary stimuli of warmth and light caused man to invent God? But Franko does not press the issue, and the questions raised do not intrude on the main point of the poem; rather, they give Vyshensky more facets and make him interesting beyond the confines of his time and his nationality.

Ivan Vyshensky

I

Like a pyramid of verdure
on a wavy field of blueness,
on a plain azure entire,
like a giant emerald—

thus awash in matchless waters,
under cloudless, mild heavens,
rises, proud in natural splendor
sleeps the famous Mount Athos.

Sleeps? But no; for Mother Nature
toils here without cessation,
primps, amuses without respite
this most favorite pet of hers.

Down below whence, proud and upright,
granite-grey rocks range straight upward,
from the boiling depths emerging:
walls, colossal shapes, and pillars—

down below, the wild music
offers not a moment's silence:
waves of surf crash in the boulders;
waves of silver foam splash up.

And above: the mountain ranges,
overgrown with ancient forests,
softly hum eternal music,
thinking their endless thoughts.

Yet the rock's wrapped up in slumber;
days and nights pass on above it,
like a pink and weightless cloudlet;
voices, noise cannot be heard.

And although, like snakes across it,
little pathways creep all over,
yet they never are enlivened
by gay laughter, speech, or song.

Although scattered o'er the hillsides,
in the woods and rocks and valleys,
on the lovely woodland clearings,
homes and settlements abound,

a deep silence reigns despite them,
covers every human settlement,
and the seal of silence covers
hundreds of old men's grey lips.

All is quiet, all is silent,
grey the garb, the movement measured,
and the faces drawn and somber,
the gaze sleepy, unaware.

Only thrice across the mountains
rolls the sound of bells, like cawing,
like the cries of wondrous cygnets
passing over these green hills.

And the bells give mournful utterance
to reproaches, accusations
of the people who have deadened
this enchanting nook on earth.

That this seat of lofty thinking,
that this school of bold endeavors—
perch of eagles—was made into
a sad prison for sad souls.

II

On the Athos bells are ringing
on the Sunday after vespers:
the great Prot intones the chiming,
in response calls Vatoped.

Cries of pain from Esphigmenou
then the boom Xenopotamou's,
then Zographou's and then Paulou's,
Everon floods all with sound.

9

The metallic sobs keep rolling
over every hill and valley,
drawing echoes from each cliffside,
every vale and hermitage.

And deep sighs the ringing follow,
men's thin hands make crossing motions,
and a whisper rises softly:
"May he find rest with the saints!"

The metallic sobs, the notice
that someone has left this planet,
cause here no alarm whatever:
it's a daily-known event.

Did a hermit, in his cavern,
die alone, as he had lived,
and his lonely, peaceful passing
was discovered after days—

was discovered, for the hermit
had not visited his cloister,
had not turned in work completed,
had not claimed his share of beans?

Did a monk die in his cloister,
touching up the diacritics,
cinnabar illumination
daubing in the Lives of Saints?

Or had died a humble menial,
once a lord or duke or soldier,
but here known for quite a while
as the cloister's kitchen boy?

Or perhaps a dignitary
died—an archpriest or an abbot—
here they all get equal honors:
"May he find rest with the saints!"

Or perhaps someone still living,
on his final step descending,
is deserting life and freedom
for a cave, to bide his end?

Look: up in the sheerest cliffsides,
in the steep walls made of granite,
hanging over surging waters—
could they be the swallows' nests?

No, they are but chipped-out warrens,
inaccessible dark hollows,

caves hacked out of rocky cliffsides;
shelters for the 'gulls, perhaps?

Those are hermits' hollow caverns;
it's the "final step," an utter
irreversible achievement:
to eternity a gate?

He who's served well as a novice,
known the cloister's rigid rulings
and the arduous mute toil
in the quiet hermitage;

he who wishes for achievement
of ascetic highest rigor,
fasting, loneliness, and silence,
harking only to his soul;

he, whose worldly ties are broken,
whose flesh harbors no desires,
who feels strong enough and willing
to confront eternity;

with superiors' permission,
he will pick himself a cavern,
he will pick himself a coffin,
whence there can be no return.

Then the bells resound, lamenting,
then all over the Mount Athos
old men's lips will gently whisper:
"May he find rest with the saints!"

III

On the Athos bells are ringing
on the Sunday after vespers:
the great Prot begins the chiming,
in response calls Vatoped.

Cries of pain from Esfigmenou,
then the boom Xenopotamou's
then Zografou's, and then Paulou's,
Everon floods all with sound.

The metallic sobs are rolling
over every hill and valley,
drawing echoes from each cliffside,
every vale and hermitage.

The bells ceased, yet their ringing
long yet kept the air a-tremble;

in the cloister of Zografou
heavy ropes began to creak.

The dark gates were slowly opened
and, emerging from the courtyard,
issued now a church procession,
to the sound of droning chants.

In the wind wave red church banners,
flaring up, like tongues of fire,
at the head, progressing slowly,
leads the way a wooden cross.

First there comes a group of bearded
monks in chasubles of purple;
other bearded brethren follow
barefoot, robed in coarse grey cloth.

Amidst them a bent grandfather,
wrinkle-skinned, his long beard grizzled,
o'er the bare skin a coarse habit,
in his hands a birchen cross.

Plain's the cross of unhewn birchwood;
and the breezes, blowing landward,
spread his white senescent whiskers
o'er the birchwood of the cross.

And the old man's voice comingles
with the monks' monotonous singing,
with its tone so melancholy:
"May he find rest with the saints!"

And along a winding pathway
moves along this church procession,
through the meadows, through the forest,
heading for the roaring sea.

Amidst nature's great luxuriance
echoes funeral singing;
in the fragrance of the evening
clouds of incense smoke rise up.

The procession has now halted
on a crag above the water,
over an abyss horrendous:
you look down and freeze with fear.

Like a giant wall of granite,
from the waters' thousand fathoms,
into the azure above them,
surges up plumb, sheerest rock.

From above one sees a sailboat
near the rocky wall at mooring
much resemble a white cygnet,
floating, rocking on the waves.

From below, the crowd of people
over the precipice assembled
much a drove of lambs resemble
grazing peacefully on the rocks.

From below one also notices
a black blot, in shape rectangular,
like a giant stamp impression
midway up the granite wall.

It's the entrance to live burial,
to an anchorite's own cavern;
goodness knows who first had dug it,
for what purpose, and for whom.

On foot it cannot be entered
or climbed into on a ladder;
one can swing in, birdlike fashion,
dangling from a piece of rope.

In the ridge atop the mountain
there's a groove cut by the hawsers—
an unfailing indicator
where to find the cavern's door.

Here the whole procession halted,
and the requiem chants resounded.
Where's the body to be buried?
Where's the blessed anchorite?

IV

Finally the chants are ended,
and the present monks and hermits
whisper their final prayers
for the dead on their knees.

First to rise was their abbot,
one by one got up the others,
and deep silence fell around them,
but the sea roared on below.

And the abbot spoke, addressing
the old man who stood in silence
in the covey of his brethren,
holding onto his birch cross.

ABBOT

"Brother Ivan, I exhort you
in the name of God Almighty
and before the Cross Most Holy,
in the face of the bright sun.

"Tell us honestly and truly:
whether of your free volition,
after a mature decision,
you go to the cave?"

OLD MAN

"I do."

ABBOT

"Does your heart no longer harbor
any worldly inclinations
or attachments to your dear ones,
thoughts and wishes of this world?

"Have you really quite forsaken
everything that leads the spirit
away from the one desire
of eternal rest?"

OLD MAN

"I have."

ABBOT

"Have you thought about the burden
of existence solitary,
irreversible cave dwelling,
and temptations' daily dread?

"Have you thought about the bitterness
of regret, which may yet surface;
of self-pity, that can poison
your exploit here?"

OLD MAN

"Yes, I have."

ABBOT

"May the Lord be praised forever;
Who this thought in you inspired!
May He help you now to follow
your road to the very end!

"Up to now, among the living,
You have been Ivan Vyshensky;
from now on, your name's deleted
from the rolls of life on earth.

"Thus embark upon your voyage!
And the cross that you are holding
is from us the only present;
other would be of no use!

"What you'll need to feed your body,
once a week, our Brother Purser,
on a rope, within a basket,
shall hence lower it to you.

"Fare thee well! And may I give thee
my last kiss in final parting,
and may God grant us to meet soon
in His glory's brilliant shine!"

And the abbot kissed the old man;
other monks as well, in silence,
with their kisses his hands covered
and the skirts of his rough coat.

Then the youngest two among them
wrapped a rope around the hermit,
under arms; the rope's end, finally,
they grabbed firmly in their hands.

Having crossed himself, the old man
to the very edge came boldly,
sat down there, and started sinking
into the horrendous void.

From the sea blew lively breezes,
his white beard and hair engaging,
and the old man, the cross pressing
to his body, vanished fast.

V

"Greetings, thou my domicile,
after storms my quiet haven!
Toward you incessant longing
I have felt a long, long time.

"Rocky walls are all around me:
it's my faith indomitable,
it's my home, it is my refuge,
it's my pillow, covers, too.

"This cross here is my companion,
confidant in days of sadness,
my defense against temptation,
and support in time of death.

"The blue sky that through the opening
peeks into my humble cavern
is the hope that on this highway
my soul too shall ride one day.

"The bright sun that on his rising
into my home, for a while,
showers, pours in gold and rubies
is the spirit—great, divine—

"that for happy, blessed moments
sinful, suffering human natures
gratifies with gifts of endless
paradisical delights.

"And the yonder azure waters
warming in the rays of sunshine
and against the boulders shattering,
splashing in a roar of foam,

"show our earthly life's true image:
bright and quiet and attractive
when surveyed from ample distance;
bitter, dreadful seen close up.

"It's my world. All variation
is no more. The shouts are muted,
and the noises of life's battles
cannot reach me in this place.

"Gone are trivial things and painful
that stir up men's souls' emotions
and divert mankind's attention
from the noblest Being on high.

"There remain the constant values,
only things of peace and grandeur;
peace and grandeur are the subjects
of your meditation, Soul!"

To himself thus talked the Old One,
sitting in his hollow cavern,
who once was Ivan Vyshensky,
and today dead for the world.

When he spoke, his lips were silent;
for he had for long forgotten
to employ his speaking organs:
he could hear his spirit's voice.

In the corner of his cavern
he sat down upon a boulder,
leaned his back on the cold granite,
dropped his head upon his chest.

His head was of large dimensions
and his neck so thin and sinewy
that the head drooped, imitating
a big melon on the vine.

On his chest his chin supporting,
at one point his eyes directing,
he sat thus without a motion,
as if sleeping, a long time.

First, all seemed to fade in darkness
before him; a spell of jitters
overran the gaunt old body
and the senses went to sleep.

Then a wave of warmth descended
and spread out throughout his body,
something sweet, so softly-softly,
playing 'round the Hermit's neck.

Through his soul flashed his own mother;
when he was a little baby,
how his chin she used to tickle,
and he heartily laughed and laughed.

Then his hearing was awakened:
like a thread spun out of diamonds,
drawn out, joyful, and so pleasing
ran a new and wondrous tone.

Like a butterfly, his spirit
flies, the lovely tone pursuing,
but the tones increase in number,
and they also gain in strength.

Now the harmony grows mighty,
flows along in a blue river,
the luxuriant tones embracing,
seemingly, the universe.

And the spirit of the Hermit
rides upon the waves of music,
like a swan upon the waters
of the sea: once up, once down.

In-between the earth and heavens,
soaring up and plunging downward,
floats the spirit of the Hermit;
greater speed makes joy intense.

And the grandiose music changes
to a violet shade, but only
to become azure in color,
then a dazzling purple hue.

Lo! and from the waves of purple
a gold ray has now exploded,
a volcano has erupted;
from it flow now streams of light.

Now a shoreless sea of brightness
inundates with rays bright-golden,
inundates with rays green-golden,
then with light as white as snow.

Luminous cascades are playing,
while enormous wheels comprising
all the colors of the rainbow
roll upon the heavenly sphere.

An invisible hand somewhere
issues strands of many colors,
issues tones of mighty music,
spans the world from end to end.

The hand issues, the hand orders,
blends the colors and collects them;
the whole world performs before him,
like a huge kaleidoscope.

Like a child, the Hermit's spirit
underwent complete immersion
in this sea of tones and colors;
in delight—he fell asleep.

VI

Days in regular succession,
waves of surf in a shoreless ocean,
measured breakers spell each other,
clouds chase clouds up in the sky.

In his cavern, the old Hermit
quietly sits upon a boulder,
motionless, his eyes directed
at the blue dome of the sky.

Suddenly an animate being
moved before him! On a cobweb,
from the rock came down a spider,
right across his cavern's door.

Hardly breathing, the old Hermit
watched the spider's every motion,
as one would an unseen wonder,
an unearthly visitor.

And the spider very swiftly,
stretched its thread from top to bottom
in the doorway of the cavern;
now it climbed back to the top.

And at once it started spinning,
stretching threads and intertwining;
in no time at all, the webbing
filled the entrance to the cell.

Thought the Hermit: "Earthly living
keeps on sending its spies over,
probably to keep surveillance
over me, just to find out

"if at least a strand of cobweb
still connects my soul, my spirit
with that life, to draw my thinking
by this strand toward earthly life.

"Could this spider be the Devil,
who spreads out his treacherous network,
to ensnare in it my vision,
my own dreams, my very thoughts?"

And he raised his hand already
to rip up the spider's cobweb,
when another thought flashed suddenly
through the Hermit's old man's mind.

"Seven brothers, once escaping
from their infidel pursuers,
found a refuge in a cavern,
where they soundly fell asleep.

"And a spider, in like manner,
built a cobweb in the entrance,
from pursuit the brothers rescued,
saved them for the glory of God.

"Sealed thus by the spider's network,
slept the brothers in the hollow
years three hundred, till Almighty
called them up as witnesses.

"God's word woke them up, to serve Him
as a proof of immortality,
showing that three centuries' passage
is a moment for the Lord.

"By divine command, this spider
is so busy at his cobweb;
perhaps I, too, have been chosen
to bear witness to God's deeds?"

Suddenly the faintest buzzing
shook the cobweb; in the network
a black fly became entangled,
squealing, trying to break loose.

In a hurry came the spider,
wove and wrapped his webbing speedily,
quickly tying up the insect's
legs and wings and all the rest.

Now he pounces, bites the insect,
bounces back, resumes his wrapping;
the fly fights with all his power,
and he trembles, and he squeals.

"You bloodsucker, thing of evil,"
said the Hermit. "Of all places,
you have found my cell, my refuge,
to destroy life even here!"

And he raised his hand already
to rip all the webs to pieces,
to give freedom to the insect—
but a thought then stayed his hand.

"Without our Lord's permission,
even this fly cannot perish;
and the spider's talent also
has been granted him by God.

"By what right may I deprive him
of the meal that he is holding,
which he has, after a manner,
earned by working very hard?"

He bowed low in adoration,
he recited fervent prayers,
but while praying he heard plainly
how the insect, like a child,

in the cobweb's trap was straining,
buzzing, whimpering, and crying.
The old Hermit's heart was trembling,
but he didn't raise his hand.

VII

"All night long the wind made merry,
whining on the toothy cliffsides;
the sea roared and gnawed and pounded
on and on at walls of stone.

"All night long my very marrow
felt the frightful frigid weather,
and I trembled, my teeth chattering,
as one would on Judgement Day.

"In the corner of the cavern
I hid, shaking, terror-stricken,
and in this distress, a prayer
did not stir within my soul.

"And I thought myself quite helpless,
pitiful and sick and lonely,
like a child alone, an orphan,
motherless and fatherless.

"It appeared: the earth was lifeless,
all mankind on it had perished,
and I was the sole survivor
to confront the dreadful scene.

"It appeared that God had also
died, and only a black demon
was the universal master,
and he pranced and stormed and roared.

"Like a speck of dust, forgotten,
lost from universal order,
whose existence worried no one:
devils, humans, even God.

"Now the sun is shining brightly,
midnight demons all have vanished,
furious winds have died down; softly
warming breezes waft about.

15

"The warmth entering my body
has revived my soul and spirit;
my soul has regained its Deity,
the ability to pray.

"My mind reaches wild wastelands
as it treads on tortuous pathways:
can the body get a soul, then,
from a little bit of warmth?

"In this manner, a spark issues
as steel's struck against a flintstone;
this spark is a conflagration:
heat and light and warmth and life.

"Life and warmth and light and fire,
side by side with death and ruin;
and new life and immortality—
they are God, the cosmic soul.

"Just a little warmth and brightness
raises souls in lifeless bodies,
and without this warmth, there never
can exist a soul within.

"In the soul it raises brightness,
faith, ambition—and without it,
without warmth, faith is impossible,
nor the brightness in the soul.

"And this faith is wonder-working:
it creates the greatest miracle,
the supreme, the highest wonder—
it discovers God for us.

"God reveals Himself—but strangely,
He comes always in broad daylight,
in the lands with warm, nice climates,
within thunder, flames, and light.

"When winds howl in pitch-black darkness,
in the ice, in numbing snow storms,
He reveals Himself to no one.
Verily, God is light and warmth!

"God has made it all, however:
He's created warmth and brightness.
Has He frost and ice created?
The Writ's silent on this point.

"This warmth, in a single instant,
souls creates in lifeless bodies,
faith, belief spring forth within them;
God's the flower of this faith.

"Couldn't one incline to wonder
if the soul, the faith within it,
God Himself—be mere creations
of this little bit of warmth?

"God, perhaps such thoughts are sinful!
But Thou sentest us to fathom
the whole truth. Without your willing
thoughts can never cross my mind."

Thus the Hermit painfully struggled
with his thoughts and wearily prayed,
but the former times' enlightenment
to his soul would not return.

And he wept: "Is this the purpose
of my having left the convent's
quiet cell, to end my journey
in the shackles of grave doubt?"

VIII

"What guests extraordinary
have strayed quietly to my cavern!
Of what tidings are they envoys?
From what parts brings them the wind?

"Tiny petals, tender, snow-white:
are they snow? They aren't melting!
They exude a wondrous fragrance . . .
Cherry blossoms! O my God!

"Cherry blossoms on these cliffsides?
Cherry trees here on Mount Athos?
Tell me, please, mysterious strangers,
tell me now: where are you from?

"Your sublimely pleasing fragrance
touches on my very heartstrings,
fills my soul with delectation,
wafts with something near and dear.

"Do you come from Ukraina,
from my native land's far homesteads,
which right now with cherry blossoms
are bestrewn from end to end?

"I inhale my homeland's perfume:
my old heart drums joyous music
in my breast. O God Almighty,
is the memory still there?

"Could it be that Ukraina,
flowery, joyful, paradisal,
dreadful, bloody, and infernal,
still retains her hold on me?

"Is she my concern? The struggle
she's engaged in with the Jesuits
and the Poles is a grave burden,
But I have my burden, too.

"I am also in a battle
of the kind which every human
must first wage within his being
ere he help his fellow men.

"Did I not put in her service
my best feelings, thoughts, and efforts,
to support her, to defend her
in this great and difficult war?

"Was I not her true advisor
when she faced her hard dilemma?
Did I not imbue with courage
her worn out, despondent host?

"Was I not severely wounded
in my heart by their insults,
sheer ingratitude, rebellion,
and dull, stubborn ignorance?

"Did I not feel deep revulsion
at their scornful lack of confidence?
Did I not brush off forever
from my boots their very dust?

"My white guests, my vernal orphans,
driven hither by spring breezes,
you have strayed here, to my cavern,
with your fragrance quite in vain.

"It's too late now for your perfume!
Not for me are now those distant
memories of Ukraina—
for her I have long been dead!

"Dead? Then why is my heart racing,
my blood quickening, pulsating,
my thoughts cruising like a plover
over the orchards of our towns?

"Birds tweet, tweet; the grass, the flowers . . .
Cherries bathed in milky blossoms . . .
Willow trees, like strange green hayricks . . .
Smoke ascending from thatched roofs . . .

"Nightingales in the viburnum
warm the heart with their trilling . . .
Children playing . . . In the orchard
girls are singing there somewhere . . .

"Go away, you far off visitors!
You have brought me, to my haven
of calm peace—distress, turmoil;
to my grave—the whirl of life."

IX

Dusk is falling. An enormous
shadow of the rock reposes
on the sea; and way out, ripples
flare with fires of red and gold.

From the rocky nest, the Hermit
gazes calmly o'er the waters;
from these waves of gold and purple
builds a road to distant points.

To a distant land he builds it,
through the mountains, through the valleys,
to his native Ukraina,
sends his thoughts along this road.

He dispatches heartfelt greetings,
all his love, and all his yearning,
which, it seemed, all had been buried
such a long, long time ago.

Lo! along this sunny highway,
a bark slowly is approaching;
from the oars and from the rudder,
gold and purple splash sprays out.

The warm breezes of the evening
billow out the sailboat's canvas;
like a swan, the bark floats, heading
toward Mount Athos gracefully.

Are those monks who are returning
from far lands where they went begging
for alms for their monasteries?
Or mere peddlers with their wares?

Are those people pious pilgrims,
faithful orthodox believers,
coming here to pay their homage?
To the Prot an embassy?

The Old Man's eyes followed closely
the bark's path until it vanished,
entering the island's harbor;
then the Hermit heaved a sigh.

The Old Man no doubt imagined
Cossack coats inside the sailboat,
Cossack headgear topped with crimson;
an illusion, to be sure.

X

Night came; then another morning;
time for prayers, genuflections;
the Old Man's soul felt but anguish;
doubt and distress dwelt in his mind.

Suddenly, he heard a knocking:
up above, as was the custom
someone knocked against the granite;
the Old Man returned the knock.

On a rope began descending
his provisions in a basket;
white upon the basket's bottom
lay a letter with a seal.

The old Hermit's hands were shaking
for the letters were familiar—
cursive Ukrainian writing—
and the old, familiar seal.

"To Ivan, the honored Hermit,
who, secluded on Mount Athos,
treads the difficult narrow pathway
on the road shown us by Christ.

"We Orthodox Ukrainians,
in the town of Lutsk assembled
in a joint fraternal council
greet you and request your aid.

"We thank our Lord Almighty:
He forgets us not a moment
and most difficult temptations
sends on us for our own good.

"His hard blows on us, we know it,
harden us the same as iron,
all impurities removing,
temper us like unto steel.

"We thank our Lord Almighty
and those blessed men who carry
Christ's cross now on their shoulders
on behalf of their kin.

"Through the prayers of the pious
and Almighty's holy mercy,
to our faith we still hold firmly
and do not abandon hope.

"The implacable foes strike us
in the open and in secret;
treason, lies, and provocations
undermine us and divide.

"The world's mighty, knights and nobles,
have abandoned us completely:
their Christian flocks deserting;
they are chasing Mammon now.

"Our own spiritual shepherds,
now, like wolves, have turned against us,
clawing at their Christian brethren,
pouring poison in their souls.

"Like a hungry mountain lion,
our enemies' derision
roars at us in our sorrow:
'Where's your God? Where is your strength?'

"Therefore we, a tiny vessel
on the waves of stormy waters,
have assembled, tearful, praying,
to decide what must be done.

"Mindful of Christ's words that only
hard work gains the Heavenly Kingdom,
and that only those who labor
may win entry into it;

"Mindful also of your teaching
that in case of a betrayal
by our shepherds, the flock must then
take good care to save itself.

"We debated various measures
how against this storm to shelter
with at least a tiny bulwark,
our holy Mother Church.

"We've decided to assemble
all our forces in one center,
so that our common, noble
cause may flourish and mature.

"Thus we send out our brethren
to you, Sir, our honored Father,
to convey to you our prayers:
be the pilot of our boat.

"Return to our Ukraina,
and your word will warm our spirits,
as bonfires serve the shepherds
watching over their flocks.

"A bonfire warms the body,
at night gives illumination,
frightens off ferocious creatures,
and gives cheer to living souls.

"Be you our spiritual father,
set us all a lofty standard;
be the sound of our prayers,
and in war our battle cry.

"And consider: constant failures
rancor breed in our spirits;
and continuing derision
seals most eloquent of lips.

"And consider: lies, injustice,
like a she-wolf in her lair,
in her evil-smelling hideout,
breed ferocious wolf cubs.

"Mind: hypocrisy, betrayals
destroy truth in all expression;
he, whose heart is full of poison,
only poison can spit out.

"Father, Father! Bitter troubles
have warped some of us already;
little wolf cubs, although toothless,
crawl already in our midst!

"Father, Father! Hard blows smite us,
bend our spines and lower foreheads;
in our souls a dreadful poison
seethes and fills them to the brim.

"Show yourself among us, Father,
an old fighter, undefeated!
The first sight of you will straighten
our bent backs and give us strength.

"Hark! Your native Ukraina,
our dolorous old mother,
with a plaintive voice is calling
her dear child to her side.

"Evil days portends the future,
she shall soon stand on the crossroads,
and who is to show her whither
she ought to direct her steps?

"Don't disdain our entreaty!
Hasten to defend your Mother!
Your voice and your mind may turn yet
all in favor of our side."

On the outside of the paper
was a postscript: "The Rus envoys
for an answer will wait till 'morrow;
then they'll be up on the rock."

XI

Pacing up and down his cavern,
the old Hermit whispers prayers,
presses to his breast the crucifix,
trying to forget the writ.

"The Cross is the only value;
the Cross is the hope I live for,
the Cross is my only suffering
and my only native land.

"All outside it is deception,
diabolical temptation;
there's one path to salvation,
the true blessed road—the Cross.

"What's this voice, and what's this letter?
Sent to whom? To Hermit Ivan.
The monk Ivan is no longer;
he is dead for everyone.

"Should the Ukraine concern me?
Let her seek her own salvation;
I'll be lucky if I manage
to squeeze through to Jesus Christ.

"For I'm weak, and I'm a sinner—
no great star, and no Messiah;
I can't save them from perdition;
I may perish in their midst.

"No, I won't betray my Savior,
I won't break the pledge I've given,
and the Cross's heavy burden
I will carry to my grave.

"The time's nigh. That's why the breakers
roll at me the final impact;
for this reason, the road's end is
full of hardships, full of pain.

"Not much time left. God Almighty!
Help me lighten my last burden!
Illumine the path I'm treading,
now uncertain in the mist."

All night long the Old Man suffered,
prayed, and washed his face with teardrops,
his old breast pressed to the crucifix,
as a child his mother hugs.

He wept, whispered, called, but darkness
all enveloped in its blanket;
in his soul was fearful darkness
and enlightenment would not come.

At the sun's new resurrection,
he sat there in apprehension,
waiting for the stone to hammer,
for the voice above to speak.

There: the dull thud on the granite;
the Man started at the knocking,
but his hand was not extended,
he said nothing in response.

"Father Ivan! Father Ivan!"
calls the voice, its timbre sounding
like a cry of pain and anguish,
like someone who begs for help.

"Father Ivan! Father Ivan!
We're the men from Ukraina.
We're your unfortunate children!
Father Ivan, answer us!"

His breath bated, the man listened,
his ear hungrily absorbing
the loved sounds of Ukrainian,
but he did not answer back.

"Father Ivan, Father Ivan!"
long thus called the deputation;
down below the waters pounded,
and Ivan did not reply.

XII

Dusk was falling. Like a dove-grey
carpet, shadows decked the water:
from behind the mount, the sun rays
sank obliquely in the sea.

A gold highway stretched out evenly
from the animated waters
to the highest point on Athos;
the surf surged on at the rock.

In the cavern's very entrance
sat the Hermit over the letter,
stooping over it, re-reading,
sprinkling it with bitter tears.

" 'Hark! Your native Ukraina,
our dolorous old Mother,
with a plaintive voice is calling
her dear child to her side.'

"Her dear infant! Aptly spoken:
one who at the bleakest hour,
in this grim, impenetrable crisis,
leaves his mother in a lurch!

"One, who in his senseless blindness,
only wants his own salvation,
leaving his distressed, poor brethren
without succor and advice.

"By what right may you aspire,
you half-broken earthen vessel,
to your personal salvation,
with a million lives at stake?

"Think of what Christ said about it:
'A good shepherd will give gladly
for his flock his life.' Consider:
are you not their shepherd, too?

"Think of what Christ said about it:
'He who says I love God dearly
but neglects to help his brother
weights his conscience with a lie.'

"After all, for all the people
who'll give up in desperation,
whom you could have helped to courage,
God shall ask you to account.

"After all, your proud monastic
dreams of personal salvation,
here, away from all temptation—
are temptation, a mortal sin.

"You're not treading on God's pathway;
you're in fact the Devil's servant,
who wished in his pride to equal
his Creator, the great God.

"This is not God's way! If somehow
you contrived to enter Heaven,
and your native land and people
perished here without your help,

"Heaven should for you turn into
Hell! The very thought, 'I could have
helped them when my help was needed'
would turn Heaven into Hell!"

Mortal fear descended on him,
gripped the Old Man's heart with terror;
he could hardly breathe; a cold sweat
suddenly covered his whole face.

He looked out upon the water,
where the outline of the mountain
on the blue was trimmed with golden
edging of the setting sun.

Lo! down in the Athos harbor
a bark slowly is departing,
heading for the sunlit region,
leaving now the harbor's shade.

A Turk's steering the small vessel,
men in Cossack coats his riders,
their hats are topped with crimson,
gold is spraying from the oars.

Those are Ukraina's envoys!
The Old Man's heart started trembling;
in alarm and confusion,
he stretched out his thin old arms.

"Halt! Halt! Turn around, I beg you!
I am still alive. As always,
I love our Ukraina;
I'll give my last days for her!

"Halt! Halt! Turn around, I beg you!"
But in vain! They cannot hear him.
On the golden waves, the vessel
floats away, away, away.

The Man wrings his hands and presses
his old aching heart in anguish;
he prostrates himself, addressing
from the floor the Crucifix.

"Jesus, Thou hast left the highest
principle for us to follow:
first of all to love our brethren,
to give life for our kin.

"Jesus, look at me, have mercy!
Don't allow me here to perish
in abysmal, hopeless suffering,
in the depth of sheer despair.

"Grant me now to love my brethren,
to give them my whole existence!
Let my eyes see this one last time
my beloved native land.

"Look, this is the thread that ties me
to my work, the last incentive;
don't allow it to be broken;
turn the vessel back to me!

"Cause the winds to blow adversely!
Raise the sea in giant breakers!
Or allow me to fly downward
from this mountain, like a bird.

"Thou art merciful, Almighty!
And if all my labors, prayers,
all my silent meditations,
my achievements, my fasts

"ever had a grain of merit,
a mere speck of dust of import,
then I'll gladly, O Lord Jesus,
give it up without regret.

"I'll surrender all; I'm willing
to boil in hot pitch forever;
only cause me now a miracle:
bring the vessel back to port.

"Or allow me, in birdlike fashion,
to attain the bark by flying,
or else let me run toward it
on a bridge of sunlight gold.

"Thou didst also, as a youngster,
run on sun rays from the temple;
in a storm, Thou didst walk also
on the sea, as if on land.

"Grant me, grant me, this one miracle!
Only once, this very minute!
Do not leave me thus despairing,
like an infant in distress!"

Thus prayed our Ivan Vyshensky,
hugged the cross with all his power;
and he felt, all of a sudden,
from his anguish strange relief.

He became completely tranquil,
wild distress he felt no longer,
clear assurance spread out over
his renewed and freshened soul.

He was sure that God had granted
all he'd asked for in his prayers;
that the moment of a miracle
and enlightenment had come.

That which he so long had hoped for
spread around him, like light breezes,
like harmonious cosmic music,
paradisal holy scent.

And he rose with joyous feelings,
thrice he crossed himself, and blessings
he bestowed upon the sun path
that obliquely touched the sea.

Now to all he was oblivious,
save the golden rays of sunlight
leading to the bark, far yonder;
he stepped out and disappeared.

In the Hermit's cave lay only
the white cross, of all illusions
skeleton, of dreams and yearning;
and the sea roared on below.

1900

Ivan Franko's Religious *Weltanschauung*

Louis J. Shein*

It is the central thesis of this paper that Ivan Franko's religious, or more accurately, spiritual *Weltanschauung* (Dukhovnyi svitozor), was deeply rooted in the Bible, which was for him a perennial source of moral and spiritual inspiration. Franko's interest in the Bible dates back to his early boyhood. Although he did not read it in his own language, he had access to the Church Slavonic Bible as well as to Polish and German translations. His interest was not restricted to the Old Testament where he found many themes for his poetry; it extended to the Gospels and the Pauline Epistles. However, it was the moral and spiritual ideals preached by the prophets which formed his religious *Weltanschauung*. The prophets influenced Franko's search for Truth, Justice, and Freedom. Franko's religious *Weltanschauung* may be defined in the ideal expressed by the eighth-century B.C. prophet Micah, "What does the Lord require of you, to do justice, to love mercy and to walk humbly before God."[1] Franko's life-long struggle for justice, truth, and freedom for his people has its source in the prophetic mission he felt he had to carry out. This deep sense of mission found practical expression in his literary, social, and political activities.

Asher Wilcher, whose work *Ivan Franko and the Bible* is an important contribution to the already extensive literature on Franko, sums up his views on Franko's interest in the Biblical ideals in these words: "Spiritual values, summoned from the corners of the Bible, enter his (Franko's) philosophy of life to find an ideological as well as an artistical expression in great works of reflecting his national thought and his outlook on the ways and means that are to bring about national progress and success in his homeland."[2]

To be a prophet entails frustration, rejection, and even stoning. Yet, the Hebrew prophets, who felt themselves called to denounce injustice and oppression and to preach the principles of truth and justice, did face the consequences of their call. When Isaiah heard the call in the temple at a time of national crisis, "Whom shall I send? Who will be our messenger?" his response was, "Here I am, send me."[3] For his willingness to go to his people who were not interested in his message, Isaiah paid with his life. Tradition tells us that Isaiah was placed in a hollowed log and then cut in half. Other prophets met a similar fate, mostly by stoning.

Franko, like the prophets of old, felt himself called by destiny to liberate his beloved Ukrainian people from ignorance, injustice, and oppression and to bring them into the "promised land" of freedom and justice. I therefore do not hesitate to place Ivan Franko in the honored tradition of the eighth-century B.C. Hebrew prophets, Amos the Shepherd, Hosea the farmer, Micah the proletarian, and Isaiah the aristocrat, generally referred to as the "prophetic quartet."

Franko, because of his deep commitment to his task as prophet to his people, put his moral and religious ideals into practice by becoming involved socially and politically. His pen became a mighty weapon in his struggle for justice and freedom. When Mykhaylo Drahomaniv lost his professorship in the University of Kiev and emigrated to Geneva, Franko identified himself with Drahomaniv's democratic and progressive ideas, which were based on moral principles. Franko disseminated these views through the pages of the periodical *Druh*. The authorities at the time could not countenance such progressive views, and in 1887, Franko, Pavlyk and the whole editorial staff of *Druh* were arrested because of their affiliation with Drahomaniv's views. Franko was imprisoned for eight months until his trial and then sentenced to another six weeks imprisonment. Two other arrests followed later in his career.

---

*Louis J. Shein is Professor Emeritus at McMaster University, Hamilton, Ontario.

These experiences marked the beginning of the many frustrations and rejections he had to face from his people. Upon release from prison, Franko was treated like a criminal and a social pariah. He was shunned by both friend and foe alike. He expresses his feelings at the time in these words:

> My fellows have forsaken me!
> They all, whenever they draw near,
> Pass on and look askance at me . . .
> What is it that my fellows fear?[4]

Franko complains bitterly of "the senseless prosecution which fell on me like a tile falling on a person's head in the street and which ended in my condemnation, although there was not in my soul a shadow of the crime of which they accused me . . . I was a socialist merely by sympathy like any peasant, but was far from understanding what scientific socialism was—this was a fearful and grievous trial to me."[5]

Jeremiah the prophet expresses similar feelings when he was thrown into a dungeon for his prophetic message. He wanted to leave his people who refused to listen to his message:

> Who will find me a wayfarer's shelter
> In the desert,
> For me to quit my people,
> And leave them far behind?
> For all of them are a conspiracy of traitors,
> They bend their tongue like a bow;
> Not truth but falsehood
> Predominates in the land;
> Yes, they go from crime to crime.[6]

But he could not run away from his people, because he loved them despite the bad treatment he received at their hand:

> Who will turn my head into a fountain
> And my eyes into a spring of tears,
> So that I may weep all day, all night,
> For all the dead out of my people?[7]

Franko, like Jeremiah, despite the treatment he received at the hands of his people, could not forsake them. Had he been willing to compromise his prophetic call by forsaking his people, Franko could have had the appointment to the Chair of Ukrainian Language and Literature in the University of Lvov for which he had excellent scholarly qualifications. He could have enjoyed a serene life of an academic with all the honours and material benefits entailed in this position. But his love for his people far outweighed his personal gains. His position is clearly stated in these words:

> If I feel myself a Ukrainian and to the best
> of my powers and strength work for the
> Ukraine, it is not for reasons of sentimental
> character. A feeling of doglike obligation
> forces me to it . . . My Ukrainian patriotism . . .
> is a heavy yoke laid by fate upon me. I can
> shudder, I can quietly curse the fate that has
> laid such a yoke upon my shoulders, but I
> cannot throw it off . . . For I would be ignoble
> in my own eyes . . . [8]

Franko was very often a "voice crying in the wilderness" of ignorance, hatred, and misunderstanding. Yet, he never gave up in the face of heavy odds against him. Although life "gave me enemies who cursed and persecuted me":

> Yet over all I value most
> the cup of unjust suffering
> Life gave to me, that truth and light
> I might perhaps to others bring.[9]

In his frustrations and despair, his deep religious faith sustained him. He could echo the famous words of the Apostle Paul:

> We are handicapped on all sides, but
> we are never frustrated; we are
> puzzled, but never in despair.
>
> We are persecuted, but we never have to
> stand it alone; we may be knocked down
> But never knocked out![10]

Like St. Paul, he "knew how to live when things are difficult and I know how to live when things are prosperous. In general and in particular I have learned the secret of facing either poverty or plenty."[11]

What prompted Franko to get himself involved politically was the intolerable situation facing the Ukrainians in Galicia. The Ukrainians, who made up 93 percent of the peasants, were deprived of their rights as citizens. They did not own the land which they tilled and were exploited by the landowners. We get a glimpse of the situation there in many of his poetic works, but the *Hireling* sums up the situation quite vividly:

> Born as a serving man, once magnified as free
> By heroes of his folk,
> In wretchedness with no escape, in misery,
> He bows beneath the yoke.
> To live, his life, his liberty, his strength he sells
> Just for a crust of bread,
> Which adds naught to his strength and scarce
> His hunger quells nor straightens up his head.[12]

We find an analogous situation in Judah at the time of Amos and Micah. Assyria had embarked upon a program of military expansion, threatening the West. Syria had already been conquered in 732 B.C.; the northern kingdom of Israel had suffered a similar fate. This left Judah in the south in a precarious situation as the first line of defence against the aggressor. The prophets, who had the power of discerning the signs of the time, could not remain silent. They realized that their country faced the Assyrians without and the enemy within—the greedy rich who were bent upon "ripping off" their poor. Amos pointed his accusing finger at this enemy who:

> sold the righteous for silver, and
> the needy for a pair of shoes—
> They also trample the head of the poor
> Into dust of the earth, and turn aside
> The way of the afflicted.

They turn justice into wormwood
And cast down righteous to the earth.
Therefore because you trample upon the poor
And take from him exactions of wheat,
You have built houses of hewn stones,
But you shall not dwell in them.

Therefore, Let justice roll down like waters
And righteousness like an everflowing stream.[13]

As a genuine patriot, Franko felt duty-bound to take practical steps to bring about a change in the situation in his country. Thus we find him working out a program for the Galician Laboring Community, whose aim was to make the land available to the communities working on the land. He also actively participated in the Ukrainian Party which came into being at the Congress in Lvov in 1890. The purpose of the Party was to effect social and economic reform. Franko was particularly concerned with the elimination of indirect taxes as well as land taxes, and the establishment of co-operation of all classes of society for the improvement of their social and economic situation; and he was against the proletarization of the village as advocated by Marxism.

The founding of the Ukrainian National Democratic Organization in 1899 along with Mykhaylo Hrushevsky and other prominent Ukrainian leaders had as its purpose the promulgation of economic and social justice among the Ukrainians. These aims were based on the religious and moral principals inherent in Franko's religious *Weltanschauung*.

The aim was both just and practical as enunciated by the leaders of the Organization:

We are striving to make our people free
in production, credit and trade from
dependence upon other peoples and lands,
so that they may have in their own hands
the necessary means of production; first
of all its land, and can develop its own
history, trade and credit. The basis of
the economic prosperity of our people is
their own labor, the energy, initiative
and frugality of each individual.[14]

Franko's socialism was deeply rooted in the religious and ethical ideals of the prophets—the principles of Truth, Justice, and Freedom. The God of the prophets like that of Franko, could not be enshrined in a ritualistic and cultic straitjacket. He was a God of love, mercy, and justice. Franko, like Amos and the other prophets had the courage to stand up for these moral principles. He states:

I never belonged to that sect of the faithful
who founded their socialistic program on the
dogmas of hatred and class warfare. And I had
courage enough amid sneers and abuses of such
adepts openly to carry the standard of a true
humanitarian socialism aiming at the ethical,
broadly humanistic education of the popular
masses for progress and general enlightenment,
for personal liberty as well as national, and
not for party dogmatism, nor for despotism of
leaders, nor the bureaucratic regimentation of
all phases of everyday life, nor for a
parliamentary chicanery to bring in the hoped-
for future.[15]

It must be emphasized that Franko's involvement with Drahomaniv and others was for the purpose of developing a healthy peasantry. His political activities were based on the principles of justice and freedom preached by the prophets. Franko viewed man *sub specie Dei,* i.e., man as a child of God, who must never be treated as a means to an end. Franko knew that the true definition of man is his freedom. Man is free in his decisions from a formal point of view. Each encounter brings man into a new situation, and each situation is a call claiming him as a free man. If man is to be free in his decisions he must also be free from his past. In his effort to bring freedom to his people, Franko was painfully aware that generally man is not able to liberate himself from his past, indeed, that he does not even wish to be free but prefers to remain as he is. But to exist as a human being means to live in freedom. Freedom is not an abstract idea but it is inextricably bound up with the principle of love. It is the kind of love that was described by St. Paul: "Love is not jealous or boastful; it is not arrogant or rude; love does not insist on its own way. Love is patient and kind; love bears all things."[16] Love, like freedom, grows out of definite situations in encounters with other people. When Franko attacked the Nationalists and Russophiles in his foreward to the *Galician Sketches,* which appeared in a Polish version, the Dathans and Abirams unleashed a barrage of abuse against him, which caused him a great deal of anguish. Like the prophets of old, Franko felt that he had to tell them the truth even if it was unpleasant to the ear. In his reply to these attacks, he made them aware of the meaning of true patriotism and genuine love. In *Life and Word,* Franko expressed his views in aphorisms, such as, "Love is not obligatory, but the sense of obligation is obligatory." "He who asserts that he loves his people, yet fulfills not his duty towards them, asserts a lie." (Cf. "He who says that he loves God, whom he has not seen and hates his brother whom he has seen, is a liar and the truth is not in him.") Franko berates his accusers in these words:

> Thou, brother, lovest Rus'
> As thou dost love beefsteak;
> But I do naught but bark
> To keep Rus' wide awake.
>
> Thou lov'st the glorious past
> Of Rus' history;
> While my heart only bleeds
> O'er all her misery.[17]

Franko's "confession" was a cry of spiritual anguish for his people more than for his own frustrations and despair.

Those who accused Franko of atheism and radical socialism failed to see, or did not want to admit, that his socialism was rooted in the ideals of the prophets who were concerned with justice, truth, love, and freedom. Franko's socialism was an ideal for work and not a political program of the Marxian type. Hence, his economic, political, and social activities were rooted in his religious *Weltanschauung.* The poem *Blazehennyi muzh* is undoubtedly Franko's Manifesto for freedom. This poem, as we know, is based on Psalm 1. However, Franko reverses the ideas into positive action. It is the task of the righteous person to go into the enemy's camp and fight for justice and righteousness.

> Blessed is the man who goes where evil reigns
> And raises there his voice for righteousness;
> Who, unabashed, the lawless ones arraigns,
> And, unafraid, plucks at their consciences.
>
> Blessed be all those who did not fear the cost,
> Whenever truth and justice were at stake;
> Though to men's memories their names be lost,
> Their blood shall all men's blood more noble make.[18]

Franko was not afraid to raise his voice for righteousness and freedom and was willing to suffer diversion and rejection for his efforts to bring about a just society among his people.

> Forty years like a smith at their hearts
> And their conscience I hammered,
> And to this it has come: that I flee
> From their stones and their clamour.
>
> Forty years have I labored and taught,
> Plunged in Thee to the limit,
> To make from these slaves a true nation
> In Thine own image.[19]

We have tried to show that Franko's literary, social, and political activities were deeply rooted in his religious Weltanschauung whose source was the Bible. Franko was a true prophet in the Biblical sense. His legacy not only to his own people but to mankind as a whole is that of justice, truth, and freedom. He was a truly Christian humanist and genuine patriot. His place is securely assured in the annals of human history. Let me conclude this paper in Franko's own words:

> I always attached the greatest importance
> to the attaining of common rights, for I
> know that a people engaged in battling
> these common human rights will by so doing
> also conquer national rights for itself.
> In all of my activity I have desired above
> all to be not so much a poet, a scholar,
> or a publicist, as to be a man.[20]

Franko was all these: a great poet, a scholar, a publicist, but the greatest attribute is that he was a man in the true sense of the word!

NOTES

1. Micah 6:8.
2. Wilcher, Ascher, *Ivan Franko and the Bible: A Study of His Pre-Moisei Poems.* Ph.D. thesis, Dept. of Slavic Studies, Ottawa University, June. 1977. p. 170.
3. Isaiah 6:8,9.
4. Franko, Ivan, *Forsaken,* tr. by Percival Cundy, in *Ivan Franko,* Philosophical Library, New York, 1948, p. 112.
5. *Ibid.,* pp. 36-37.
6. Jeremiah 9: 1-3.
7. Jeremiah 9:1.
8. Stachiv, Matthew, "Social and Economic Ideas of Ivan Franko," in *Ukrainian Quarterly,* Vol. 12, June, 1956, pp. 136-137.
9. Ivan Franko, "What Life Gave," tr. by Percival Cundy, p. 110.
10. II. Cor. 4:8-10, J. B. Philips translation.
11. Philip. 4:12-13, J. B. Philips translation.
12. Ivan Franko, "The Hired Hand," tr. by P. Cundy, p. 101.
13. Amos, 2:6,7.
14. Stachiv, Matthew, *Ibid.* pp. 139-140.
15. Ivan Franko, quoted by Cundy, *Ibid.,* p. 39.
16. I Cor. 13.
17. Ivan Franko, quoted by P. Cundy, p. 73. *Ibid.*
18. Ivan Franko, "The Righteous Man," tr. by P. Cundy, p. 255.
19. Ivan Franko, "Moses," tr. by P. Cundy, *Ibid.,* p. 226.
20. Ivan Franko, quoted by Cundy, p. 13.

Yahweh and Yahwism in the Poem *Moysey* by Ivan Franko

Oleksander Dombrovsky*

In the poem *Moysey,* two qualities of Franko's genius merged: the brilliant talent of a great poet and the erudition of a scholar, to display expert knowledge of the civilization and the ethos of ancient Israel. Franko's interest in the Semitic cultures probably was one of the motives which led him to the writing of the poem, or at least created the needed psychological atmosphere in which the concept of the poem was born and became crystalized. The poet clad his expertise with rhymes and rhythms, infused it with the breath of his poetic soul, penetrated with full profundity of his contemplative spirit the historic role of Moses, who became leader and lawgiver of the Jewish people, thus fashioning Moses' imposing stature on the background of his era.

Yahweh's characterization in several places of the poem sheds a light on the cult of Yahweh during the time of the Old Testament. Reproaching the Jews for their disregard of the Prophet's words, who is Jehovah's spokesman, Moses warns them:

> Beware, or else He'll speak to you
> in His own manner;
> He shall speak more terrifyingly
> than the roar of thunder in the desert.
>
> Mountains tremble at the sound of His Word,
> and the earth gives (subsides),
> And your heart, like leaves in the fire,
> will flare up and shrivel up.

Yahweh is a mighty God, Lord of Nature, and as its Creator may use elements of Nature in His actions. In the lines above, we find not only anthropomorphic features in Franko's depiction of Deity, but also realistic tendencies, which appeal to human beings, in the painting of outward features. This is no dead and impotent Deity, behind concealed walls and marble columns of some Egyptian or Babylonian temples, which, to use a Biblical expression, "has eyes but sees not, has ears but hears not, has a mouth but speaks not." This is the living God of Israel, at whose command the seas part, water springs from rocks, and the foundations of Sinai quake. Yahweh is capable of speaking one hundred times louder than thunder in the desert. From His words "mountains tremble and the earth gives," and the human heart wilts from fear. Such a presentation of Deity is, without a doubt, a fragment of the naturalistic religion during the announcement of the principles of the Decalogue.

*Oleksander Dombrovsky, Ph.D., is a historian of the ancient world. He has held several research and teaching positions in Europe and the United States. He is a member of several learned organizations. This paper was first delivered at a session of the prestigious Ukrainian Schevchenko Society in 1961 in New York. Dr. Dombrovsky's articles on various problems of antiquity have been published in English, German, Italian, Russian, and Ukrainian. This paper has been slightly abridged in my English translation; it has been approved by Dr. Dombrovsky.

We come across other naturalistic tendencies in the characterization of Yahweh in the verses where the Hebrew children ask Moses to tell them of his adventures:

> Well, tell us about when you were young,
> how many wonders you saw,
> when you herded the flocks of your father-in-law
> on the highlands of Horeb.
>
> How you beheld that thorn bush
> which burned but was not consumed,
> and how you heard a voice from the bush
> which made you jitter with fear.

The last mighty chord of naturalistic tendencies in Yahwism is that place in the poem where Yahweh speaks to Moses. Expelled from the camp of the Israelites, the Prophet climbs a high mountain and there converses with Yahweh in a mute prayer. After this conversation in solitude, the exhausted Moses falls on the ground in a faint. In this somnolent state, he fancies hearing the voice of his mother, which at first lulls and calms him, but later infuses doubt into his heart as to the correctness of Yahweh's commandments. Then Moses has a vision of the historic future of his people. Having seen the thorny future path of Israel, from the seizure of Canaan to the Diaspora, the Prophet succumbs to dispair, disillusioned with Yahweh's promises, and blasphemes:

> And he fell with his face to the ground:
> "Jehovah has deceived us!"
> And demoniac laughter was heard
> as an echo of his words.

A powerful reaction to the words "Jehovah has deceived us!" is Yahweh's reply, preceded by natural phenomena:

> Thunder. There suddenly shook
> the deepest foundations of the mountains,
> and one after another took off
> Yahweh's predecessors.
>
> To the ceiling of the Heavens rose
> a black cloud, like a wall,
> as though Mother Night's face had turned grim
> with menacing hatred.
>
> And she blinked rapidly with her fiery eyes
> in the darkness,
> grumbling like a mother who is
> chastising her bad daughter.
>
> And with terror Moses was listening
> to the talk of darkness and lightning:
> no, his heart could not hear yet
> the voice of Jehovah.

Thunder roared above the mountains:
hair stands on end from fear,
his heart grows faint in his breast, but no:
this is not Jehovah's voice.

Winds howled among the cliffs,
and the angry sounds
clinched the soul, like a groan, but in them
Jehovah's voice was not yet audible.

Now rain rustled with hail,
and the cold gripped;
in its impotence, the soul
is sick and ready to surrender.

In this variant of Yahweh's characterization, Yahweh does not speak through thunder, but mighty natural phenomena precede his mysterious soft speech:

All became silent, only waters purl,
like someone sobbing with sorrow;
from the soft breeze came a draught
of terebinth and almonds.

And this warm breeze contained
mysterious language;
and Moses felt it with his heart:
it was Jehovah speaking.

Franko's examples of naturalistic tendencies in Yahwism are confirmed in the Old Testament. We find an analogy in Kings 19:11–13:

11. And he said, Go forth and stand upon the mount before the Lord. And, behold, the Lord passed by, and a great and strong wind rent the mountains, and broke in pieces the rocks, before the Lord; but the Lord was not in the wind: and after the wind an earthquake; but the Lord was not in the earthquake.

12. After the earthquake a fire; but the Lord was not in the fire: and after the fire a still small voice.

13. And it was so, when Elijah heard it, that he wrapped his face in his mantle, and went out, and stood in the entering of the cave. And, behold, there came a voice into him, and said, What doest thou here, Elijah?

The archaic phase of the Old Testament Yahwism is characterized, among other things, by strong and dynamic naturalism as an expression of nomad life of Israel's tribes in the desert. In subsequent phases of Jewish history, this naturalism is subdued and polished, and after the time of Exile, it surrenders its positions to motifs of settled life, mostly urban in character. One of the examples of urban motifs in Yahwism is Isaiah 2:3:

And many people shall go and say, Come ye and let us go to the mountain of the Lord, to the house of the God of Jacob; and he will teach us of his ways, and we will walk in his paths: for out of Zion shall go forth the law, and the word of the Lord from Jerusalem.

Therefore: not under conditions of naturalistic staging, not amidst thunder and lightning and earthquakes, but from Jerusalem, from the Temple built by Solomon. During the nomad desert life, when the Jews moved from place to place and had a portable Arc of the Covenant, Yahweh remained amidst nature and surrounded himself with natural phenomena. After the conquest of Palestine and the erection of the magnificent Temple, Yahweh finds a new abode, exchanging old naturalistic props for the urban setting of Jerusalem. In Zechariah 8:3 we read:

> Thus saith the Lord; I am returned unto Zion, and will dwell in the midst
> of Jerusalem: and Jerusalem shall be called a city of truth . . .

In this we see a complete transition from nature to the city. The same happens in the area of Biblical eschatology, where the Paradise of Genesis, located amidst lush vegetation, changes in John's Apocalypse, in the New Testament redaction, to New Jerusalem.

Furthermore, it is *apropos* to mention anthropomorphic qualities in the depiction of Yahweh. These qualities are found in the Old Testament, and Franko, as an expert in ancient Jewish folklore, used it in his poem.

> But jealous (is) Jehovah, our God,
> and fierce and angry;
> to whomever He gives his love
> he cannot be loved by others.

In Exodus 34:14 we read:

> For thou shalt worship no other god: for the Lord whose name is Jealous, is a
> jealous God.

In Deutoronomy 29:29: The anger of the Lord and his jealousy shall smoke (King James Version). Luther translated it into German as " . . . *dann wird sein Zorn und Eifer rauchen* . . . "

Moses, reproaching the Jews for the stoning to death of God's messengers and prophets, says in *Moysey*:

> Every drop of the blood of those servants
> of his best flocks,
> Jehovah shall revenge on you
> and on your descendants.
>
> He shall beat and torture you
> until you weep with pain,
> and in your sorrow you shall swear
> to obey His righteous will.

In Exodus 20:5, in the Ten Commandments, Yahweh says:

> . . . for I the Lord thy God am a jealous God, visiting the iniquity of the fathers
> upon the children unto the third and fourth generations of them that hate me . . .

The anthropomorphic qualities listed here are a product of the age, in which human beings had not yet purged themselves of animism in religious practices, and ascribed human qualities to deity. Here we also find other attributes. Yahweh is not only strong, mighty, before whom natural forces tremble, but also righteous and omniscient. The last quality is particularly stressed, and belongs to the stronger moments of the poem.

> Man of little faith, you had not yet been conceived
> in your mother's womb,
> when I had counted your every breath,
> every hair on your body.
>
> Abraham had not yet left the Land of Ur
> and the plains of Haran,
> when I knew all descendants of his
> to the very last day.

"CHOSEN PEOPLE"

Talking to the Jews, Moses reminds them how once upon a time Yahweh called Abraham from the Chaldean Ur to Palestine.

> Was it for the sake of peace He called
> from Ur and from Haran
> Abraham and his tribes
> to the meadows of Canaan?
>
> Did He for the sake of peace lead them
> over the Jordanian lowlands,
> or drive them by hunger of seven years
> all the way to the banks of the Nile?

We see from these lines that the poet touched upon the Biblical concept of Jewish ethnogenesis based on the patriarchal principle, according to which "*Urvater* Abraham" forms the departure point for the Jewish ethnogenesis. In connection with this idea, Franko puts words into Moses' mouth which draw an analogy between Abraham and his descendants. Just as Abraham lived constantly in a tent and knew not the complete peace of a settled life, the people of Israel must not dream about a peaceful, comfortable life, because Israel

> . . . is an arrow pointing to a target,
> sharpened for battle.
> Is it seemly for the arrow to say:
> I desire peace?

This is the Yahweh arrow on the taut bow, which has its own eternal goal. This apt analogy of Israel to a pointed arrow is the poetic overture to the brilliantly conceived and presented rhymes which develop the notion that Israel was a "chosen people," and that ancient Israel had a special mission. Having explained through Moses how the Thorn had become king of the trees, Franko gives an explication.

> The trees are the peoples of the earth,
> and the king in their midst
> is God's chosen, His son and servant
> of the Lord's will.

Like the Thorn among the flora, so is Israel among other peoples the most humble, because "Jehovah did not choose the proud and the loud, whose thoughts bombard the heavens" nor the "rich nabobs who plunder the whole earth" nor the "handsome gallants who strum their lyres."

> Thus the people chosen by God
> is a pauper among other peoples,
> where there is splendor and honors, to him
> the thresholds are too high.
>
> He is no wise man among the sages,
> no warrior in war,
> he is a guest in his homeland
> and a universal nomad.

Instead of power, riches, and glory, the chosen people have a treasure in their hearts. They have to be "the salt of the earth," "like a beacon in the darkness" (a phrase which is repeated in the Old and the New Testaments in several versions). In another place, Franko says through Moses: "Woe unto you whom God has made the bonfire of humanity," or in another variant of the same thought:

> But Jehovah put into its heart a treasure,
> for He knows human hearts,
> so that it might be like a light in the darkness,
> the treasurer of His Word.
>
> For the endless life's journey
> He gave it support:
> His commandments and promises,
> as though bread for the road.

As cited above, the idea of a chosen people, or Messianism, has here a transcendent character, but the end brings a tendency to politicize the idea, that is, confusion of the messianic idea, transcendent in character, with political aspirations.

> O Israel, you are the messenger
> and a future king of the world!

However, almost immediately comes another stress on the transcendent nature of the idea of a chosen people:

> Your kingdom is not of this world, and not worldly your glory!

Yet the phrase "future king of the world" produces a strong worldly dissonance on the background of the transcendental idea of a chosen people, which itself is free of ulterior motives of politicized religion. It is hard to decide whether the poet inserted this motif of political aspiration consciously, in line with politico-religious ideas present among the ancient Jewry, or in a moment of poetic inspiration. Either is possible for, on the one hand, Franko knew well the mentioned currents; on the other hand, an analysis of the poem will reveal elements of pathos.

It is perhaps to the point to mention that in the books of the Old Testament we come across two kinds of Messianism: the soteriological idea of the coming of a Messiah; and popular Messianism of the chosen people among the heathen, where the chosen people would spread the word of God in the protoevangelic sense of those times. In this case, we are dealing with the second, popular, Messianism, whose aim was to become "the salt of the earth," "to obtain grace for all," "to free the world from suffering, division, and fear." Again we have a confusion of metaphysical concepts with worldly concerns, because the phrase of freeing the world from "suffering, division, and fear" may also conceal political aspirations on a universal scale (in the narrow sense of the ancient world, of course), although this protoevangelic action might bring to the pagans not only eternal but also temporal benefits.

The idea of a golden age of mankind is very ancient, and at different time segments of ancient history it appeared in different redactions. The Palestinian boondocks did not escape its impact, the more so that it found here a suitable psycho-religious soil in the shape of popular and even soteriological Messianism, of which the latter also contains the idea of a golden age, which was, without a doubt, the main generator of this Old Testament eschatology, without which Yahwism would have been mere religious—dead—formalism. That's why the idea of a golden age is dear to the world of eschatological concepts. In the books of the Old Testament, it appears in the form of politicized religious concepts, or in the form of theologized political aspirations of ancient Jewry. Along with the process of crystalization of national consciousness and attempts at statehood, the popular Messianism evolved more in the direction of politicized religion. These two elements, religious and political, intertwine on the background of the idea of Messianism, so that often they are hard to separate from the ideas which animated Jewish multitudes in antiquity.

Therefore in *Moysey* they appear intertwined, with the qualification that Franko has given precedence to the idea of popular Messianism of transcendental character. It is also possible that Franko circumvented the historical principles of time and space and spanned several scores of centuries, from Moses' age to his own. In this case, we would be dealing with an actualization of politico-social postulates through association of concepts. This is not impossible in Franko's *Weltanschauung*.

SEMITIC DEMONOLOGY

In addition to the descriptions of Yahweh and some ideas of Yahwism, demonology plays an important part in the poem *Moysey*. Demonology, an element common in all the religions of the world, seldom appears in the books of the Old Testament, and not very clearly at that. Only a microanalysis of the texts reveals allegorical hints. In Pentateuch there are two such occasions. The first one speaks of the temptation of Adam and Eve (considered by Pan-Babylonian scholars to be a copy of Babylonian originals). In Leviticus 16:21–22 the Lord instructs about sacrificial ceremonial, and mentions Azazel, the scapegoat on whom all the sins of Israel are placed, whereupon the goat is chased out into the desert. In addition, in Ezekiel 28:13–19 we find a hint about a fallen cherub, then other mentions of demoniac intervention are in the Book of Job, Chronicles 21:1, Psalm 109:6, and in Zechariah 3:1–2. Characteristically, angels are more strongly represented in the Old Testament than demons.

The majority of researchers agree that after the Babylonian exile, under the influence of Persian dualism, the demonological element is more pronounced on the fabric of Yahwism. Franko, well versed in these circumstances, took the demonological element in his poem from the archaic redaction, i.e., from Pentateuch, about Azazel, the most appropriate choice for the chronological background of the poem *Moysey*. The demonological motif appears twice.

Walking from the camp to the mountains, Moses hears at first a mysterious voice, "like the hissing of a snake," which tries to awaken doubt in Moses as to his being called by Jehovah to lead the Jews out of Egypt. When Moses refers to the fire on Horeb, he receives a painful reply.

> Perhaps the fire on Horeb did not burn on Horeb, but in your determined heart, bent on an audacious strike?
>
> Perhaps the voice that led you out on this unfortunate march did not come from burning mounds, but was your own, internal?
>
> After all, passion blinds the eyes, and desire is magic that generates for the eye a world and gods, like a mirage in the desert.
>
> That desire which, like a jackal howled in your soul—it alone made you their chieftain and prophet.

At Moses' question: "Who are you, enemy?" the mysterious voice betrays its identity: "I am Azazel, the dark demon of the desert."

However, the doubt placed in Moses' soul by the demon does not break the Prophet's spirit. After he had prayed and fallen on the ground in a faint, the dark power of the demon attacks him again with poisoned arrows of doubt. Now the demon suggests to Moses not only doubts about the validity of his mission, but questions the power and omnipotence of Jehovah, in the voice of his mother, but Moses knows the voice and unmasks it at once.

Having showed Moses the smallness and poverty of Palestine, the demon reveals before his eyes the sad vision of the future of Israel, its difficult struggles, political splintering and disunity, and finally dispersal. Such was the fulfillment of Jehovah's promises, and such happiness was to come to the Jews in the land toward which Moses' prophetic spirit had been striving! This time the demon's attack was not in vain. Exhausted and drained by doubt and despair, Moses speaks the blasphemous words: Jehovah has deceived us. The demon has achieved his goal. Having led the Prophet, the leader of a chosen people, astray, the demon has cause to rejoice.

While the contents of the first demonological motif are human auto-suggestion, the calling of voices, or simply schizophrenia, the tenor of the second demonological motif is clearly the struggle of two hostile elements from the religious-ethical dualism: Good and Evil. Under the influence of poetical inspiration, Franko probably infused more meaning into archaic Old Testament concept of demoniac activity than it had had during the chronological period underlying the poem. The sharpness of the conflict suggests to the reader of the poem substitution of Yahweh and Azazel with Iranian concepts of Ormuzd and Ahriman, the more so that the dynamically naturalistic trappings of the poem support such a view. But Franko adheres to the orthodox concept of Biblical demonology. In his poem, Yahweh and Azazel are not equivalent deities, as Ormuzd and Ahriman are in Iranian dualism: Yahweh is the stronger of the two.

From the foreign cults under whose influence the Jews fell from time to time, the poem mentions Baal and Astarte, or Ishtar, from the Phoenician and Babylonian pantheons.

From the mentioned material, from the characteristic of Yahweh and the ideas of Yahwism, the gold thread of monotheism breaks through everywhere. We find no monolatric elements here. Yahweh is the ruler of the world and all its peoples, and not a local deity of the Sinai or the object of a local cult of the Jewish people alone. Franko accepted the idea of monotheism because it appealed to his view of the world.

There is no mention of Levites in Franko's poem, and Moses is the only intermediary between Yahweh and the Israelites, as attested in Jeremiah 15:19. The function of the Levites was strictly ceremonial.

Moses

Prologue

O People mine, divided, deathly tired—
A cripple sitting at a highway juncture—
With human scorn, as though with sores,
    bemired.

My soul's distressed by prospects for your
    future;
The shame to sear the hearts of your
    descendants
Robs me of sleep and pains me beyond
    measure.

Is it indeed engraved on iron tablets
That your fate is to dung your neighbors'
    acreage,
To be the draught for their speedy chariots?

Must you forever hide your fury savage,
Feigning instead submission hypocritical,
To everyone who through deceit and outrage

Put you in chains and swore in to be loyal?
Are you alone by Fate denied a labor
Which would reveal your infinite potential?

In vain so many hearts have burned with
    ardor
For you, with purest holiest affection,
Laying their souls and bodies at your altar?

In vain your land has known the saturation
With heroes' blood? Is she not to exhibit
Good health and freedom, beauty and
    perfection?

Do in your language sparkle to no profit
Humor and strength, intensity and softness,
And all the means which elevate the spirit?

Is it in vain your songs so flow with sadness
And ringing laughter and the pains of loving—
A radiant riband of your hopes and gladness?

Oh, no! 'Tis not the tears alone and sighing
To be your fate! I trust the spirit's power,
The resurrecting day of your uprising.

If only one a moment could discover
When words were deeds, and words that
    blessed moment
Would come that heal and belch life-giving
    fire!

If one could find a song—inspiring, fiery,
    potent—
To rally with the multitudes of people,
To give them wings, to lead toward atonement.

If only . . . We, careworn from constant
    struggle
And rent by doubt, despondent from
    opprobrium,
We are not fit to lead you into battle.

The time shall come; in the free nations'
    gremium
You'll take your place—resplendent and
    perfervid;
You'll echo freedom on the Mare Nostrum—

The Pontus; sash-like, you'll gird on the
    Beskid
And shake the Caucasus; your gaze
    proprietary
Shall scan your land, the homestead you
    inhabit.

Accept this song, although its tone is dreary,
Yet full of hope; it's bitter but veracious;
Toward your future—a downpayment teary;

My modest festive present to your genius.

20 July 1905

I

Having roamed forty years through the sands
Of Arabian deserts,
Moses came with the people he led
Up to Palestine's limits.

Here the sands are still red as the rust—
The Moab: rocky, barren—
But beyond them are meadows and groves,
The blue waves of the Jordan.

In the meager vales of the Moab
Camps the Israel nation;
To advance beyond those barren peaks
It feels no inclination.

In the shade of torn tents, indolent,
The whole nomad camp dozes;
In the thistles and weeds roundabout
Feed their oxen and asses.

That a wondrous land promised to them,
That gems—emeralds, hyacinths—
Glitter close on that side of the ridge
Not one of them gives credence.

Forty years long the Prophet had preached,
So majestically, nicely,
'Bout a homeland long promised to them:
Wasted words, spoken idly.

Forty years long the rare vale beyond
The blue waves of the Jordan,
Like a desert's illusive mirage,
Drove the tribes and allured them.

"Our prophets have lied!" people said,
Their faith tried to the limit.
"We must live our lives out in the sands;
Waiting longer won't change it."

So they stopped their blind forward drive;
Fond hopes dashed, they abandoned
Sending scouts out, guessing what is concealed
Beyond red, rusty highlands.

Day by day, in the Moab's ravines,
When a scorcher oppresses,
In the shelter of their shabby tents
All of Israel drowses.

Their women alone spin and bake,
Roasting goat meat in ashes;
Their donkeys and oxen chew on
In the thistles and rushes.

Their children, though, playing outside,
Do invent strange amusements:
They build cities, they play waging war,
Or fence in their gardens.

Many times shake their heads in surprise
Their somnolent fathers:
"Where on earth did they pick up these
        games?"
They keep asking each other.

"For they never see them around here
Or learn them in the wild.
Have the prophet's words entered the blood
And the heart of each child?"

II

But one man in his tent submits not
To the general torpor;
On the wings of his cares and his thoughts,
He surmounts the high border.

It is Moses, the prophet denied,
In his feeble senescence;
Without kin, flocks, or wives, he now stands
In the fall of existence.

All he had in his life he gave up
For a single ideal;
With its fire he shone; for its sake,
He knew torment and toil.

Like a storm, he had snatched out his folk
From the yoke of Misraim;
From constriction of life outside walls,
Led the slaves out, to freedom.

As the soul of their souls, he rose up
Many times since departure,
To supernal, celestial heights—
Inspiration and rapture.

On the waves of their tempest-tossed souls,
When they faced doubt and trial,
To the slough of despond, many times,
He went down with his people.

Now his voice has turned brittle and faint,
Gone's the old inspiration,
And no longer his words hold appeal
To the young generation.

To them words of a great promised land
Seem a fairyland story;
Their flocks' meat, butter, and cheese—
Their ultimate glory.

That their elders had sent from Misraim
On the march the whole nation
They consider both folly and sin,
And the tribes' ruination.

Over them Abiram and Dathan
Today run herd as leaders.
They respond to prophetic remarks:
"Our starved goats need fodder!"

To his call to get ready to march:
"Unshod are our horses."
To the promise of glory in war:
"Their troops are the fiercest."

When the new land's attractions he named:
" 'Tis not bad right here, either."
At the mention of God's own command:
"Keep your mouth shut, you trickster!"

When the prophet then uttered the threat
Of Jehovah's new strictures,
Abiram then debarred what he called
Sacrilegious speeches.

At a meeting of Israel's sons,
Who'd first worshiped Baal's idols,
The vociferous Dathan pushed through
A new statute, as follows:

"He who likes as a prophet to pose
And whose talk lacks coherence;
Who holds out to the ignorant mob
Divine mercy or vengeance;

"He who dares agitate our folk
And incite to sedition,
Luring people beyond distant hills,
Toward final perdition,

"As a scary example he'll serve,
To our crackpots a warning:
First we'll cover the man with our spit,
Then he'll perish by stoning."

III

Dusk was falling. Abated the heat
Of the daytime entire.
Over a mountain the sky was ablaze
Like a distant big fire.

Like gold rain, heaven-sent on the earth,
Cooler air brought refreshment.
Signs of life now appeared in the tents
Of the nomad encampment.

Slowly, fluidly stepping along,
With their earthenware vessels,
In a queue on the pathways of stone
Walk the black-eyed Jewesses.

On their heads they bear pitchers they'll fill
At the rock spring with water;
In their hands they hold bottles of skin,
To milk ewes grazing farther.

Older children, like rabbits, play games
On the flat empty barrens:
They run races and holler, or shoot
From the bows their arrows.

A faint whimper is heard from a tent,
Or a girl's lusty laughter,
Or a song that's so sad as the sands
At the night's blackest hour.

Now the elders—grandfathers and dads—
Venture out in the open;
Their eyes scan over the hills
And the sands, flat and barren.

Are no enemy riders concealed
In the yellow mist's curtain?
Is a sand hurricane set awhirl
By the southerly *shaitan*?

All is well, and the talk turns toward
What concerns neighbors daily:
"There is less and less milk from our ewes,
And the lambkins are tiny.

"Our jennies do not find enough
Of the thistles for fodder.
We shall have to move camp to somewhere
Where the pasture is better.

"Abiram points toward Madian,
Dathan likes farther regions.
What says Moses? He'll hold his tongue
After last night's decision."

All at once the encampment is filled
With commotion and babble:
From their shelters run out, big and small,
Every manner of people.

What has happened? An enemy raid?
A beast caught in a snare?
No, it's Moses! Behold, he's come out
From his tent over there!

His back arched with the weight of his years,
Age and worry in tandem;
Like two lightning bolts inside a cloud,
His eyes burn on despite them.

Though his hair is as white as the snow—
A senescent adornment—
Yet two bunches still proudly stand out,
Like two horns on his forehead.

He proceeds to the place where the points
Of the tent of the Covenant
To the four main directions on earth
Jut their horns out, defiant.

In the tent stands the heavy, strong Ark,
Hammered out of pure copper;
Therein lie God-Jehovah's commands,
Signs of freedom and splendor.

But the sacred confines of the tent
Have for long been avoided;
Fear stands guard over them day and night,
As a dog guards a threshold.

A large stone lies against the east side
Of the tent-tabernacle.
Custom wills that from this stony perch
One may speak to the people.

Moses steps on this stone, and the crowd,
With dismay and annoyance,
Flinches: Will he now preach
And soothsay, in defiance?

Like a log rotted through from inside,
Must they smash up and shatter
Whom their ancestors came to regard
As their whole nation's father?

At the head of the crowd—Abiram,
His face angry and crimson.
To the middle ones whispers Dathan,
The community's demon.

IV

"Yesterday, my poor children, you held
A conclave—dumb and simple.
This I wanted to tell you at once
And forego a preamble.

"Both my lips and my soul you would still
With a tight seal of silence.
For this reason I must now speak up
To you all in defiance.

"Understand it and keep it in mind,
O you blind generation:
Stones will speak if you manage to rob
Living souls of expression.

"Yesterday you conspired to turn
A deaf ear to all preaching;
Not my own, not from these lips of clay,
But Jehovah's own teaching.

"But beware lest he speak to you now
In his own mighty mannner,
With a voice hundredfold stronger than
Desert crashes of thunder.

"Mountains quake at the sound of his voice
And the earth gives and buckles,
And your hearts shall, like leaves in a blaze,
Flare up briefly and crumple.

"Yesterday you heaped oaths on revolt—
But they weren't effective,
For your hearts are recoiling against
All this mindless invective.

"For Jehovah has placed in your hearts,
Like in bread dough a leaven,
Causal forces. To the place that He chose
By this force you'll be driven.

"Yesterday you regarded repose
The most blissful condition.
Did your Lord and your Master concur
In your present decision?

"Did He too for the sake of repose,
From the towns Ur and Haran
Summon Abraham and his whole clan
To the meadows of Canaan?

"Did he lead to the Jordan lowlands
So that they languish idle,
Drove them on after seven lean years
To the shores of the Nile?

"Had he wanted to leave you at rest,
Like a corpse in a coffin,
You'd have slaved in Egyptian yokes
To this day, like grey oxen.

"Thus I shall speak to you not from me
But by higher commandment,
To persuade you that to fight God
Is to yield to poor judgement.

"For Jehovah's bow ready to shoot:
The bow string's tense and supple
And an arrow rests on this taut string—
You're this arrow, my people.

"When an arrow is sharpened to pierce
And is ready to fire,
Is it right for the arrow to say:
'It is peace I desire'?

"And because yesterday you all swore,
Like effeminate creatures,
Nevermore to pay heed to my threats,
Forewarnings, and strictures—

"So I purposely want to bring out
All these things in the open.
I shall promise you what is to come
And admonish and threaten.

You must listen although you'll be pricked
By the cold sting of anger.
Whose hand will raise itself against me
With the first blow, I wonder?"

V

"Since you've sworn not to listen to words
Of God's mercy and glory,
I'll treat you as childlike, naive,
To a fairyland story.

"On a broad plain one time, there convened
All the trees' congregation.
'Let us chose us a king,' they proposed,
'In an open election.'

" 'May he shelter us and lend prestige,
Offer hope, aid when needed,
Be at once our servant and lord,
The goal sought and the method.'

"And one group said: 'Let us elect—
For one we'll vote together—
May he ever remain our king:
Our Lebanon Cedar.'

"And the trees all agreed and began
To appeal to the Cedar:
'O descend from your proud lofty heights
And become our leader!'

"But the Cedar declined and remarked:
'How excessive your wishes!
Do you want me to leave for your sake
All my hills, rocks, and ridges?

" 'You expect me to leave for your sake
The sun's glitter and freedom,
For such hodgepodge to give my consent
To a new life of serfdom?

" 'You have brought me an honor—a crown.
What a beautiful moment!
I am Lebanon's crown anyway
And the whole world's adornment.'

"And the trees next approached a Palm Tree,
In their quest for a sovereign:
'You're from here, you are our kin;
Come among us and govern!'

"And the Palm Tree responded to them:
'What a notion, my brothers!
To rule over you, keep things in line?
I must leave this to others.

" 'To keep order among you, would I
Have the strength to abandon
The perfume of my blossoms, my dates—
Sweet as honey and toothsome.

" 'Should I let the sun's rays warm in vain,
Day by day, my sweet juices?
Should men's eyes and the beasts' look in vain
For my succulent produce?

" 'Take whomever you want for your king;
I decline your throne's offer.
I prefer to provide shade to all
And nutrition and succor.'

"And the trees then all bowed their heads,
Full of thoughts grave and dismal
That the Palm and the Cedar as well
Had refused honors royal.

" 'Let's appeal to the Rose!' But the Rose
Is to everyone's liking.
Though uncrowned, she's the queen of the
        plants
And God's special darling.

" 'Let's appeal to the Oak!' But the Oak
Is in love with his riches:
He's engrossed with his roots and his trunk
And his acorns and branches.

" 'Let's appeal to the Birch!' But she is
A white silk-clad young lady.
She lets down her luxuriant plaits,
Her head down, her mien broody.

"But someone, as a jest, said such words
As an infant might utter:
'There's the Thorn yet unasked if he would
Entertain our offer.'

"And as one, all the trees echoed it,
In concordant opinion,
That the Thorn Bush should be approached,
Offered royal dominion.

"And the Thorn Bush responded: 'Someone
Has advised you correctly.
To your throne I'm prepared to ascend,
Resolutely and promptly.

" 'Not as tall as the Cedar am I,
And the Palm Tree's more comely.
My self-love's not as strong as the Oak's;
The Birch's more melancholy.

" 'I shall gain new ground for you, although
I crave not for new regions;
While I spread out, hugging the ground,
You can soar to the heavens.

" 'I shall bar every access to you
With my bell-metal briars;
I'll adorn all the wasteland around
With my milky-white flowers.

" 'I shall shelter the hare and the bird;
May you steadily flourish,
While I, giving refuge to all,
By the roadside shall perish.' "

VI

In deep silence the speech was received
By the Israel nation . . .
"That's the story," said Moses, "and now
Comes the tale's explication.

"All these trees are the tribes of the world,
And the king, their champion,
Is God's son, chosen by Him to be
His Divine Will's custodian.

"As Jehovah created mankind,
Like so much vegetation,
He looked into men's souls to divine
Future fate of each nation.

"He examined the mainsprings by which
Their natures were driven,
To determine which nation of all
As a son should be chosen.

"He did not take the proud and the loud,
With thoughts cosmic in grandeur;
With an iron heel over men's necks,
They keep mankind in terror.

"He did not take the well-heeled nabobs
Who the whole world despoil,
Who, as mortar for their own crypts,
Use mankind's gold and toil.

"He took not those who twang on the strings,
All so handsome and gallant,
Who attempt, both in stone and in songs,
To preserve their talents.

"He disdained all the glory and shine,
All the earthly puissance,
All the wisdom affected in books,
Of the arts all the fragrance.

"As the thorn, when compared with the trees,
Is so drab, ordinary,
And cannot lay a claim to renown
For its flowers or berries—

"So's the people elected by God:
Among nations—a pauper;
It finds thresholds too lofty to cross
Where it sees pride and splendor.

"Among the sages, it is not wise;
It's no fighter in combat;
It's a guest in its own fatherland,
A ubiquitous nomad.

"But a treasure's been placed in its soul
By Jehovah, heart-expert:
Like a beacon, to shine in the dark,
To be his wisdom's steward.

"For the endless life's journey, He gave
For his people's refreshment,
As though bread to sustain on the road:
His paroles and commandments.

"Yet how jealous is Yahweh, our Lord,
Fierce and dread in his passion:
To the one that he loves no one dare
Show the slightest affection.

"In a cloak of his fondness he clad
His elect among peoples:
Inaccessible, prickly, as though
It were bristling with brambles.

"And he made it corrosive and sharp,
As the nettles are—mordant,
So that only He may inhale
The perfume of its spirit.

"And a mission he put in its hand,
Seven-sealed dreaded orders,
To be borne into far-future time,
To the hate of its brothers.

"Woe's the messenger who's so inept
To doze off on his errand,
Or to fracture the seal on the writ
And profane Yahweh's warrant.

"For another shall take the dreaded writ
From the sluggard's possession,
To proceed on the course and run home,
Shine at his coronation.

"Lucky's he who the message with faith
And dispatch due will carry,
For the Lord shall place laurels on him,
Grant him measureless glory.

"You're this messenger, O Israel,
And the world's future sovereign!
Why d'you stray from your mission in life,
From its precepts and cannons?

"Your empire is not of this world!
Not yours earthly attainments!
Woe unto you if you're ensnared
By this world's entertainments!

"You'll become—not the salt of the earth—
But mere ash, wretched, lowly.
Having failed to obtain grace for all,
You'll be of it unworthy.

"Having failed to free all of mankind
From pain, horror, dissension,
You'll resemble squashed up little grubs
In the throes of extinction."

VII

And sarcastically said Abiram:
"My dear sir, Mister Moses,
You've excited and scared us to death
With the story you've told us.

"Be a thorn among peoples! Indeed!
And for this giant favor
It makes sense to acknowledge your god
Our master and savior.

"What an honor his errands to run!
Into dark, unknown future
To deliver sealed missives; this part
Most appeals to our nature.

"It's exactly the fate of the ass
Who tied-up bags of fodder
Lugs around, suffers hunger itself
For the joy of another.

"But the Hebrews have not lost their minds,
They're of better life worthy,
Which they'll get if their prayers are sent
To Baal and Astarte.

"Let Jehovah on Mount Sinai rocks
Keep on thundering merrily;
Baal shall give us the riches and might
In a large territory.

"Let Jehovah regard spiky thorns
Nice and handsome as posies;
Ashtureth's hand shall show us the way
Toward myrtles and roses.

"Our destiny is in the East,
In Senaar and in Haran.
We won't move one small step to the west,
To your favorite Canaan.

"All that's clear, and to waste further talk
There is really no reason,
But what are we to do with yourself
After last night's decision?

"Should we stone an old ruin? A waste
Of much effort and trouble.
He may yet be of use in some things
To the Israel people.

"To spin tales, to blow bubbles—his skill's
Masterful and uncanny.
Let's assign him therefore to the kids:
A community nanny."

Thus he spoke, and the mob answered him
With a loud, vulgar cackle;
Next to laughter—a hail-laden cloud—
Came from them a dull rumble.

"As you say, Abiram; So be it!"
Moses answered, unshaken;
"He who's destined to hang later on
Cannot drown in the ocean.

"You shall never behold Canaan's lands
Nor proceed further eastward;
Not a step shall you move from this place,
Neither forward nor backward."

Deathlike silence descended at once
On the lips of the people.
Abiram froze with fear and turned pale:
He expected a miracle.

There's no miracle! And Abiram
Laughs! Along with his cackle,
Over the crowd, like a hail-laden cloud,
Could be heard a dull rumble.

VIII

The relentless Dathan rose to speak:
"Don't you augur and threaten!
When I tell you the truth, then perhaps
You may not care to listen.

"Now admit it! The schools you went to
In the Egyptian Kingdom
Taught you how to enslave, when grown up,
Our honor and freedom.

"Now admit it: did you now attend
High Egyptian councils,
To connive with their sages and priests
At betrayal of Israel?

"Now admit: there's a prophecy there
Since the ancient ages:
The Egyptian power would die
From an oak and twelve branches.

"What the oak and the boughs signified
The priests knew all the while:
They were Israel's one dozen tribes
Prospering on the Nile.

"They were shocked that in spite of all toil,
Tortures, cruel oppression,
This Israel grew and increased,
Like the Nile inundations.

"Each time a Hebrew mother gave birth
To her very first offspring,
An Egyptian firstborn must die
On the very same morning.

"No one knew how to remedy this,
How to ease their sorrow;
Only you, turncoat, threw yourself down
At the feet of the Pharoah.

"And you said to him: 'If you permit,
To the desert I'll lead them.
I'll weaken them, dry them all up,
Make them humble, obedient.'

"And you did keep your word; you led us,
Like a dumb drove of muttons,
Through the sands, to the Pharaoh's great joy,
To our sorrow and penance.

"And how many the wilderness claimed!
In these rocks and sand barrens,
Sons of Israel found their graves
By the hundreds of thousands!

"And today, when from all our bands
There remains but a handful,
In the sands has been lost the dread might
That was once mighty Israel,

"And so weak as a feeble small babe's
Is, once brave, our spirit;
In our hearts, like a hunk of wet clay,
Our courage is flaccid.

"Into Canaan you're leading us now,
As though to a wolf's lair!
But the Pharaoh is sovereign over
All the princes out there!

"It is madness for us to press on
Toward a trap voluntarily!
Are we going to fight Misraim
Or for mercy beg humbly?"

"O Dathan," Moses spoke up again,
"Don't you worry, my young one!
You're not destined to bend your proud spine;
You shall never see Canaan.

"One more thing I would like you to know,
O Dathan of ill fortune,
At your death, not a palm span of earth
Shall be present to stand on."

"Hey, you Hebrews! You've pledged to Baal!"
Dathan hailed to assembly;
"The decision you made yesterday
Is forgotten so quickly?

"Grab your stones! He is mocking us now
As on many occasions.
Better he perish now than bring death
To our whole population!"

"Let us finish him off here and now!"
Catcalls came from the rabble.
Not a single hand, though, made a move
To pick up a stone missile.

And Dathan changed his tune on the spot:
"You must clear out this minute,
Or we may shed your blood at nightfall
And besmirch our hands in it!"

And the mob roared insanely: "Clear out,
And don't wait till the morning!"
And their clamor boomed over the plain
Like a twister approaching.

IX

But now Moses, with furious heat,
Raised his voice in great anger,
And his words rolled out over the plains,
Like wave-crashes of thunder.

"Woe betide you, ignorant slaves,
Piteous in your bluster;
Like blind men, you are being led by
Fools and confidence tricksters!

"Woe betide you, mutinous minds!
Since our Egypt defection,
Running counter to our common good,
You foment insurrection.

"Woe betide you, passionate men,
Frenzied, headstrong fanatics!
Your intransigeance, like a sharp wedge,
Cleaves asunder your beings.

"Like the nettles, you sting the same hands
That promote you and nurture;
Like a bull, you gore shepherds who search
For superior pasture.

"Woe unto you whom God has made
The humanity's beacon,
For this highest gift shall be for you
A dread bane and a burden.

"For whenever God's grace shines on you
With His mercy and brilliance,
All His prophets and envoys you'll stone
Till they die, in each instance.

"For each drop of the blood that you shed,
For the blood of His faithful,
On yourselves and your grandchildren shall
Our Lord make requital.

"He shall scourge you and smite you until
You cry tears in your torment!
You shall pledge, in your grief, to obey
Every holy commandment.

Once the punishment's over, your necks
Will grow stiff with defiance;
They will turn the full circle again:
Sin—punition—repentance.

"Pity you who'll be forced to endure
In this school many ages,
Till you learn to read fluently from
The great Book of God's wishes.

"I see you: a herd peels in the woods
Some agaric for tinder.
Now he soaks it and dries it in turn,
Pounds it hard with a hammer,

"Till the sponge turns as soft as the down
And acquires the fettle
To receive lively sparks from the flint
When the stone meets the metal.

"You're this tinder, O Israel!
You must suffer God's dressage
Till you're soft as a sponge and prepared
For the spark of His message.

"You'll advance toward your fate without zeal,
As an ox drags a harrow . . .
If Jehovah's big fist strikes your neck,
You'll know nothing but sorrow.

"You delve into the past, and you try
To scan future's horizons,
While you bloody your feet on the thorns
In your nearest environs.

"To a precipice you gallop on,
Like a crazed wild stallion;
You may yet don a yoke in exchange
For the crown of God's champion.

"Take good care lest Jehovah revoke
All the pledges He's given;
Lest your willfulness cause Him to break,
In your case, His word even.

"Lest He shed you, for all men to see
As a horrid example,
Like a motley snake crushed underfoot,
In its final death rattle."

They stood there, heads bowed down, listening:
Grim and silent and downcast.
But a dull wheeze escaped their breasts:
The first gasp of a tempest.

X

The gigantic red disc of the sun
Neared the mountainous border;
Like a swimmer and hero, it was
From fatigue going under.

Murky sadness there floated above,
In the cloudless sky's ether;
Jackals' howling throbbed painfully on,
Like a festering ulcer.

Something human and soft stirred just then
In the heart of the Prophet
And his lofty thought paused in its flight,
To descend for a moment.

Must he always bode wrath and remain
To his folk a bad omen?
All at once, like a sick hungry child,
Something sobbed in his bosom.

"O Israel, if you but knew
Wherewith this heart is brim-full!
I love you more than words can express!
If you knew it, my people!

"You're my family, you are my child,
All my honor and glory;
My own future reposes in you,
My soul, beauty, and country.

"For I gave you my life and my toil,
I was fierce and undaunted;
Through the centuries you'll go through life
With the stamp of my spirit.

"No, it isn't self-love that makes me
Feel affection toward you;
I've imbued you with all of the best
And the highest of value.

"These blasphemous words I shall speak,
O Israel, do not remember:
But I love you more perfectly than
Does Jehovah, our Master.

"He has millions under his care,
To keep warm and humectant,
But I have you alone for myself,
And to me you're sufficient.

"While you, from among multitudes,
Have been chosen to serve Him,
Though unchosen, I have come to serve you
From love only and yearning.

"While He lays a claim for Himself
To your working potential,
From you, Israel, I don't expect
The least thing, the most trivial.

"While He is demanding incense,
Praise, respect, adoration,
Unthankfulness I'll take from you,
Wounds, as well as derision.

"For I love you not solely because
Of the good in your essence;
None the less for your evils and faults,
Though decrying their presence.

"For that pride of the spirit you have
And your blind willful nature;
Having chosen your own stupid course,
You invite Yahweh's censure.

"For your glib and mendacious tongues,
For a conscience that stretches;
Like tenacious roots, you cling to
Your material riches.

"For the shamelessness of your womankind,
For its ardent lovemaking,
For your speech and your customs and ways,
For your laughter and breathing.

"O Israel, children of mine!
Pray God Shaddai may right it!
Though my love for you is without bounds,
I must leave you despite it.

"For my hour is drawing quite near,
That mysterious last one,
And I must, I must come without fail
To the borders of Canaan.

"I had wished so to enter with you
To the horns' mighty thunder,
But God's humbled me and I'm obliged
Alone Canaan to enter.

"I am willing to give up my life
By the Jordan this instant,
Only so that my bones may repose
In the Land of the Covenant.

"There I'll lie and keep gazing toward
The Moab's hilly prospect,
Till, like children behind their mom,
You will follow my footsteps.

"I shall send all my longing to you;
I will tug at your clothing,
As a dog when it wants to go
With its master a-hunting.

"Like a flood in the spring—that I know—
All of you will come over.
In your glorious campaign, of me
Do not ask or remember.

"Let your march keep on surging ahead,
Like a fast flowing river!
O Israel, children of mine,
May you fare well forever!"

XI

When he left the campsite, the hills blazed
In the last sundown radiance;
The hills lured to the purple-hued road,
To the goal in the distance.

From the dark mountain valleys, the gloom
Rolled the lowlands to cover;
Something wept in the exile's heart:
"I am leaving forever!"

Hebrew children playing outside
Of the nomad encampment
Came to Moses, touching his hands
And the tails of his garment.

"Oh, Grandpa! Are you leaving at night?
O Grandfather, stay with us!
Take a look at the wall we have built
And the gates and the towers!"

"Very nice; carry on with your wall.
But my dears, I can't linger,
For the wall that divides life and death
I am due to look over."

"We have killed a bad scorpion, Grandpa,
In the canyon's crannies;
In the briars, we've captured—no less—
Than all three of these bunnies."

"That's good, children! Keep bravely on
Killing scorpions vicious!
It's to people's advantage, although
It is not wholly righteous.

"It's not right, for the will to survive
Is no less in the scorpion
Can they help it if their tails' ends
Have a sting full of venom?

"But the bunnies you must take right back
To the place where you caught them.
Did it not cross your minds that perhaps
Their mom's crying for them?

"Toward everything living, you must
Be compassionate, gracious,
Because life is a jewel; is there
Anything that's more precious?"

"Bide a while, Grandfather! Don't go!
Please sit down with us children.
Tell us all the adventures you've had,
We'd love so to listen.

"Tell us how it was when you were young,
And what marvels you saw then
When you worked for your father-in-law,
On Mount Horeb, as herdsman.

"How a thornbush you saw was ablaze
But remained whole as ever;
How a voice from the bush spoke to you,
Which did chill you with horror."

"There's not time, my dear children, right now
To enlarge on this story,
For the eye of the day's growing dim,
The night's mists make all blurry.

"But the time will come too in your lives,
Amid valiant efforts,
When a fiery bush you'll behold
As I did as a shepherd.

"At that instant momentous, you'll feel
Very solemnn and pious;
And the voice you will hear from the flames
Will be mighty, tremendous:

"Shed the shell of your daily concerns
And approach without quaking,
For I want you to go and take part
In a great undertaking.

"Don't put out the celestial flame.
When the summons is tendered,
You can truly respond: 'O my Lord,
I am wholly prepared.' "

For a long time the children gave thought
To the Seer's pronouncements,
While he, to meet nighttime and gloom,
Slipped away, mute and noiseless.

For a long time, among the mute kids
Reigned both sorrow and sadness,
Till his dim silhouette could no more
Be discerned in the blackness.

XII

"Solitude has enveloped me now:
A sea—infinite, boundless;
And receiving its breath is my soul,
Like a sailing ship's canvas.

"This protectress, for long, very long,
Has been my true companion.
I have walked my life long all alone,
In crowds and in seclusion.

"Like an errant star, I plummet through
A mysterious void;
One hand's touch yet I clearly perceive:
A strange contact with Godhead.

"All is mute, all the words are sealed shut,
Lips are sealed with a muzzle.
In my innermost heart, Thou alone,
O Jehovah, art vocal.

"My heart thirsts after Thee, O my Lord,
In nostalgic desire;
Speak to me once again, as Thou didst
Once on Horeb, in fire.

"Now the journey commanded by Thee
Has been fully completed,
And I stand before Thee all alone,
As I did at the outset.

"I have toiled forty years, I have taught
In Thy Word's full immersion,
To create in Thy image, O Lord,
From low slaves a real nation.

"Forty years, like a blacksmith, I forged
Their hearts and their conscience;
At the end of all that I must run
From their jeers and their violence.

"All this happens when we should have been
In our promised land—Canaan . . .
O Omniscient, didst Thou foresee
From the start such an outcome?

"Worry gnaws at my heart, and I think
Perhaps I was deficient;
Perhaps I failed to carry out well
Every holy commandment?

"O Jehovah, I tearfully prayed,
I'm tongue-tied, I lack vigor!
Give another rather than me
Thy Word's terrible grandeur!

"Now doubt pierces my heart, pressing home,
Like a cold steely bodkin . . .
Art Thou satisfied with me, O Lord?
O Almighty, say something!"

In heartrending distress, Moses walked,
Prayed to Yahweh for guidance;
Softly twinkled the bright stars above;
The wilds answered with silence.

XIII

Then he heard a subdued laughter, as though
From someone at his elbow;
Though no footsteps were heard, someone still
Seemed the same path to follow.

And soft words could be heard from one side,
Like the hiss of a serpent:
"Folly's flower always gives fruit
To barbs only, and torment.

"When the weight of the fruit proves too great
To be borne its full season,
Then it's best in such cases to dump
On a god the whole burden."

Moses:

"What is this? Does my own bleak despair
Cause me now to hear voices?
Or am I being jeered at out here
By demoniac forces?"

Voice:

"Of your work as reformer, you've had
Certain doubts only lately?
Forty years you were certain and led
Although blindly but boldly."

Moses:

"Who is speaking? And why does my brow
So profusely perspire?
Fear? It's not! Yet it goes through the heart
Like a red-heated wire."

Voice:

"In your boundless conceit, you have steered
Off its course your whole people;
You've reshaped it to suit your own whims;
Should you fear now and tremble?"

Moses:

"Who are you, O Strange One? I can't see
Nor get rid of your presence;
I feel only your eyes bite into
My soul's innermost essence."

Voice:

"Could my name be so vital to one
Who the sea once commanded?
Not the *who* but the *what* matters here;
Are my words not well-founded?"

Moses:

"It's not true that it was out of pride
I embarked on my mission!
But my heart ached whenever I saw
My own kind in subjection."

Voice:

"Flushed with shame, you reflected you were
Kin of slaves, low and abject;
Hence the wish to change them, for your sake,
To a pleasanter aspect."

Moses:

"Yes, indeed; from the depths dim and grim
I so wanted to raise them
To the very bright heights where I stood,
Of true honor and freedom."

Voice:

"Of your Maker, who'd put them down there,
You did not first ask counsel;
You call Him for relief in your plight
Only now, after downfall."

Moses:

"I was prompted to act as I did
By His mighty commandments,
For the fire on Horeb brought in
To my dark soul enlightenment."

Voice:

"Well, perhaps Horeb's fire did not
Burn upon Horeb's summit,
But in your own audacious heart
Bent upon a mad gambit?

"Perhaps the voice that induced you to start
On this ill-fated journey
Came from no burning bush, but from you:
Was it your own, internal?

"For emotion obscures human sight,
And desire works magic,
Conjures up desert phantoms, to fool
Our senses, our optic.

"This desire which, jackal-like, howled
At that time in your bosom
Was the sole thing that made you their chief
And a prophet among them."

Moses:

"From these words, I feel my solitude
Hundredfold more. O Spirit,
Who art thou?"

Voice:

"I am Azazel,
The dark fiend of the desert."

XIV

It was dark. Only vivid bright stars
Shimmered up in the void.
Moses made out his way in their shine,
Heading upward and upward

Without paths. In his progress, strange clues
Showed the way in the darkness:
A hyena would wail in the gorge;
Snakes would make rustling noises.

He walked on without rest, like a knight
To his ultimate battle,
But his heart was already engaged
In a different struggle.

Something shouted in him: "Was this urge
Born of pain, shame, and outrage
The real fiery bush that bid me:
'Free your people from bondage!'?

"Was this fire—the desire in me—
The real causative agent
That created Jehovah in me
And Jehovah's commandments?

"This desire—to aid brothers of mine,
To relieve their anguish—
Is a sin I've earned banishment for,
Nay, for which I must perish?

"It's no sin! You must not disregard
Your own conscience judgement!
This desire is holy! Perhaps
Sin crept in, like a serpent?

"Were you not their chieftain and lord
Who controlled them completely?
Didn't power eat up in your heart
These desires, so holy?

"Were you not a new Pharaoh to them,
One much harder to suffer?
Their conscience you tried to control,
With their psyche to tamper.

"It is dangerous to change the course
Predetermined by nature;
It is easy to pass off your whims
As Jehovah's own strictures.

"What if these forty years you've been ill
With illusions of godhead,
And instead of God's plan, you've imposed
Your own scheme, narrow-minded?

"P'raps in Misraim they would have grown,
Amidst pain, despite misery,
Gaining vantage ground as they increased,
To control the whole country.

"As you led them away from the land
To these wastes' desolation,
Did you think: It's a hideous crime
I commit through this action?

"To a landless mob freedom hold out?
Does this promise hold water?
Is it not like uprooting an oak,
To let float down the river?

"They'd left their old nests, said Dathan
(Was he really mistaken?);
To gain new ones, there was now no drive
Or desire among them.

"O Jehovah, respond, answer me:
Did I act with Thy guidance,
Or was I just a plaything of my
Sorrow, anguish, and blindness?

"O Jehovah, the use of Thy voice
Doest Thou only acquire
In the passions and dreams people have,
When our blood is on fire?"

But Jehovah was silent; one heard
But ill-ominous noises:
A hyena wails in the ravine;
A snake slithers and rustles.

XV

Like a purple wheel, over the wilds
The sun's disc was ascending;
Arrow-like, its rays went through the dark,
Penetrating and piercing.

In their shine, seemed Mount Nebo a queen
Clad in her purple raiments.
Over the neighboring peaks rose the bare
Ribs of her grim escarpments.

On the peak of the mountain, above
All the rock scree and ledges,
Stands a motionless man, like a giant
From the ancient ages.

There—above all the feuds of the world,
All alarums and stridor—
He stands still, his arms fully outstretched
Toward Heaven in prayer.

In the sky-dome's aurorean glow,
In its purple effulgence,
In the desert, his huge silhouette
Is seen far in the distance.

Anxious looks fly from Israel's tents
To that illumined mountain,
As though couriers bearing a word
To that ancient titan.

"It is Moses," they shyly repeat
As they meet with each other,
But the twinge in their hearts they all feel
Their lips fail to utter.

It is Moses conversing with God,
Praying there on the summit.
And his prayer the Heavens assaults,
Like a fiery trumpet.

Though no words issue forth from his mouth,
For his lips are compressed,
Through his heart, both with words and with
    cries,
Is Jehovah addressed.

The sun climbs. Now the vault of the sky
Is completely on fire;
In his stance Moses seems like a rock,
Immobile in prayer.

Now the demon of midday spreads 'round
Through the wilds heat and weakness;
As though propped up by somebody's hands,
Still stands upright Old Moses.

Now the sun is inclining at last
To the Fasg's very summit,
And a huge shadow falls from the ridge
On the low lands beneath it.

For the last time, as though a farewell
From the Prophet, their parent,
His huge shadow fell upon the tents
Of the Jewish encampment.

And fear spread in the camp: "At this time,
Should he cast an enchantment—
God! The Prophet's curse upon us
Would be strangely potent.

"From such prayer, the earth's very core
And foundations would wobble;
Rocks would melt; the primordial throne
Of Jehovah would tremble.

"If he curses us now, and the sun
Sets on such malediction,
Tonight this land'll disappear without trace
And its whole population."

XVI

Moses struggled and strove, feverish,
Toward his destination.
As night fell on the mount, he collapsed
On the ground in exhaustion.

Under him shook the mountainous rock
And the peaks on its table,
And insensible he lay, as though
In his own mother' cradle.

Melancholy soft strains of a tune
Filled the ether around him,
And a hand downy-soft, white as snow
Rocked the crib he reposed in.

And soft words he could hear next to him:
"My poor son, precious treasure!
Look what life has done to you within
Such a tiny time measure!

"Was it long ago I nursed you, son,
By the hand led you, darling?
Did I send you out into the world
To endure such great suffering?

"Myriad wrinkles now cover your brow;
Your frame's wilted and feeble;
White as snow is the hair on your head
I would stroke once and fondle.

"Once you eagerly left me to join
Every battle and tourney.
What an end you've come to! And the wounds
In your heart: are there many?

"O my poor, my unfortunate child!
You have suffered much anguish!
Today, too, in the sun all day long . . .
What good did it accomplish?

"And in prayer! Of your people's past life
And the future they're destined,
You attempt understanding through prayer.
O you innocent infant!

"From a precipice I'll shove a stone,
And it shall keep on falling,
Rock to rock and ravine to ravine,
Splitting, shattering, bouncing.

"Here it smashes against a sharp ledge,
Into fragments to shatter;
There it knocks down a stone in the way,
To fall with it together.

"One chunk here, one chunk there comes to
    rest,
As they fall, as they rumble;
Who can know and predict where each piece
Comes to rest in its tumble?

"I assert: and Jehovah cannot.
Despite all your orisons!
For whenever a fragment must stop,
It'll stop there for certain.

"It contains its own guidance and rules,
It contains the puissance
That determines its place in the world,
That has caused its existence.

"And however strong Yahweh may be,
He can't alter these forces:
He cannot stop these rocks in midair
From pursuing their courses.

"Here's a mere speck of dust, and your eyes
Barely notice its presence,
But Jehovah can't cause it to turn
Back into nonexistence.

"He cannot order it to embark
On a course that is different
From the one it eternally runs
Through the forces within it.

"That's a dust speck; but take a whole tribe,
Many souls' congregation,
Each contributing some of its flight
To the total mass motion!

"Have you heard yet the story about
The blind giant Orion?
He embarked on a hike to the Sun,
To recover his vision.

"On his shoulders he carried a guide—
A young lad full of humor—
Who continued to show him the way:
A new one every hour.

" 'To the sun point the way, my good lad!'
He'd lead east in the morning;
Toward the south at midday; at sunset
To a westerly crossing.

"And Orion walks on and walks on,
Full of faith and assurance,
Full of thirst for the light which at last
Must burst into full radiance.

"Through the mountains and seas, giant steps
March relentlessly, steadily.
He knows not: to the boy on his back
He's an object of mockery.

"This Orion's the whole of mankind:
Optimistic, aggressive,
With a huge effort rushing toward
An unsighted objective.

"It loves that which cannot be attained;
It trusts the enigmatic;
Trampling down the familiar, the near,
It pursues the fantastic.

"It makes plans with inadequate means,
Aims beyond its potential.
At its plans laughs the while the young lad:
The hard facts of the actual.

"Like that strange sightless man who relied
On another man's guidance,
It attains ever unwished for goals,
Quite at odds with its tenets.

"And you pray! My unfortunate child!
Where's your sense? Where's your power?
You are grasping at begging the froth:
'Stop the flow of the river!' "

XVII

There was something at first in these words
Like transparent pure waters:
Cooling air emanated from them,
Spreading freshness and goodness.

But at length it grew stiflingly hot—
The simoom's stuffy closeness;
He felt fear, like a child in the night,
Without light in the darkness.

Moses shuddered and raised himself up
With great effort, to comment:
"I'll be soon in my grave; ere I go,
Why not spare me the torment?

"You're not Mother! I sense no warm love
In the tones of your dictum.
You're not Mother! You are Azazel
Desperation's dark demon!

"Go away! I adjure you to go
With the four-letter symbol!
You're a liar, and I trust you not,
Even though you're immortal."

And soft words came to him in response:
"What an ignorant infant!
You curse me in His name, but I am
Of His power a segment.

"What's your poor oath to me? I am sure,
You'd die from desperation
If you knew but a fraction of what
Is within my cognition.

"Now you curse, for your blindness was
          touched
By a spark from that furnace
In which I live and He—beyond bounds
Which time and space encompass.

"Well, I'll open the curtain a crack
To your limited vision;
Behold now the land promised by him
To your forefather Abram."

And the whole west exploded in light,
And the whole Palestina
Could be seen from the mountaintop then,
Like a broad panorama.

Now spoke up once again, in soft tones,
His invisible escort:
"There's the Sea of the Plain; notice now
Down below the black mirror?

"On the far side are peaks that range up
To the vault of the heavens.
It's the ridges of Carmel stretched out
In rows, tortuous patterns.

"Now note Zionese highlands up north:
Jebusites occupy them;
Amorites would be likely to hear
A loud shout from the mountain.

"With the Sea of the Plain, the bright band
Of the Jordan stream merges;
Near the mouth of it lies Jericho,
Which exacts crossing charges.

"Only one vale runs next to its banks,
And in it crowd together
Ammonites on this side of the stream,
Canaanites on the other.

"In the west you see mountains: high peaks,
Alpine meads in their purlieu,
There's a tiny lake up in the north,
Then high mountains continue.

"This accounts for the whole Palestine—
The land of mutton and barley—
All could fit in the palm of your hand:
From Kedesh down to Carmel.

"No wide highways are there to be found,
To the sea no connection;
Can a people develop and grow
Under such poor conditions?"

"He drew water from stone," Moses said.
"I daresay He'll be able
To transform into Eden this land
For his favorite people."

XVIII

Stifled laughter was then heard again:
"Faith, they say, will move mountains!
But behold these new images now:
This is destined to happen.

"See, your tribe is advancing across
The Jordanian waters,
Conquers Jericho, and everywhere
Wades in gore, bloody rivers.

"Now for centuries fighting goes on
For this small Palestine:
Amorites fight and Hebrews; Hittites,
Amalik, Philistines.

"Here's the realm of the Hebrews! The price
Paid in blood and in torment!
Like a fly on an ox is its weight
On the fate of this planet.

"Then it all begins coming apart
Without reaching full splendor,
Bit by bit to fall into the maws
Of its powerful neighbors.

"See what dark clouds are racing across
From Damascus and Hala?
Assur's bearing new ruin and death
To the people of Judah.

"Behold, corpse upon corpse everywhere
And the fields painted crimson:
Bent on Judah's destruction, the host
Of dread Babylon's risen.

"Yahweh's temple in flames . . . And the
        crowd . . .
Flies aswarm in the compound . . .
Into serfdom are led the half-dead,
Bound in groups of one thousand.

"Do you hear someone weep in the ruins?
It was their sole wise man.
His advice was: give in to the foe
And eschew thus the coffin.

"How the emptiness stinks! But wait now:
A dawn spells the gloom dismal.
Of the multitudes who went away
Now comes back but a handful.

"At the ramparts of Salem, again
New life's stirring—small, feeble:
A new god, a new temple, new men,
A new latent potential.

"It grows, battling in dire distress,
And it clings to the soil,
Like the thistles—tenacious, low—
And forever a rebel.

"Over the heads of these people pass through
Tempests—terrible, cosmic;
Like grim phantoms, first rise and then fall
All the bodies politic.

"And meanwhile a steadfast resolve,
In its nooks, it keeps fiercely;
Only loathing it has for them all
And unfailing contumely.

" 'It's because of a new god,' they say,
That they feel greatest hatred.
See how they loiter now and crowd there,
On the Temple's great threshold.

"It engenders but hatred. Now look!
By the will of a despot,
To root out your whole tribe once again,
Comes a brute force of jackboots.

"Here the thud? It's the thud of the feet
Of those terrible legions;
They are trampling down Judean land,
Turning fields into barrens.

"Hear the splash? Shedding Judean blood
Are the enemy swordsmen.
Hear the screams? Judah's girls dragged
        behind
Wild steeds of the Roman.

"Here's a mother who's eating the fruit
Of her womb, from starvation.
Thousands are crucified over there—
The elite of your nation.

"Yahweh's Temple's ablaze once again,
And this rings down the curtain,
For whatever's knocked down by this hand
Shall not rise from the ruins.

"And once more the survivors stream out
Into serfdom, like rivers.
There's no homeland for them after this:
They are leaving forever.

"Israel's star shall be snuffed out for good,
And it won't be rekindled,
But the temple-grown hate shall live on
To roam hence the whole planet.

"Sound incredible? Can't you believe?
But I know, you are able.
That's the paradise, the promised land
Which awaits all your people.

"You have labored toward it. Pray tell,
Was it worth all your labor?
To speed up its advent, would you still
Pray to Heaven with fervor?"

Moses lowered his head and exclaimed:
"Woe is me in my misery!
Are my people not ever to break
Their shackles of slavery?"

His face pressed to the ground, Moses cried:
"God-Jehovah's deceived us!"
And demonical laughter rang out
To re-echo his sentence.

XIX

Thunder crashes. The mountains shook hard
In their bedrock recesses;
One by one, from their crannies took wing
Yahweh's old predecessors.

Like a wall, rose up black thunderheads
To the sky's very ceiling:
Mother Night's frowning visage, as though
Overcast with dread loathing.

Blinking her fiery eyes in the gloom.
She continued to mutter;
Thus a mother, displeased, might behave
To upbraid her bad daughter.

With an anxious ear, Moses harked
To the lightning, the darkness,
As they talked, yet his heart failed to hear
Yahweh's voice in this discourse.

His hair standing on end from the fear
At the crashes of thunder,
Though the heart felt so faint in his breast,
This was not Yahweh's timbre.

Round the cliffs, the winds started to howl
Their melodies furious;
Their groans gripped the soul, but in them
Yahweh's voice wasn't obvious.

With the hail came the patter of rain,
And the weather turned frigid.
In its impotence falters the soul,
Feeling helpless and morbid.

All turned calm, but the rivulets purled,
As though sobbing with sadness;
Soft, warm breezes brought a whiff of the scent
Of terebinth and almonds.

And within this soft breeze were contained
Imperspicuous tidings;
Moses read them at once with his heart:
Now Jehovah was speaking.

"So Jehovah's deceived you? Did we
Strike together a bargain,
Sign a contract, and drink on our deal
Before public opinion?

"Have you seen all my plans? Of men's fates
Have you read in my codex?
Seen the ultimate ends? Do you know
I have not kept my promise?

"Man of little faith, you weren't yet
Inside your mother's bowels
When I counted your every breath,
Every hair on your noddle.

"Abraham wasn't leaving Ur yet
For Haranian lowlands
When I knew, to the end of all days,
All his future descendants.

"So your land is poor, narrow, and small,
Glitters not with gold baubles?
You forget: small and narrow as well
Are the greatest one's cradles.

"When the time comes, I'll lead you from here
Toward conquest and labor,
As a mother weans a child from her breast
When the time's right and proper.

56

"On the land here that's scanty and lean,
Like the thorns on the gravel,
You'll grow up hard as iron and tough
For the coming upheaval.

"Oh, I know well this nature of yours:
Never sated and sessile;
On good soil you would multiply
In the manner of thistles.

"With your bodies and souls, you would suck
At the furrows, like leeches;
Mammon would catch you soon in his nets,
Like extremely fat fishes.

"With your neck in the yoke, nonetheless,
You gorged yourselves, like gourmands;
Now for ages you'll eructate from
Those Egyptian viands.

"Having taken off from your own land,
Having broken all fetters,
You'll disperse to lay siege to the world,
All its juices and treasures.

At the same time I'll place a firm curse
On all your acquisitions;
Like a snake on a hoard, I'll give you
From them grief and afflictions.

"He who gains all the wealth of the world
And above all will love it,
He shall also become the wealth's slave,
Lose the wealth of the spirit.

"At the price of great torment and blood—
Lord and slave of possessions;
To increase his wealth, he must destroy
Their very foundations.

"Like the leech that sucks blood, curing ills
But must die when its over,
Thus the ocean of gold shall strand you,
In the end, on a sandbar.

"In the ocean of gold, by the thirst
You shall always be haunted;
Not one time in your life, with gold bread
Can you ever be sated.

To this planet's four corners you'll go
As a living exhibit:
Of all people I choose for my own
Those who nourish the spirit.

"He who feeds you on bread shall at once
Turn with bread into carrion,
But he who aims your spirit to feed
Blends with me in communion.

"There you'll find the land promised to you,
Without bounds, full of glitter;
You have served on the road to this goal
As my folk's sightless leader.

"There's the best of all lands to be found,
Your own home, shiny and radiant,
And this Palestine's but a small pledge,
The initial downpayment.

"It shall be just a memory, a dream,
An undying desire;
In its search to attain it, my folk,
Global might shall acquire.

"Since the nature of my commands
You did doubt for a moment,
Having seen Palestine from afar,
You won't enter your homeland.

"Here your bones shall decay into dust:
A deterring example
For all those who pursue lifelong goals
And succumb in the struggle."

XX

Sad nostalgia stalks the bare mount,
Like mists over the deserts,
Casting over the land's length and breadth
Its desires and concepts.

It spreads flowers and leaves that became
Long since yellowed and wilted;
In one's soul raises voices that now
A long time have been muted.

What but yesterday counted for naught
Is esteemed now, beloved;
What was trampled down and spat upon
Has become wholly sacred.

In the Hebrew camp they spent the night
In acute apprehension;
As the dawn broke, they looked: Is he still
On the rocky projection?

He was not! And this "not" was as cold
As the terror of dying;
They had lost something dear without which
They could not go on living:

That intangible, invisible thing
Which had once burned among them,
Had infused them with purpose in life
And could warm and enlighten.

Boundless sadness descended upon
Their hard-bitten conscience;
The whole camp, as though magically, felt
Stupefaction and faintness.

Into each other's faces blood-drained
They continued looking,
Like some murderers who'd killed in sleep
A beloved human being.

They rush somewhere; they herd their
          flocks . . .
Is a foe on the warpath?
They are driven by nameless alarm,
God's invisible digit.

Hungry spirits and solitude's dread,
The old pit of despondence . . .
But Joshua shrilly commands:
"On the march! Get your weapons!"

Joshua's cries rose above the mute crowd
Like the wings of an eagle;
And their echo rolled up to the hills:
"On the march! Into battle!"

One more moment: they shall be awake
From their stunned stupefaction;
And no one shall know what induced
Their sudden conversion.

One more moment, and Joshua's call
Finds a myriad echoes;
Lazy nomads this instant transforms
In a nation of heroes.

Hooves shall thunder; the sands underfoot
Into mud shall be kneaded;
In a stoning shall die Abiram
And Dathan shall be hanged.

Like a bird, they'll swoop over the hills,
Splash the Jordan in droplets;
They'll melt Jericho's ramparts, like ice,
With the sound of their trumpets.

Filled with yearning and stricken with fear,
They'll go into dark ages,
For the spirit paving the road,
Dying, too, in the process. . . .

Lvov, January to July, 1905

Lordly Jests

Translator's Note: The poem Lordly Jests *describes the events in West Ukraine, then known as Austrian Galicia, shortly before the abolition of feudal servitude for the peasants, on April 22, 1848. West Ukraine was part of Austria-Hungary from 1772 to Nov. 1, 1918.*

I

People's and lords' jests—
The squires of old—
Gambling and hunting

Go on and jest; God keep you, children;
Now you're allowed to do it all.
But when we lived as feudal subjects,
Of such cruel jesting we were objects
It is a horror to recall!
Then for the slightest misdemeanor:
You'd nudge an animal from the Manor
Or strike a dog that tries to bite
Bread from your hand or speak up crossly,
Upset a horsecart, bind sheaves poorly—
The flunkeys then would tan your hide.

The gentry then were really something,
Not like today—of no account!
Although expensive rags they're wearing,
Although, like hogs, they're blubber-bound,
They walk on eggs despite it; canny,
Lest some new troubles might emerge.
They snoop around, forever search
For someone who would loan them money.
Their heads are filled with thoughts unfunny:
On credit eat, on credit lodge,
And in your pocket not a penny.

It was not so in feudal bondage!
Then every lord appeared so pompous
And spoke so haughtily among us
As were he king, had he one village
Or a whole string. No one envisaged
Or hoped for in his wildest dreams
The age-old rule would change a smidgeon.
The lords and feudalism, it seemed,
Had merged in every vital thing,
To be inseparable and synonymous.

Then it was really worth the price
To see a lord. The peasants' eyes
Would simply wilt when they beheld
Their lord, although he didn't scold
Or shout. Bad for your blood such anger . . .
No emperor struts now, I wager,
So proudly through his capital city
As lords walked then across the village.

This widow's daughter's very pretty—
Into her house! A man has managed
To build a fence. "Hey there, you hick,
For your new fence you've used my sticks.
Pull it apart, take to the Hall,
Or else you pay for them in full!"

Whether it's lordly wrath or favor—
Like some unfailing words of God—
Fell on the peasants, meek, untaught;
Don't shed a tear or dare to mutter!
The gentry's eyes were bright and smiling,
The manors boomed with joyous parties,
And through the woods went hunting sorties,
By day and night resounded singing.
That was the time when our worthies
Were eager for caprice and jesting.

And how they used to bet at card games!
They play today as well, you're right,
Sit in a stupor day and night;
Without these games are not the same
The gentry's parties. But I venture,
You'll never see in your own future
Such players as in our day!
He'd fill with sovereigns a glass,
To win or lose on just one chance;
He'd lose and never bat an eye.
He'd never pale, he'd never shiver,
His tone of voice would never quiver;
At worst he'd shake his *porte-monnaie.*

My children, this is not surprising!
For it's from our sweat and pains
The golden harvest had been flowing
For centuries to lordly hands.
The chivalry, the martial glory,
Historical achievements gory,
All riches, splendid ostentation,
All vileness and all corruption,
Those lordly whims and cards and hunting,
All kinds of frenzied wild tricks,
And lordly favors, lordly jesting—
The peasants bore them on their backs.

II

Innovators—Conservatives—Uncertainty

A curious thing: the times were nearing,
Where'er you looked, from every side,
More boldly, loudly there resounding
Were harbingers of a new tide.
The words like equal rights and freedom . . .
Manor-born scions, far and wide,
Were taken by them, too, and often
Took to the people words of cheer,
For the afflicted. And there were
Even among the lords, though seldom,
Men who had formed a clearer notion
Of the events; although with caution,
They grasped at novelties. The system
Of servitude, they felt, would fail.

When in the woods you lose your bearings
And strain your throat and lungs for nothing
In shouts and calls to no avail,
The lords were quite as unreceptive
When they heard others new thoughts speak;
In fact such talk was but productive
Of obstinacy, touchy pique.
Among them also were such others
Who spoke up plaintively to strangers:
"We're living now through hellish times—
Not only peasants, but the gentry.
This feudal work obligatory
Soon shall leave us without a dime."
As though from ledgers, they recited
What various profits they'd derive
If they were paying for all work.
But even they had no intention
To change the antiquated system
And free from bondage their folk.

No wonder, either! Own dominion
Is most attractive, and the doubt:
God knows what change would bring about
The newly free domestic regimen?
Although some prophets made predictions
Of direct governmental action,
To wipe all feudal bondage out
In a few years. "But," mocked the gentry,
"The servitude is private property.
Then by what right the government may
Take private property away?"

The gentry lived in this assurance
Until the very final hour;
And their customary arrogance
Diminished not in any manner.
And, as it happens in the summer,
When the west portion of the sky
Is black with thick clouds, like a wall,
Which grimly threaten, drawing nigh,
With thunder seething, distance-dull,
But here the scorching sun keeps shining,
Straining to give us its full measure—
The lords thus kept up their pressure
To the last moment most severely,
When men were on their way already
To ring the bells in joyful tidings.

III

Lord Myhucki—Cui bono?

Thus from this period distressing,
From my old memory is served
A dreadful and unseemly happening
From the likes of which may God preserve!
How Lord Myhucki, I remember,
Played on the village his mean jest;
I recollect the tears and clamor
Which of this jesting were the cost.

But listen now! 'Tis not the reason,
When I of past events now speak,
That you, perchance, upon the children
For their blind parents' vengeance wreak.
God judge them! They've had their penance
For their own blindness. Look, to wit,
Of our Lord a mere rememberance
Is all that's left; and look at that
Great manse of stone that we assembled,
Of which our Squire sometimes said

"My fortress"; where his subjects trembled,
Where oftentimes musicians fiddled
And gentlefolk the whole night gamboled,
Is now an inn; in rooms once noble
Today Jew-jabbering is heard.

It's God's revenge for our misery!
And when today of lordly knavery
I thus relate, it's not because
I'm trying to arouse your ire
And let thoughts of revenge bemire
This hallowed gain in freedom's cause . . .
My good old dears, the sole intention
Of your old father's recollections—
A history of modest length—
Is meant to boost your pluck and strength.

For evil's not asleep completely!
Once loudly-boldly, and once softly,
It creeps toward our towns in stealth.
Who knows, but you may yet be living
Through such distressing, dreadful days,
It may appear to human beings:
Now we must surely lose our lives!
Truth has been lost, good life's succumbed,
And people's will has been enchained;
Injustice everywhere prevails.

At such a moment, my dear children,
Recall my present narrative
And keep in mind these words of wisdom
Which I from my experience give.
The very time injustice cruel
The highest rears its vicious head;
The very time when flesh in shackles
Hurts most severely, and when people's
Opinion's mute, as though struck dumb,
And all around is darkest gloom,
No hope a new day shall dawn soon—
Precisely then, keep up reliance
On hope; stay firm in the assurance
That into dust shall crumble the prison.
Don't countenance evil and injustice,
Don't drop your hands in sheer despondence,
And from a yoke find ways to freedom.

IV

Lord Myhucki's qualities—The leasee—
"Someone's agitating"

Myhucki was a rich landowner,
Although one village was his base;

His family background was unknown here.
Because the peasants he could squeeze,
Exacted tribute without mercy,
Kept count of work days exemplarily,
Would never give them a free spell—
His people destitute; he's wealthy—
The Lord was famed among the gentry
As one who ran his business well.

At times, as often in the winter,
The fields and barns provide no labor,
For all is done, no wood to cut;
Since he might forfeit corvee days,
The Lord would order: "Plow the ice!"
Lest peasants sleep in their huts . . .

He cared for the peasants, be it stated;
His oxen, horses got the same.
Three wagonloads of wood he granted
In winter: warmed the peasant's frame;
In springtime, with bread grains supported,
Lest summer hunger make them faint.

He loved when peasants had their vigor,
To work and talk were quick and eager,
And loved to dance and sing and laugh.
He hated peasants too well-heeled
And taciturn and full of zeal,
And literate peasants drew his wrath.

"When the peasant knows his farming chores,
Can whirl his wench around the floor,
And knows the basic texts Divine,
To teach him letters there's no need;
For when the peasant starts to read,
Who'll tend the manor's herd of swine?"

Although he seems to have insisted
That every serf keep up to snuff,
He kept distilling booze despite it;
And every batch he'd divvy up
Among the village households all.
Each dwelling got as many pecks
As it had souls: both boys and girls,
The oldsters counted, children small.
The price of this unwanted booze
Was duly charged against each home—
A feudal burden to be borne;
You pay in labor or in crowns.
Throw the stuff out, if you so choose,
But don't you ever dare re-sell.

The lord had a leasee as well
Who with the Lord made common cause.
He drew the people to the inn
With music. And the population
Lost here its wits and overcoats
And boots; the girls, their innocence,
And married women—chicken eggs;
The Elder's court was here in session.
The Jew, delighted, smacked his lips.

Year in, year out in similar manner,
This manor enterprise did bloom—
But suddenly the inn got quieter:
The serfs were overcome with gloom.
To the Lord's distress, they showed a knack
Toward uncertain brooding moods:
They do their work, and bear their load,
Each one attentive, each one quick
(If not, the whip shall score your back.)
But somehow quiet, taciturn,
Nay, even grim, as though within
Their inmost souls, there gnawed a worm;
As though a new mysterious cause
There were astir in murk obscure:
Its touch is noticed everywhere,
The eye, alas, can't see a thing.

The music doesn't seem to please
The young; now at the inn there are
Only those whom long feudal training
Has penetrated to the bones.
The Jew runs to the Lord, complaining:
"How can I pay the rent?" he groans.

Indeed; for some time now, the Squire
Observed the change that came about
In people; beatings, raving, shouts
Changed nothing. Soon he had no doubt
This was indeed no laughing matter.
The Lord knew well: when peasants drink
And sing and work without a rest
And laugh and jest, in many a thing,
They bear resemblance to the beasts,
Which all their lives in harness spend,
Are overjoyed when men augment
Their fodder with some grains of grist.
But when their mood turns to dejection,
Their heads hang down in sheer despair,
When they brood over their condition,
Consult their friends about solutions—
Then better tremble and beware!

For thought and popular enlightenment
And of like-minded men agreement
Are dreaded enemies of those
Whose wealth and comfort and contentment
Are based on human sweat and tears.
The Lord thus gravely cogitated
Over this puzzle day and night,
Once angry, then again dejected,
As though his heart sensed future plight.
Then he leaped up and even shouted:
"There's agitation here, I bet!"

V

Who's responsible for agitation?—
Polish emissaries—
Ukrainian people—
"The Priest agitates."

"It's agitators!" God in Heaven!
Who wasn't suspect in those days!
Officials put some lords in prison
And charged them with subversive action.
The lords broadcast their accusation:
The peasants were in government pay,
With orders all the lords to slay.
One group tried to accuse the Jews,
Some others dragged in Jesuits,
Still others set to spread the news:
"It's Democrats! It's Communists!
It's emissaries!" Rumors buzzed.

Amidst these rifts and arguments,
The peasant stood, his shoulders bent,
Both mute and blind, yet still a threat.
For after centuries of peace,
The peasant-hurricane looked dread
And seemed to strike without a cause.
He rose and with his brothers' blood
His native land he painted red.

There was abundant evidence:
A dirty hand, to us still hidden,
On purpose reached the very bottom
Of people's souls, with impertinence,
And godlessly dredged up most wicked,
The wildest passions, to befool
Men's reason, and to render dull
Men's feelings; and it pressured, guided
Uncomprehending hands to action.

Although since Tarnów's* conflagration
A year had passed; although kept count
Cengliewicz† of his days; Dembowski†
By the Vistula ‡ rotted in the ground;
On Gallows Hill at Lvov ** had found
Eternal rest the rebel Wiszniowski†—
But still there passed across the nation
Cold shivers, constant vigilance,
Expectance of fresh violence.
Each morn to God they offered grace
The night had passed without explosion.

It was as if a feverish patient
After a serious operation—
Who trembles sleeping and awake,
Who jumps and wakes at nary a touch,
Knows not himself what scares so much,
Reacting merely to his aches—
After the carnage, for two years,
Our country lived through difficult times;
It bore in agony severe
The old world's difficult demise.

Another interesting feature!
Although throughout those dreadful days
Ukrainians weren't quick to slay—
(Of Horozhana, I shall venture,
The gentry came to grief out there
Primarily because they bore
The guilt for the attack on peasants.)—
And even sometimes took a stance
In their local lords's defence
Against Mazovian insurgents;
In spite of this, in our parts,
The peasant wasn't looked upon
By gentry any kindlier than
He had been in Mazovian lands.

They thought, of course: what happened there
But yesterday may happen here;
Much worse, for this is alien ground.
Thus wild rumors wouldn't cease,
Kept up the mood of tense unease;
Bad jitters, too, affected all.
It was as though the darkest clouds
Hung over the village, with lightning bolts
About to strike; that year, our lords
But mutinous serfs had on their minds.

Thus is was not surprising, when
Myhucki saw his subjects' humor
And heard how peasants all began
To skirt his inn, from drink abstain—
"It's mutiny!" he cried with fervor.
Who was behind it? In succession,
He went through all the younger, braver
Men, a long time under suspicion,
But none of them, in any manner,
Had given lately any reason
To be held guilty in this matter.

Did a commissioner through the region
Pass lately? Or perhaps a letter
Someone from town to them did bring?
Or did the serfs, by any chance,
Convene a secret conference?
No one had heard. "O damn this thing!"
The Squire figures this and that,
Standing mute there in his salon.
Frustration showed in his drooped head;
He whistled from the mental strain.
Then he jumped up and with his hand
He struck against his forehead twice:
"I'm stupid!" quoth he. "Here I stand;
In agony, I wrench my mind
As to who spoils the populace;

*Tarnów is a city in Poland. In 1848, the city belonged to the Austro-Hungarian Empire as a result of the division of Poland in the 1790s, between Austria-Hungary, Russia, and Prussia. A scene of disturbances and demonstrations during the last days of the Metternich regime, 1846–48, immediately before the abolition of feudal servitude in Austria-Hungary.

† Cengliewicz, Dembowski, Wiszniowski—Polish terrorists in the fight against Austro-Hungarian oppression. Cengliewicz was jailed in the fortress of Kufstein (Tyrol) and Dembowski and Wiszniowski were executed for their activities by the Austrian authorities.

‡ The principal river of Poland, Wisla (Vistula).

** Lvov, a city in Ukraine; capital of West Ukraine. During the Austro-Hungarian rule, Lvov was the principal city of the Province Galicia, seat of the provincial government.

From beyond chains of distant hills
In fancy hostile penetration,
And yet here, on the spot, I fail
To stem the source of insurrection!
The emissary is not far;
Right here's the principal instigator.
O sapperment! Warum nicht gar!*
The Priest is our agitator!"

VI

The old Ukrainian Priest—
The Priest as the teacher—
The Priest's audience with the Lord

Our Priest was of the old and meek,
Old-fashioned, poorly educated,
In Lutsk or Kholm † yet consecrated,
Accustomed both to live and work
Among the serfs; who glanced with terror
In the direction of the manor,
And bowed low when he saw his Lord,
And ever sensed from his demeanor
That he was alien; no friend.

Although there was no plain avoidance,
The Lord maintained his usual distance,
Disdained religious observance,
And when there happened an occasion
To see the priest for a discussion,
The Lord would call him to the hall,
But keep outside his mansion's walls.

The only thing such priests then stood
To gain from all this serf priesthood
Was freedom from the feudal burdens.
With other peasants land they shared
Took for church fees what people spared,
Earned daily bread with their own hands.

The oldster, our priest, had never
Thought or envisioned in his dreams
That he would live to see the hour
When to the master of the manor
A rabble rouser he would seem.
It was to be! A childless widower,
He'd lived among us many a year
Before the thought in him did stir
That he should be an educator.

Although himself of little learning,
But when the labor in the field
Became too much, he felt a yearning
At least to teach the young to read.

No sooner said than done; at once
He summoned to him all the children:
In summer to the fields and woods
And to his dwelling in the winter.
At first he didn't make them sit
With books, to study their letters—
It could have been that in the writ
He seldom pored himself, or thought
That bookish learning didn't matter—
He roused the children's interest
With fairy tales and little stories
And drew attention to this blest
Great God's creation—our world,
In his repeated observations.
At every step, he always could
Find things that called for their attention.
Whatever it was, a word or two
He'd say about it, and he knew
From life to tie in fitting instants
Or to derive a useful lesson.
He could bestir thus all the infants,
Take their hands and give direction,
Awaken their minds to thought,
Provoke them till they would respond—
In consequence, the little tots
Flocked to him, tattered and barefoot,
As gladly as, consumed by thirst,
Sheep run in summer to a pond.

'Tis not the tale in its entirety:
For to the quarters of the priest
They came not wholly in the quest
Of learning; more for the hospitality
Of cheerful, happy noon repasts.
At a table set in spacious quarters,
The priest, domestics, all together,
Like one big clan, were seated jointly,
And all the servants bantered freely.
Like their own dad, the Reverend
Would here admonish, there instruct,
How to do things, or how to act.
The children listened, and to them,
At home accustomed to behold
And bear the smoke and dirt and cold,

*Damn it! And why not?
†Ukrainian Catholic seats of bishops.

64

And hear the knock each morning early,
The flunkeys' shouts: "Is necessary
The knout to make you come along?"
Accustomed to the never ceasing
Parental sorrow and heartrending
Sad sighs that were the only song—
But in this corner all gleamed bright;
In cozy, tidy calm unbroken
Unpleasant words were never spoken.
The infants' breast expanded wide
And somehow their minds grew strong.

They rise and go outdoors to play,
Then settle down and rest a bit.
The priest then teaches them to read:
From willow twigs, the children lay
Gigantic letters on the sand,
And then a booklet of some kind
He brings outside; at once they crowd,
Peer in the volume on display,
Familiar letters they make out,
Into familiar words array.

It is in God's domain, no doubt,
To grant these various gifts to people:
One man receives a clear, strong mind,
In the whole world without an equal;
Another's swarming thoughts remind
Of cloud-ascending soaring eagles;
Still others get such golden hands:
The eyes can see, the hands can fashion;
But what endowment get the men
So capable of teaching children?
Methinks, into their treasure trove
Was placed the greatest share of love.
Among the people, many a year
I lived, and teachers crossed my paths,
But of a teacher I didn't hear
Who could behave with little tots
As did our now departed Father.
And in the village: what a feast,
A double treat he served for Easter,
When our boys sang in harmony
In church, and then each boy in turn
One paragraph read from the Acts,
Reciting from the choir loft.
The folk buzzed like a swarm of bees
In summer. Mothers shed a tear:
"We never saw a thing like this!
Look at our boys! Not fruitlessly
They eat their porridge! The old dear
Has really taught them!" Orderless,

The people formed a joyous crowd.
The fathers, in deliberation
How to show their appreciation
To their Priest. Ere of one mind
They were, a flunkey with the news
Ran to the hall, to tell his master.

The Lord came not to church because
He wouldn't stand with 'cattle' together.
The service ended, then was blessed
The Easter bread; but lo! there comes
A manor messenger to the Priest:
"The Lord will speak to you at once!"
The Priest set out. The congregation
Fell silent, saddened and depressed.
An unknown evil's visitation
Was imminent, though no one sinned.
They all were going to escort
The Priest, but he declined, to say:
"There is no need to gall the Lord."
He crossed himself and went away.

He's gone. With blessed bread, provisions,
Outside the church awaits his flock.
After a while, he comes back.
"God love you, people! Christ is risen!
Now all of you go home, d'you hear?
It's nothing serious; have no fear!
The Lord but asked me, how dared I,
Without official permission,
To start a school; and I replied,
There is no school, and only I,
Quite privately—no compensation—
Am teaching children how to read.
"I have no power to forbid
This thing," replied the Lord at length.
"But I advise you as a friend:
Why don't you drop this pointless matter?"
"This work I never would have started,"
Thus I the gentleman retorted,
"If there had not been sent a letter
From the consistory to me:
'Not only teach all village children,
When possible, new schools, too, open.' "
"Indeed? About this we shall see!"
His Lordship said, and with his hand
He gave a sign that for today
The talk was over. "Go in peace!
Don't be afraid! And all you boys
Come to my house for the holidays!
Now go; don't stand around like this.
Christ's risen! Now be on your way!"

And from that very morning on,
Between the village and the Lord
A constant silent war began.
It was the first time that we'd heard
That there were things he couldn't deny,
Although he owned the village land.
And we, for centuries on end,
Had lived, and like a field of rye,
Continued with the wind to bend
To the mighty blast of lordly words.
It never even had occured
To serfs to counter lords' decisions;
And if one could no longer stand
The slavery, the persecutions,
He chucked it all and fled abroad,
And left his family behind,
To face more horrible privations.
But suddenly: "I can't forbid."
This meant: above him was a might
Of which he also was afraid,
And not allowed to disregard.

On hearing this, our congregation
As though regained its second breath.
Throughout the Easter, in the huts
Went on most lively group discussions:
"We must have schooling for our kids;
This thing the Lord dare not forbid!"
So boldly now the peasants rumbled
Who yesterday with terror trembled:
"A school is badly needed here!
Are we indeed among the last
That our own children even must
This heavy yoke forever bear?"
But—I cannot conceal the truth—
There were men older, circumspect
Who tried such noisy talk to quell:
"Why are you raising all this fuss
And keep repeating this one phrase:
'He daren't!' Just you wait a spell,
And he will show you how he dares!
Be quiet, rather, and beware
Lest mortal flesh be called to pay
For all this foolishness!"

Dejected

On hearing this were hearts most stout.
On some of them had not yet healed
The bruises from the lordly knout.
Yet this time they just couldn't hide
From wolves and stay out of the woods,
So in the end they did decide

In town to seek advice and aid
From the Commissioner: if they could
Set up and run a village school,
Contrary to the lordly will.

We had a German Commissioner,
Of mature years a gentleman,
And comical. When his affairs
At a late hour brought him here,
However close, the Hall he'd shun,
Stop at a peasant's house. On jelly
And *borshch, varenyky, lohaza*
He'd dine, and chat. "I'll tell you truly,
I love your peasants," he'd profess.
"Ten years long Ukrainian bread
I've eaten. You've won my regard,
Good people, but your lords are bad.
It's worrisome, I'll tell you, though;
If the Lord leans on you too much,
Come see me—all the rest I'll know—
And I shall deal him such a blow
He'll chew his fingertips with rage."

I don't know why, with vicious fury,
With his whole being, all his blood,
The man could not abide the gentry;
Perhaps because he never could
Attune himself to their quirks
And felt a stranger among them,
Whilst they had lofty looks for him
And their arrogant quips that irked
With which to humble the poor man.
Behind his back, they also whispered
He'd once had a predicament
In which from gentlefolk he suffered
Fear, injuries, embarrassment.
A fact must, surely, back the rumor,
That for no reason but his humor,
A lord had served him with a lager
And almost brought about his end.

He was, of course, a young man then,
Had just been given his promotion,
He worked with squires hand-in-hand,
For he'd developed close relations
With one who had a little girl,
No only child, yet so lovely,
To boot, so playful, always jolly,
And to him not at all unfriendly—
A mischievous delightful doll.

The commissioner being well acquainted

With the lord was often entertained.
He came officially at first,
Then was invited as a guest.
While amusing the young misses,
Minding decorum, proper distance,
To Mania once he did confess
The greatest yearning of his life:
For Mania to become his wife.
Maniusia's color heightened slightly,
She smiled wordlessly and sweetly,
And finally responded softly:
*"Pomów pan z mamcią,"** and was gone.

The man was left alone to wait,
But soon he heard a heavy gait:
Milady entered the salon.
"Wiem, to pan ma się to Maniusi.
To bardzo dobrze, ale musi
Pan z ojcem mowić, bo bez niego
Nie decyduję sama tego."†

In half an hour's time he sat
Already in the squire's chamber,
But all he did was watch and wait
As guests at table bet and played
One hand of whist after another.
He waited thus two hours at least
Before the game broke up at last.
The gentry left. And then the master
One of his servants summoned up:
"Hey, Michael, here, come, hurry up!
Fetch me a bottle of strong ale,
Two glasses, and some *wurst* as well;
Alert the stable boys, to say—
I mean, tell Hryn, the groom, of course—
To saddle the Commissioner's horse
And ready it without delay."
The man fulfilled the lord's desire,
And very cheerfully, the squire
Beside his guest pulled up a chair,
Of this and that began to chatter.
In silence sat the Commissioner,
Waiting; the host refreshed his beer,
But of the very delicate matter
The Commissioner had sat afoot
The squire said absolutely naught.

The glasses drained; the groom reports
The steed's awaiting their pleasure;
His lordship charmingly insists:
"But drink, sir, please, just half a measure!"
The Commissioner drank up than and rose;
After a silence, this he posed:
*"No jakże pan dobrodziej myśli**
W tej sprawie co mówiła pani?"
"O proszę, proszę, towar tani!
Dziś jeszcze, teraz, zaraz w nocy
Zarządzę wszystko, co w mej mocy,
Byśmy na dobre oba wyszli."‡

And letting things remain at that,
He walked the German to his steed,
Into the saddle gave a boost,
And patted on the back, so friendly,
Then mumbled something indistinctly;
Without a warning, in a trice,
A nettle plant of moderate size,
Under the horse's tail he thrust.

"Farewell, then, sir! And may God bless
And lead you home without distress!"
He said and whistled. The horse snapped
The bridle, jumped and tore away.
The Commissioner had no time to pray,
To bid farewell, or thanks to say;
He merely grabbed the horse's mane
And left the yard, like a hurricane.

The race was smooth on the level plain,
But soon he ran across a ditch
And left the saddle, the poor wretch,
And here passed out from cruel pain.
There on the morrow he was found,
In a cart driven to his town.
A severe fever he endured,
Long to a colic he was prone,
He coughed then for five years at least,
And for the future he vowed fast
Never to mount a steed or mare
And leave all Polish girls alone.

From that day on for evermore,
An unconcealed fierce rage he bore,
Residing in his inmost being.

*"Sir, talk to Mommy."
†"I know, you, sir, like Manusia. That's very nice, but you must talk to her Father. Without him I can't make such a decision."
‡"Well, sir, what is your opinion in the matter Madam mentioned?"
"Of course, please, the merchandise is chéap! Today, this very night, I'll order everything in my power, so that it's favorable to both of us."

On lordly thresholds he ne'er tread,
Involved the gentry where he could
In legalistic skirmishing.
In regional administration,
His voice much as the prefect's weighed,
And there was hardly e'er a day
That didn't bring to his attention
Some nasty twisted altercation:
The lords and serfs in an affray.

In many instances—no wonder—
He touched the gentry where it hurt!
To seek from his advice and succor
From every village flocked the serfs.
The squires did whatever they could
To oust him, to get rid of him:
On the governor called, to intercede,
Denounced him, rumors spread abroad:
He riled the serfs; that of their own
The gentry was unsure; soon would
The peasantry again shed blood;
They scorned their feudal obligations.
Such letters vanished without trace,
Brought the Commissioner no disgrace,
Could not besmirch his reputation.
For the whole region was at peace.
The lords, in the eyes of the government,
Earned failing marks in deportment;
The Commissioner ignored all this.

It was to him that we appealed
For help. He gasped in admiration
When our peasant brain creation
Was bared to him. "Go on and build!
Don't be afraid! Let the Lord dare
To stop you; then he'll get to hear
Things not heard ever in his life.
Build! For it is royal will
That every village have a school;
Peasants must learn to read and write!"

These words so pleasant were to us
As to the thirsty water fine;
As though grace truly real, divine
Shone on our village. Men at once
Began to meet and hold discussions,
Collecting school fees, contributions,
As though the Lord existed not.

Well, we were to discover soon:
Into the fire from the pan!
The lord found out exactly what

They buzzed about; and twenty prominent
Leaders of the "scholastic movement"
He summoned; saying not a word,
He had each one of them stretched out
And ordered that they be dished out
Each twenty good ones with the rod.

He said then: "It has reached my ears
You're building now a school, dear sirs!
Right on, I say! You're doing well!
You've even started a collection?
This, on account, is my donation.
Was it sufficient? Pray tell!"
Smiling, he slowly through his teeth
Forced these words; then his face turned
    white,
His body shook, his lips a slit,
His eyes burned with an ominous light.

"You mugs," he shouted, "bloody vipers!
You need a school? Your real intentions
I know too well! It isn't letters
You crave—but freedom! Bloody peasants!
You snakes think, 'we shall get a taste
Of schooling; then who'll dare to chase
Us to corvee work.' Now be gone!
Avoid my clutches, unless bitter
Trouble you want; and if the news
Reaches me that you choose to waste
Time on this stupid school, by Zeus,
I shall then really cook your goose
So thoroughly, your heads will spin."

This time these tactics didn't pay:
To scare with beatings he had tried;
Instead, he stirred us more. "We'll die
If that's our fate," we raised a cry,
"But this time he won't get away!
We won't abandon our truth!"
For grave and wilful battery,
They filed a complaint forthwith
Against the Lord. An inquiry
Came from the state. He'd rave and shout
But wasn't generous with the knout
Our school became reality.

But here our troubles didn't end.
To find a teacher—the next step;
Our priest alone just couldn't cope.
As soon as we a man could find,
The Lord in no time, one-two-three,
Would draft him in the military,

Or else cause him to change his mind,
Take manor work or scare him away.
Sometimes he would on a school day
Send manor men who were instructed
That learning children be disrupted
And to the orchards to be sent,
To pick bugs, caterpillar tents.
Nor stood we for the Lord's transgressions.
We kept on sending our petitions.
The Commissioner stood us in good stead,
Got often under the Lord's skin.
The Lord placed all the blame on him,
Grew as an arch-foe to regard
"The Kraut." The enmity thus seethed
Between them long, until Fate wished
To mock them most maliciously:
In a strange house they faced each other.
Seeing "the Kraut," he instantly
Leaped at the man and took a swing;
Before the other guests could hinder,
He slugged the German on the chin.

A scandal!—and who can discover
How the Lord ever smoothed it over?
But as for the indignity—
Deferring, waiting for a chance,
The Commissioner did get his revenge
On the Lord, with great severity.

Two years continued the turmoil.
Quite a few changes came meanwhile
Within the village. The innkeeper
Died, and a new man took it over,
One hellish shrewd. For it was he
Who caused the Squire to agree
At lower rates to sell the booze.
"The rate of drinking will increase;
And in a drunk community
All insurrection will soon cease."

Through such Jew trickery, indeed,
Many of us fell for his ruse.
The Jew himself, down at the inn,
To drunks his word keeps dinning in:
"The priest tricks you. Shame on you all!
Why do you send to school your kids?
Why do you bicker with the Lord?
Insisting on this school's no good!
To hell with it! Who needs this school?"

Thus the contagion commenced
From the inn, slowly, and moved hence
From house to house. There never would
Be now concordance anymore
In our ranks. Fewer than before
Attended school. The neighborhood
Seemed somehow silent and morose—
Save for the drunken songs, of course—
Dragging the yoke of servitude.
The noble movement, it appeared,
That had the populace bestirred
Had gone now with the wind for good.

VIII

Sobriety in the village—
The Lord and the Priest—
A sharp exchange—
The Priest's conscience—
The Lord travels to Lvov

Then suddenly, out of the blue,
The village witnessed something new:
The inn stood empty; singing ceased.
Somehow the people lost their cheer,
In silence their suffering bore.
The Lord at once saw that all this
Boded no good; though at first sight
He knew not nor could even guess
What kind of and where from this blight
Came blowing on the populace.

Still, sure the Priest's the only one
Who sowed the seeds of discontent.
He was informed of the extent
Of all the work the Priest had done:
Whether a christening the occasion,
A burial, birthday celebration,
The Priest received an invitation
To all the functions; and at table
The conversation was the same.

"My children, now you must be able
To quit the inn. In heaven's name!
Through drink you're losing all your wits!
It is the devil's evil brew!
Pity yourselves! Come winter frosts,
And you have not a pair of boots;
Swelled, like a leech, though, is the Jew!
Now at your children cast an eye!

Ignorant, hungry, ill, unclad!
What's to become of them? Today,
In the world light, not gloom, holds sway.
It's not enough to turn the clods
Of furrows over; you must learn
To talk to men in human terms.
Demand of others a fair break!
Stand up for own and common weal,
For how can one with life's strife deal
When he's untaught—an ignorant drunk?"

Reported those of manor servants
At times on Sundays in attendance
How the Priest over and again
About sobriety intoned,
The inns, the Jews, the booze condemned,
And said, now really was the time
To give up totally all drinking.

The Lord stopped, as though struck by
    lightning,
When he heard this. "So, that's the gist!
He wants to stop all their imbibing.
Why should I bother to distill?
P'raps pour it to the pigs as swill?
It's all the same to our Priest,
But not to me, he may be sure!
Into my pocket he sees fit
Quite openly to stick his mitts
The source of income most secure
He undermines! Hey, reverend father.
Satan himself won't stand such bother!
Get me the Priest here, right away!"

And while waiting, highly wroth,
He paced the chamber back and forth,
He spat, he sat, he rose again.
The parson came, made his obeisance,
And halted humbly at the entrance,
And in his hands he held his hat;
Alarm and shyness in his gaze,
All color drained from his white face,
As though his pluck sank to his feet.
As one regards some stray brown mutt—
Such a poor figure the Priest cut—
The Lord gazed down with a stern look
Upon the priest and spat. Relaxed,
Twice more his room the Lord traversed;
The Priest stood, held his tongue, and shook.

The Lord came near the Priest at length
And over him his tall frame bent,
And spoke in strident tones and harsh:
"Hey, padre, have you lost your smarts,
Or have you had no brain from birth?
Or have you heard some balderdash?
Why of free choice d'you stick your head
Into the very nets I spread?
Is this why your authority
Has made you parson of this place,
So that you rouse the populace
Against me to insurgency,
And teach to steal my property?"

The Priest sagged visibly at this,
Atremble made the sign of the cross,
But looked straight in the Squire's eyes.
"Your gracious lordship has been lied to,"
He answered shyly.

                "How lied to?
Is it a lie, then, would you say,
That you in church and out do prattle
To the peasants here most senseless twaddle
And do harangue them every day
That they should stop all their drinking?"

"That's true."

                "But if the peasant pay
Attention to your words, then what
Am I to do with my distilling?"

"That's not my business."

                "That's the point!
You wash your hands! To undercut
My income, stir the peasant's wrath,
Is that your business?"

                "My own will
Matters here not; I beg your pardon.
My priestly office does compel
To do my duty. On the farm,
In peasant work in house and barn
And storeroom, I don't interfere;
To care for their souls, to lead
On paths of moral rectitude,
That is my business, my dear sir!"

"Ah, esteemed sir, such fiddle-faddle;
All that is merely empty babble.
This is my word, I won't repeat it:
On this dumb temperance not one word
After today I wish to hear.
Not I; not people! Better drop it!"

"I'd gladly drop this whole affair—
Would not have started the whole matter—
Had there not been a direct order
From the consistory, very clear."

"What devil is this?" With a curse,
The Lord jumped, as if on hot coals
"Those filthy prelates have resolved,
It would appear, that our whole class
Go beg for alms. Just let me see
This order now. So God help me,
I'll see that their end is sealed!
On the expenses I won't stint,
Expose them to the government,
To the Emperor even I'll appeal!"

And quoth the Priest: "The mentioned order
From the consistory can't be shown.
It went 'round as a circular letter;
I failed to jot the number down."

"Aha, you pope," the Lord cried angrily,
"You lie! I have exposed quite clearly
Your lies! Of course, there was no letter
From the consistory on this matter
Which would have ordered such a deed.
You know: on pain of punishment,
Your cantor brings such documents
Each time one comes, for me to read.
That's how you are! To the peasantry
You give rebellious, lawless talks,
Then you invoke authority
And try to hide behind its back.
And what a pose he strikes: so saintly,
'I wouldn't have started the whole story!'
But just you wait; you will be sorry
That you have challenged me so slyly."

But strangely, though, this voice irate
And all these stinging, painful words
Designed, it seemed, to devastate,
To bend, and to humiliate,
To knock the priest down to the earth,
Had a contrary consequence:
Infused the poor wretch with new life.

He straightened out; his countenance,
Ere now aquake, turned luminous.
He faced the Lord. A courteous
Great bow he made and spoke up: "If
I've acted in a way contrary
To law, I'll answer without fail.
I only do what God's great glory
Commands me. At my age I stand
With my life drawing to an end,
Thus I am not concerned at all
With any threats. I do not worry.
My conscience transcends it all."

Having said this, once more he bowed
And then withdrew, composed and slow.
The Lord, however, gnashed his teeth.
"Pope, wait a while! For this trick
You'll feel my hand yet on your back,"
Over and over he'd repeat
And curse and wish the Priest in hell . . .
After regaining self-control
In his mind he began to weigh
How he would carry out his boasts
And threats. From rage almost
Real teardrops welled up in his eyes,
When he discovered that the parson,
For all his teaching and his sermons,
Could not be punished readily.

Should he to the consistory
Appeal, to make the man desist,
Get relocation for the priest,
Or punishment? He was averse.
Or at the district chancery
Complain about him? There's no reason
To hope to find there friendly ears.
The Commissioner's there, who gladly would
Rip the Lord's last shirt off his back!
"No," the Lord thought, "I see the track
On which this matter must proceed:
We'll go to Lvov! There, after all,
Are contracts, and the Land Assembly,
Parties . . . The mustard seed I'll sell
And thus get hold of ready money.
My wife shall find amusements,
For long the poor thing's voiced complaints:
She's wilting from *ennui* at home.
The governor I'll see personally
And tell him most exhaustively
Of everything. I knew him when . . .
Some years ago he was oft here
When he was stationed in Sambir

As the Commissioner. Wait you, peasants!
And you pope, too! For times unpleasant
Await you! I'll turn on the heat!
There shall be for you no recourse,
No help from begging, God, or tears,
Or from that bloody toothless Kraut!"

IX

The Lord and his lady left so fast
For Lvov, they stirred a cloud of dust.
The people's spirits were uplifted,
As though a close miasmic pall
Had quit the town. Although, exacted
By flunkeys in sheer pain and toil,
They'd pay tomorrow. That's humanity:
It yearns for change. After daylight bright,
Its only wish: to see the night.
It cannot stand monotony.
Let it be worse, but different.
The servitude may still torment
Without the Lord much more, and yet
In every house, in every street,
You talked and breathed with less restraint.

Meanwhile the parson is no slouch,
Of total abstinence does preach,
And presses hard his flock to pledge
To give up drinking altogether.
In silence, they mull matters over.
It all appears to them so strange:
How can the peasant quit all liquor?
Some were afraid that the Lord may
Force them to break the solemn oath.
"Who knows for certain here, forsooth,"
These poor unfortunates would say,
"That manor rules do not prescribe
That every peasant must imbibe?"

The Priest explains it all in vain.
An oath, you see, is a dreadful deal:
You may well forfeit your body and soul.
The priest saw that he couldn't sway
Them this way; so he turned elsewhere:
Namely, he asked the Commissioner
To come and visit them one day.
The Commissioner jumped up from his chair
At the good news he got to hear.
"*Ja, so*! That's it! That is the way!

You should have done it long ago!
You're good, sincere, and modest folk!
But if for *vodka* is their love,
*Vergeblich** will be all your work."

The Commissioner, then, in combination
With the Priest agreed just what to do,
Then left a generous donation.
But secretly he was so glad
How it would undercut the Lord
When peasants ceased to drink his brew.

Thus once on Sunday, after Mass,
The people coming out of church,
Then men stood as was customary
Along the edge of the cemetery,
All eager for the local news.
But lo! not far we all espied
The Commissioner's gig and recognized
Him, heading straight for our group.
In uniform including a sword,
He greeted us and spoke these words:
"How are you? All is well, I trust?"

"We thank you, sir."

        "Now, well, well, well . . .
I have a word I'd like to tell
To you—a tiny word at most.
They tell me that your Reverend
Has talked to people over here
That *vodka* drinking you forswear.
That's very fine! Full steam ahead!
Have courage! You're afraid to face
Your Squire's wild shouts and noise?
Nix draus!† Let's see what he can do!
Did you imagine that the Lord
Can force you all to drink his brew?
Nix draus! Now fear not! God forbid!
I'll tell you: The Imperial will
Decrees that peasants be content,
With flocks, abundant fields to till,
And toward schooling show a bent.
Our emperor wants—now, do you hear?—
To set you free, to free you all!
But if you drink this alcohol,
He'll say: 'These people aren't worthy
To be set free yet.' Understand?

*In vain, for nothing.

†Nothing doing.

Now you go back to the work at hand!
Do as you please! Good-bye, all! Cheers!"

It is beyond me to express
How powerfully did he impress
These words on the minds of all the serfs.
"The Emperor says personally
'Don't drink!'—he wants to set us free!
The Lord, the inn, are naught to us!"

It was as though across the village
Thunder had rolled; now no one ate
The news seemed to intoxicate:
They'd soon be free. To the parsonage
In a solid wall, they all were borne.
Our Reverend Father's humble dwelling
They jammed soon, like a noisy swarm.
In the hubbub there, there was no telling
Who spoke or what they said, at all.
They chanted: "Father, freedom, freedom!"
"We shall be free!" and "Down with serfdom!
Our woes be gone! Our bodies and souls
We pledge to the emperor; he accords
Us freedom! Let the bells ring now!
Come now and lead us in our vow!
From this day on, both small and sere,
We pledge before you and our god:
Not a drop for all eternity.
We want to deserve our liberty!
Now, let us go, O Father dear!"

The poor Priest paled, for he was frightened.
He knew not what this change had wrought
In the people. Joy and cries concordant
Attested that we were in truth
Performing an important act.
He had not heard of any freedom.
Instead, the Lord had really driven
Fear into him; and in his threat
To see his Governor, the King—no less—
In his attempts to find redress
Against the Priest, he sensed distress.
For to himself he couldn't deny
That to the Lord he'd told a lie.
There was no writ from the consistory
Which would have ordered him to teach
Sobriety—to boot: to inveigle
The peasantry an oath to pledge.

The Oldster's heart could well foresee:
The Squire, if he were inclined,
Could really cause a deal of trouble.
And at St. George's* no one would lend
The least support; nay, his superiors
Would cast the first stone and condemn
The work he had done as "improper."
The Priest himself they would abandon
To public scorn. That was the reason
For all his fears. If there, today,
Among the serfs were a commotion,
The Lord would not proceed to weigh
The causes that the folk could sway,
And set disturbances aflame.
He'd say: "It is the pope; no question."
And the poor Parson'd bear the blame.

His hands at rest upon his crook,
He stood there silent. It took long
To still the noise of the village throng.
"What ails you?" finally he spoke.
"Hey, children, what, by God, is wrong?
What are you up to? Where's the freedom?
Surely, it's dreams, imagination?"

"No dreams," the people spoke in unison,
"It is in truth a revelation.
Mr. Commissioner came along
Not long ago and personally
Told us of it. Officially.
He wouldn't tell us what is wrong!"

"What kind of message did he bring?"

"He said the same as you do, Sir:
That we should drink no alcohol.
Then added that the Emperor
Would like, he said, to free us all."

"Well, and what else?"

                    "That's all he said."

"Fools, fools! And this has made you glad?
You really are prize muttonheads!
The Emperor wishes—God in Heaven!
Of course he does! But whether he can?
And right away? You wait, poor man!

*St. George's Cathedral (*Svyatyi Your*) in Lvov, the seat of the Metropolitan Archbishop of the Ukrainian Catholic Church (1740–1946).

Here's a thing for you to ponder:
At home a father has three lads.
He wants their future to assure,
But three sons at once can't marry, for
They can't be dealt their equal shares,
While their father, in the winter
Has no provisions. So's a country:
Three sons as well has its King-Dad,
The serfs, the army, and the lords—
All equally in royal favor,
For all of them to royal glory
Contribute, and to national power.
The King to each extends his aid,
But cannot do it all at once.
To give you freedom would be great,
But who knows if the gentry might
Rise in revolt in consequence."

"What? A revolt? Let them but stir!
Satan won't know how they'll disappear.
Was last year's Lent too little yet?"

"Now, see how childishly unwise
You are; how little you would prize
This freedom, when such awful threats
You utter. No, my dears, relent!
Do not rely on your own strength!
No vengeance and no bloody knives
The Emperor wants. Your destiny
Entrust to him! He'll set you free,
Most surely, when the time arrives.
Believe me, dears, that shouts and commotion
Shall aid your adversaries only,
And you yourselves shall gallop blindly
Along the road toward destruction."

Downhearted, saddened were the peasants,
For what they heard rang so unpleasant
In their ears. But was there, then,
A thing to do? True, though unwelcome,
These words: the Emperor would give them
    freedom,
But it's uncertain if he can.
Many were saddened and downhearted
Because on their bodies smarted
The welts from their Master's whip.
Their skin, of course, advised them softly:
"Don't you, my friend, be over bold
Until in black on white you're told
That you no longer are a serf."

Thereupon groaned the whole assembly:
"What must we do then, Reverend Father?"

"Well, children, pray to the Creator,
Stay calm, and humbly wait in peace.
It won't be long now to endure!
And keep in strictest confidence
The things that the Commissioner
Has said today."

       "So be it settled!
But from today we'll drink no more.
The Emperor wants to test our mettle,
So we will show him, and therefore,
We are prepared today, right now,
To swear eternal abstinence."

"May God help you to keep your vow,
Defeat temptation's every chance.
My dears, there is a great deal to it—
It is no joke an oath to swear—
But do you know how you must do it?
St. Phillip's fast is almost here.
Each to yourself you make the vow
To drink no more; in peace and love
To live with people; harms and wrongs
Neither remember nor inflict.
Fight all the devilish temptations,
With constant patience put up with
All God sends for our transgressions.
Then just before the Christmas Holy,
Who is still eager, willing, stout,
Come to confession; then shall follow
The swearing of the solemn oath.
This is the test you must endure:
Two months' hard trial first for you.
You'll pass through it in order to
Prepare yourselves and enter pure
The coming year. And what this year
Brings in its train, who can now say?
Thus if you wish this oath to swear,
Come to our church on New Year's Day!"

They thought about it a few instants,
Then said, while making an obeisance:
"So be it your way! We are game!
We will endure some more misfortune,
But even if we're killed or tortured,
We'll never touch hard drink again."

X

The end of 1847—
The Lord and his lady return—
The Lord and the Manager—
The Lord and the Leasee

The end of the Forty-seventh year
Stood bright and clear. The deep snowfall
Was frozen hard as a threshing floor;
And every foothill's stream and rill
Through to the bottom was icebound.
The trees were cracking from the frost,
And every day there could be found
Wingéd things dead in snowy dust.
The present year was almost over,
With dire omens; we were fearing
That our hideous social order,
Firm and unshakable, shall rack
Our substance and persist forever.

Behind the ridge the sun was sinking
When we first heard the jangling bell.
On the bridge from behind a hill,
The Lord's sleigh showed, like a magic trick.
Wrapped up in blankets and in furs,
Their Lordships were now coming back.
The sound and the sight spread everywhere
In homes involuntary fear,
As chicks fear when they see a hawk.

The village passed the word around
"He must have brought with him some news.
Where did he tarry? Did he press
In fact some charges, blaming us
Before the Governor? What, in turn,
Did the Governor have him know?"
Thus whispering voices spread abroad
Among the people dark alarm;
Everyone cringed, expecting woe.

Meanwhile, over at the mansion
All hearts were seized with palpitation.
The servants there—pale, out of breath—
Ran in confusion back and forth,
As flies in boiling water dart.
For each one in his inmost heart
Was well aware of many sins,
The saints imploring silently:
"Let scales fall o'er his ears and eyes,
Lest he find out and hear and see.

Just this one time, the only time!
I'll pay for matins, Masses prime,
If Thou protect from harm poor me!"
The Lord arrived morose and frowning,
In wolf-like manner glared ahead.
He had lost weight, his color bad,
As though his substance city dwelling
Had sucked off him, or in its grip
A worry held him. On the carpet
He paced a bit, as was his habit.
He swung his hand, as if he held
In it the handle of a whip.
Thereupon with a bell he called
One of his servants to come up.
"I want the Manager right away!
Get going! Hold it, dummy, stay!
After the Manager you have seen,
Get me the leasee of the inn."

The Manager came.

                    "Well, any news?"

"Your Lordship, everything is fine.
The wheat and rye, with help Divine,
In a week's time shall be in bins.
Of the twenty calves born just within
The last few days, in stalls, I plan . . ."

"All right, that's splendid, my good man!
About all that we'll talk again
Tomorrow. Could you tell me, please,
What do you hear of village news?
How with the peasants you got on?"
"God blessed us, and there was no trouble.
The village was subdued and humble.
And they worked well. If I complained,
I'd sin."

                    Now pouting in disdain,
The Lord seemed to dislike such news,
As he walked round in his salon.
Meanwhile the Manager went on:
"But with woodcutting, we cannot
Yet bring the project to a close."

"Woodcutting? Where?"

                    "There is a spot
Where during summer, and then since

Worms kill the trees; you said to cut it."
"Don't tell me, you're not done by now?"
"Alas, we're not. So many chores
We've had 'round here, and many serfs
Have now worked off the time they owe,
Still others must be paid to work,
To do the job on the threshing floor.
Thus to the woods we couldn't afford
To send too many. Previously
They cut some trees, but recently
The frost has gripped us . . ."

     "That is great!"
The Lord cried out, and like a beet
He turned all red. "So that those curs
Don't catch a cold, may God forbid,
Let the worm eat up all my wood.
Well, with the splendid help, like yours,
I'll soon be rich! Well, you are free
To go; I'll check it personally."

His Lordship waved dismissal haughtily,
The Manager made his deepest bow,
And leaving the salon quite meekly,
He scratched his head, his spirits low.
"It's an upheaval for the worse!
Our Lord is furious, and no joking.
They must have really rubbed his nose
In it! Not even after gambling
Or visiting, although a loser,
He came home thus, in such a liver."

The old man caved in even further
And sank into a blacker mood
When he observed somebody scurry
With canine pleasure, feline flattery:
The Jew came up to see the Lord.
The Squire's confidant. The reason
Why he's come with an eager gait:
There is someone to calumniate.
The real desire of this demon
Is to try to trip somebody up.
How the Lord's fortune shall increase
In tandem with the Jew! We'll wait
What comes if it. But probably
Not victories, but miseries
Will come from Jewish obloquy.

The Jew, meanwhile, without the trouble
Of knocking, entered bent quite double,
Into the Squire's very presence.

The Lord stood at the window and,
His back turned, long he thus remained,
Not turning to the Jew, as though
He could not hear him. At the entrance
The silent Jew just stood and bowed,
While His Lordship watched the show
In a small mirror. After many
Minutes had passed, the Jew kept up
His act; he knew how to butter up
The Lord, to whom at last too funny
Became the bowing. He turned round:
"Well, Moshko, stop your bowing now!
Come over here! Don't stand like that!
Sit down and tell me what is what."

"The news is dreadful, honored sir;
And very soon we won't be here."

"Well, now, how come?"

     "Did you not hear?
The stirred up peasants, through the fast,
Every last Ivan of your serfs,
Abstains from drink, and like the pest
Avoids the inn. *Ach, ach, weh mer,**
I am quite bankrupt now, I fear."
"Now, now, my Moshko," The Lord joked,
"God's kind; things couldn't be too bad
When you continue to look good,
Bear no resemblance to a rake!"
And with these words the Squire stroked
His Moshko's rounded, ample paunch.

"Your Lordship makes a little joke!
But, no: the times have certainly changed.
Now both of us shall soon be tossed,
Like some old slippers, in the trash.
Have you heard, sir? The local priest
Has now subverted all the serfs!
Have you heard, sir? They plan, in church,
Tomorrow—that's their definite word—
As soon as Mass has run its course,
To swear off alcohol for good!"

"What's that? Tomorrow?" The Lord fumed,
Jumped up as though on thorns he sat.
"The pope? He still cannot forget
His whimsies? I shall get them soon!
Der Teufel drein!† The old cadaver!"

*Oh, woe is me.
†The devil.

They swear the oath in morning hours?
Just wait, I'll play a different tune."
"And you know, sir," the Jew droned on
And bowed, "Who really stands behind
This whole thing; who has lent a hand?
Ach, what difficult times have come."

"Well, who then, speak!"

          "The serfs let on,
The Commissioner stopped by at the church
And right beside it held a speech:
The Emperor wants to set them free;
This action, though, he must delay
Till peasants choose sobriety.
Oh, in the village on that day,
There were shouts, fierce insurgency;
So much so, I prepared to flee."

"Indeed? My Manager didn't say
About these happenings one word.
Well, from now on we'll be advised
Whose loyalty is to be prized.
I thank you, Moshko; I'll report
To Lvov at once. And you, meanwhile
Among the peasants use your guile
And properly sniff out the truth.
Have witnesses to everything,
And fear not what tomorrow brings.
The world's not topsy-turvy yet:
The pope can't walk all over me.
We'll trim their horns but properly!
But quietly, with skill!"

          "It's *git*!"*
The Jew said, bowed again, and left.

XI

New Year's Day 1848—
"The church is shut!"—
Lordly authority over a Ukrainian holy
day—
The Priest once more a peacemaker—
"The Priest has to do corvee, too!"

Not quite yet ready was the sun
To rise; there was a hint of dawn.
There slept the village in the gloom,
When the church bells began to boom
And bid that all the faithful come

*Good, all right.

To matins. The community
Woke up; they rose in every home.
Like stars, the little windows shone.
With measured strides, with dignity,
In sheepskin coats and lambskin hats,
Of one piece fashioned great big boots,
Toward the church the folk were heading.
From far off one can hear the crunch
Of frozen pathways underfoot.
Whole clouds of steam from their breath.
As if from chimneys, fairly belch,
Within a moment to be turning
Into ice spikes on one's moustache.
They walk in clusters, larger groups,
Subdued somehow: there is no chatter,
As though collecting their thoughts
Before they face a serious matter.

No wonder, either; for today
Is New Year's Day and their oath swearing,
And like a soldier who is marching
To battle, each of them can sense
That this oath certainly will cause
Much trouble for them; that they may
Drive numerous enemies to defeat;
That they may suffer many a scourge,
The Lord's reprisals, the Jew's revenge
Before their firm resolve bears fruit.
They're all agreed: whatever comes
They'll take it all and march as one,
Together even suffer death,
To earn their freedom prove their worth.

Well, well, that was a moment bright,
Still vivid in my memory,
When the united popular might
Grew under pressure, pushed aside
All barriers, and did negate
Its rifts, internal enmity.
One single mention was sufficient
That freedom's possible, to quicken
The people's souls. Each would have given
All his possessions at that moment,
Even his life, to gain this freedom.

Alas, it didn't last forever!
Such blessed moments are quite rare
In the lives of nations and of men.
If later, under fiercer ravage,
We had more of such moments bright,

Of similar nature and like courage,
Things would have undergone a change;
Mistakes and many an oversight
Would not give rise to late reproach.

They reached the church door. A surprise!
The door is locked! The cold is fierce,
One cannot stand it long outdoors.
"Hey, Mr. Sexton! Be so nice,
Come down and let the people in,"
They shouted up. The bells were silenced,
The man climbed down. "Make your obeisance
And cross yourselves, and then go home.
I can't unlock; it can't be done."

"What? Why?" The faithful raised a cry.
The Sexton then made his reply:
"I'd just begun my belfry chore,
When a man ran up from the mansion
And seized the keys to the church door."

They grasped. "Another misery!
What manner of new-found repression
Is the Lord using? Could he well
By it o'er us win a victory?
On the Almighty wage a war?
Lock up a church he also dare?
The belfry! Let the bells now peal!
Ring an alert! Let all assemble
Whoever in the village dwells!
March on the manor! Squire, be humble,
Or else your bones shall not be whole!"

The bells all groaned in unison,
The milling crowd used strident tones,
And anger, fire-like, gushed forth
From their movements, eyes, and mouths.
They curse and threaten and shout: "Hey,
Go fetch your sledge at once, Blacksmith!
We'll knock the whole door lock away!"
The women there began forthwith
Their death lament. Groans, shouts, and din
In the churchyard, beyond description.
And so, my children, in this fashion,
The famous forty-eighth came in.

But there, appearing round the bend,
A gang of henchmen of the Lord,
With a proud strut, their whips in hand,
And arrogant, approached the crowd.
The people ceased to cry and shout,
Waiting to hear the Squire's order.

At last their cudgel-wielding leader
Spoke: "People, tell me, what is wrong
That you are standing here in throngs?
Why do you fiercely shout and bray?"

"Unlock the church! Where are the keys?"
They shouted back with a single voice.
"Let us go in! It's a holy day."

"Are you all crazy? Who has said
Such lies? It is a day of toil!
The pope has told you. He's a child.
He hasn't even learned to read.
The Lord knows better. Now disperse!
Prepare for manor work at once!
Bring along axes, wagons too;
For logging we shall have to do."

They stood dumbfounded. What's this talk?
Is this indeed a day of work?
Had all of us lost our minds?
But no; the evil creature mocks!
And suddenly, like mighty winds
That beat like wings above a forest,
Which groans from a hail-bearing tempest,
The folk which had been dumb from fear,
Now thundered in a mighty roar:
"Bark on and lie, like the canines,
You dirty manor house lickspittle;
Don't make us all look asinine!
Our Priest gnaws not beneath the table
The bones with you, when gentry dine!
That's how you, scoundrel, have contrived it:
Do manor work on New Year's Day!
Or does your master get the credit?
Let him beware, for in this vehicle
He won't be making much headway.
He deals with God here, not with people!"

"And I am telling you: disperse!"
The Squire's minion repeated.
"The Master has the keys, he's stated,
No matter how you twist and curse,
No services shall be conducted.
If there's resistance, he'll request
A military unit; and
I tell you: now disperse, make haste,
Avoid a worse predicament!"

"Let him roll on artillery!
If this means even our lives,
We won't budge one step from this place.

What is this: daily drudgery,
And not enough time left us free
On holy days to God to pray.
Break the door! Let them do their worst;
Let them slay all of us in church!
From the door, thugs, now get away!"

But the Lord's servants took good care,
Formed a tight line before the door.
Finding themselves in a tight squeeze,
With whips they shooed the crowd away,
And failing, started to employ
Their fists . . . They squeal and scream and
    press!
Above the heads of the people now,
From behind them, large chunks of snow
Against the door began to fly.
And anger seethed; more scary, fierce.
In several hands there glittered knives.
And cries: "Let all these Judases die!"
The Nineteen forty-eighth, no doubt,
We'd have baptised with human blood,
If it had not been for the word
The Priest in time had spoken out.

With all the hubbub, cries, and noise
No one did notice, hear, or see
He had joined us—when suddenly,
With a large doorside crucifix
In his hands, facing us he stood
And raised the cross as high he could
And called to us in a loud voice:
"God love you, children! I ask whether
Today you're gripped by an evil demon?
Or are you Tartars, or Turks even,
That in the holy church environs
You are involved in this disorder?
Is this a place to start a riot?"
"We didn't start the riot, either!"
The faithful shouted. "Reverend,
The Lord's seized the church keys; demands
That we today for him do labor!"

"The Lord is wrong; I won't deny it.
It's a great sin upon his soul.
But is his wrong a reason that
You now commit a sin as great
When you allow yourselves a brawl,
Profane our holy church of God?
No, children, God loves anger not."

"We did but for the glory of God
That we raised our voice for truth!
Or should we this, too, tolerate?
If so, the Lord soon on our pates
Shall sharpen stakes for a picket fence!
This we must not allow to happen.
Tell them to get the keys at once!
But if the lord to you won't listen,
The church door shall come off by force!"

"Fools, fools, may God forgive you now
For this enormous blasphemy!
You say that Divine majesty
You wanted to protect somehow
With shouts and brawls? Could it be true
These holy words are strange to you:
Were there a need God to defend
Legions of angels He would send
From Heaven earthward in a moment?
No, children, God's Divine commandment
Tells us authority to obey
And heed its every command."

"Should we, then go to work today?
That's a mortal sin, O Reverend!"

"You are not willing, but you must;
Therefore God shan't count this as wrong."

"You, Reverend, too, shall come along,
To work with them, like all the rest,"
Spoke up the leader of the gang.

"I," cried the Priest, as though a bee
Had stung him. "I? Am I not free
From feudal labor?"

                "No, sir, Father.
The Lord said clearly: you proceed
Chase everyone to work the wood;
The pope goes with them; all together."

"Not on his life shall this happen, ever!"
The faithful roared. "No, Reverend,
Fear not! We shall stand right behind,
To back you up. We and our Elder
Will go at once to the district seat,
Fall down at the *Starosta's** feet,
And let him judge it: who is wrong!"
"No, children, no," the old Priest quoth.

*The principal district administrator.

79

"That's bad. I will not go along.
If the Lord ordered that we ought
To work today, then it would seem
That God inspired such a thought,
Allowing him in pride to preen,
Intending that he very soon
In nets of his own pride be caught.
I must say one thing to you all:
The Lord thought fit to weight his soul
With a sin on a yearly holiday:
Decided to bar us from church
And force us in his woods to work—
So be it! Those who will survive
Shall see how all of this turns out.
But children, let's not mutiny,
And on account of the Squire's pride,
Take upon our souls besides
The threat of sinning mortally.
Let's, then, to might, authority bow,
Ourselves, dears, in meekness show
That we are worthier than he.
Today you had an oath to swear.
Do you imagine that I would
Let you all swear this holy oath
If you had broken down the door?
Let us endure this difficult trial,
And I can surely prophesy:
God shall place this in your account.
In the early morn, it is well known,
Ere the rosy star begins to dawn,
The frost burns with the fiercest strength.
It makes opaque your window pane,
But that is just a sign that soon
The sun shall shine and warm the earth."

A curious change in the populace:
Their stridor gone, the will to resist,
Their posture bent, the souls downcast,
Their gaze went up toward the east,
As though in hope of the gloom's decease.
The sky, however, clear at night,
Now when it was so near daylight,
Wrapped itself up in a misty cawl;
And yonder in the pinewood forest
Resounded now a mighty howl.
As soon as the Priest had said it all,
Boding a fear-inspiring tempest,
In the churchyard, a tall elm tree
Uttered such strangely painful creaks
That shivers ran down their backs.
As one the crowd groaned cheerlessly:
"God be the judge! We'll be obedient.

Let us go get the working implements."

XII

The New Year's storm—
The Lord's greetings—
The talk between the Squire and the Priest

Wow! did we get a vicious storm!
The wind came whistling from the east,
Like a wild horse, its hobbles torn,
At once from all restraints released:
It looks about and paws the ground,
Leaps up and kicks its legs and neighs;
When galloping, it makes clods fly
Or canters in a circular way;
It neighs again, and then stops dead.

The blast ripped crusty snow right out,
Brought it to towns from the fields in squalls;
It hurt the eyes, and underfoot
Stole paths within a time so short,
And howled, roared as though it could not
At our Lord its rage conceal.

But stronger cries and howls and sighs
In peasant dwellings everywhere
Went on: old people, children, wives
Wept, and the storm increased their fear.
In it they all perceived God's hand,
An obvious sign of Divine wrath.
We said good-byes to such lament
As we went out to work the woods,
As though to death were being sent.
I won't forget it till my death.
Tears, crying were of no avail!
What the Lord orders must be done.
With threats and shouts men are assailed
By manor thugs in many a barn.
Into the drifts of the roaring blizzard,
One, then another from the barnyard,
The peasants slowly ride outdoors.
Their horses snort, shut eyes halfway,
And pant into the tempest's roar.
The men are wrapped in sheepskin coats.
The blizzard's blast may skid a sleigh
Or lurk ahead and thus waylay.
It makes it hard to catch one's breath.

The Lord's will greater power wields
Than a winter gale in the open fields.
This will, on us a pressing threat,
Like a sledge, overhead hung now.

80

Across the village formed a trail:
Empty sleighs, strung in a single file,
And their tracks filled up with snow.
From time to time, through the blizzard's rush,
The faintest hum came through—a gnat?
The sound of bells! Just fancy that!
Some have a holiday! A crush
Inside the church. The lights ablaze;
Up drifts the smoke from the incense;
The cantor sings; the populace prays.
Are we accursed? The only ones
To be denied a holy day!
Everyone hearing the bells' sounds,
From habit, puts his whip aside,
Removes the mittens from his hands,
Crosses himself, and with a sigh
Whispers a prayer.

But behold!
From the parsonage also a sleigh starts,
On it the Priest, two manor guards,
A servant, too. This means the Lord
Intends to force the Priest to work.
But by what right? Did he obtain
A permit at the Governor's seat?
He didn't tarry there in vain;
In tricks, the gents there can't be beat.
Such thoughts we had; for ourselves now
We braced for new disasters' spate.
Meanwhile, in front they shouted "Whoa!"
The Hall! We halted by the gate.

There stood the Squire: tall of stature;
Broad shouldered; Polish style shod;
In hat and fur. His prominent features:
Black eyes, mustachios. And he had
A whip in hand; as if in play,
Into the wind he cracked his whip.
He counted all the sleighs, in fact,
Which at the gate were passing by.
From his vodka flask he took small sips;
To the peasants' bows, he offered not
The slightest gesture in reply.
And then the Priest's own sleigh drew near;
Behind him quite a line of men
Whom the Squire termed as mutineers;
For long had kept an eye on them.
He smiled, came out on the road,
And shouted "Whoa!" very loud.
The sleighs then halted. They all made
A bow. The Lord maintained his beam.
Then he spoke up: "Well, gentlemen,

At least today you aren't late!
Perhaps someone has feared the storm
And with the womenfolk stayed home?"

"They are all here," his henchman spoke,
Who meek before the Lord was standing.

"That's a good show! But what a hiding
He would have gotten! In the neck!
Now all you, burghers, tell me, please,
What are you up to? Tell me, when
We'll have the village here at peace?
Not enough beatings, it would seem,
Or else you wouldn't have the birds
Inside your heads a-twittering!
Then tell me now, O honored sirs,
What have you been considering?
An oath? Do you still have a taste
For cudgel blows, or for the switch?
I'm not God's kin, but I'll be pleased
Your hides so properly to baste
That your grandchildren still shall blanch."
Having said this, he looked us over
With a hawk's eye, and then made seem
The Priest now only to discover,
And only now went up to him.
He said: "Your Reverence, a surprise!
Are you working for the manor, too?
How very nice! You are a prize,
A proper shepherd: where the flock,
Thither he goes. Well, what to do . . .
We greet you, welcome you to work!"

Now our Priest, his voice aquiver,
But with great dignity, rejoined.
"The esteemed Squire's in good humor
Today, we see. Our God has sent
Joy to his lordship. Praise to God!
But now, my kind sir, you must pray,
Lest God decide on the following day
To send anxiety in its stead."

The Lord jumped, startled, as if he
Had felt a serpent's poison fang.
"What, pope, what have you said to me?"

"I say what any Christian man
Can listen to with perfect calm.
To whom Almighty great pride sends,
Who even God Himself condemns,
It's a sure sign: not far off stands
Open before him—a deep chasm."

"On top of all, you threaten me?"

"No, honored sir, this is no threat
I only tell you God's own truth,
Which probably's unknown to you."

"You go and teach such fools as you.
You're not about to lecture me."

"To your wisdom, sir, I'll give its due
Most gladly, but my inquiry
Goes to the course that you pursue.
Was it wise a holiday to deny,
To put our church under lock and key,
And drive the people out to slave?
Sir, sir, wake up and turn to reason
And do not glory in your wisdom!
Had I not earlier in the day
Used my own breast with which to shield
Your servants here; who knows, perhaps
This moment, by the very church door,
This blizzard would be forming drifts
Over red pools of their blood.
Keep this in mind, my honored sir:
In our world, without exception,
For every act and entity,
Limits exist; these limitations
One can't transgress with impunity."

"Well, now, your sermon's really nice,
But you know, pope, you are a wonder:
For others you have wise advice,
Your own acts, though, to it run counter.
Didn't I tell you: be aware
Of your own popish limitations,
For all this schooling cease to care,
Don't feed the peasants stupid notions.
But, look at you! Now you are set
To try to make me wholly indigent!
The serfs for the oath, for freedom wait,
Won't drink my booze, no matter what.
The Jew says, he won't pay the rent.
What do you think then? Should I go
Because of you to beg for alms?
No, Pope. I tell you once more: no.
I'll deal with you with other means!
You and the bloody Kraut so chatter
Of freedom, but it's much too soon!
I'll show you now: it doesn't matter
What you may do or what you plan.
I'm master here! Now I'll expect
You to muck in, do feudal chores.

You knew how damage to inflict,
Which your own hands shall help restore."

"That you're in charge here is not news,
But there's a higher Master yet.
Today I only yield to force,
And I am stating to your face:
This is injustice; my estate
Exempts me from the feudal burdens.
Of imperial law you're in contempt."

"To talk of law there is no point;
That is outside of your mind's competence.
Did you see my inventory book?
It says therein, the pope maintains
Two fallows' land among the folk.
From this I dare to draw the inference
That it is peasant, rustic land,
From which I duly may demand
The customary share of labor."

"That would be so, but for the waiver
Appended to it—the notation:
'From all the feudal duties free.'"

"Only he is free who deserves to be!
However, if it's your impression
That you are being put upon,
Take me to court, but I'll defend
What's due to me. But right now, still,
I'm master here; therefore my will
Must be obeyed. Enough of talk!
On to the woods and get to work.
And spare no effort! Look alive!
Or else my footmen soon shall drive
With the whip zeal into the slack.
Be gone, and do now hurry up!
I'll soon be there, to look you up!"

XII

Work in the woods—
The martyred Priest—
Human anger explodes—
The Squire as a peacemaker—
The Lord's servants know no jokes—
The Priest's evaluation of the Lord's joke

The forest groaned from the blizzard's blasts,
Roared like a hungry, angry beast.
Like living arms, its darkened limbs
Waved in the wind; they thrashed and heaved,
When we, in little gloomy bands,

Arrived beneath its murky eaves.
How strange we felt, somehow afraid.
We all were at that time as though
We'd entered an enchanted world—
A land of dusk and frost and snow,
Which like a prison would now hold
Us always, never let us go.

How strange and scary was the din
We caused with our axes' blows
That echoed in each gorge, ravine,
As though commanding to convene
In covens: witches, spooks, and ghouls.
It was a feast day, we remembered,
And all this sacrilegious noise
Who knows what, and how large in number,
Would draw on us in pain and woes.
Alas, we couldn't hesitate,
Turn back, or even cogitate:
The Manor's flunkeys would prevail.
Thus we ourselves, to quiet down
Our own fears, then went to town,
Making the splinters fly like hail.
Our teeth clenched, we chopped, as though
Those trees were really our foes—
The most treacherous enemies in the world.
Some bark from felled trees began to peel,
Others sawed logs and split them small,
Then piled them up in stacks and cords.

The Priest was told by the manor thugs
The limbs upon a stack to drag,
Working together with young men.
"Good God," the men cried out together,
"Is this the right task for an oldster?
Do you possess no conscience? Then
Look here: He barely can walk,
Here we have stumps, the snow is thick.
This is a labor for the strong."

"Silence!" the leader cried. "Work on.
What the Lord's ordered shall be done!
Pull, Reverend!"

                                    We held our tongues.
And silently, in fury grim,
To the woods rush, the tempest's groan,
The work went on with feverish speed.
We watched the flunkeys' merriment
When our aged Priest, with all his strength,
With great exertion sweated blood,
Toward a pile dragging wood.

The cursed ones laugh, have no esteem
For advanced age or his priesthood.
Their hounding concentrates on him:
"Pull, Reverend! Soon comes the Lord,
And if he finds the stack too small,
There shall be trouble for us all!"

The old man drained his strength in vain:
His hands, while trying, merely tremble,
The branch's weight they cannot handle,
His feet trip up, let down his frame,
He falls, gets up, and tries again,
But for this work he is too feeble.
For long we were compelled to see
The torment and the mockery
The henchmen heaped upon the Priest.
But he had not a word to say,
Lamb-like, bowed to it and obeyed,
Giving beneath the boughs his last.

We watched: he could no longer move,
Fell, like a splinter, in the snow,
From the weight of the wood exhausted.
His old man's chest but wheezed and gasped.
Would they leave him alone? But no!
Like ravens, they surround the victim,
Now poke him, now attempt to lift him:
"Why don't you stop now trampling snow!
You've got to carry logs. Let's go!"

What triggered this amazing miracle?
Was it the blizzard's frightful howl?
Did a tree crack before the crash?
Was it the fire of a lightning flash?
Did in our hearts then break a dam
And free a thing congealed since dawn,
Which poured out through the open gate?
As though upon a clear command,
With hatchets, axes in our hands,
We rushed and shouting took our stand:
"Inhuman scum! Accursed! You wait!
You have sucked our blood enough!
You wore us out and made life rough!
The time of judgement is at hand!
Death comes but once! So, kill them, smite!"

Was it the wind or evil spirits
Accelerating our movements—
In short, it took one wink at most
For us to reach the Manor men,
As though with fencing, hem them in
With our angry, mighty chests.

The cutting steel of our axes
Close to their heads began to gleam.
We shouted: "Pray now, you accursed!
Here's a priest. If there's a sin
Upon your souls, go to confession.
Pray quickly, get your absolution.
You won't escape from here alive!"

They lost their speech and turned chalk white.
The henchmen seemed all mortified:
Such was the fierceness of our drive,
When we leaped on them, that no thought
Occurred to them our force to counter.
Alarm and fear made them distraught,
So that not one did dare consider
Resistance: were there such a man,
He would have died with certainty.
Not knowing why, the flunkeys then
Bowed their head with humility,
Proceeding at our feet to kneel.
The Forty-sixth, and the whole story,
It seems, of all the happenings gory
Revived in the memories of all.

"Neighbors and brothers, God love you!
Do you imagine that we would
Be doing this of own accord?
You know, the master over you
Is, after all, our master too."

"That is a lie!" came back loud shouts,
"While we are compelled to toil,
You people of your own free will
To the gentry hired yourself out.
Now we are neighbors, brothers too;
But what could we expect of you?
What kind of words did we hear when
The tender mercies of your hands
Used to scourge us with whips and knouts
Until blood seeped through our skin?
You've done enough! Now our cup
Is overfull! We may die here,
But we shall teach you what is fear!
Now start to pray! Your time is up!"

"Ha, ha, ha, ha! And what a pickle!"
We heard above us a loud cackle.
"Ha, ha, ha, ha! And what a joke!
Lo! Gentlemen of the *service*
Learning to crawl on their knees
Before the peasants! And good luck!
Fie, gentleman! Do show your pride!

Enough of kneeling! Now arise,
Or else you'll thoroughly wet your pants!
Why do these people stand around
Over you, each an axe in hand?
Are they about to do a dance?"
It was the Master. From nowhere
He seemed to spring; now he stood there,
In Polish boots, in his furcoat,
And in his hand he held a knout;
Haughty as always, but not cross;
On the contrary, a jocose
Smile was flickering 'round his mouth.

We froze. Our group a thunder bolt
Would be less apt to stupefy.
The insane rage that our eyes
Had newly blinded was well-nigh
Cooled off. Of own accord we felt
A sense of shame, almost as though
At thieving we'd been caught red-handed.
As though on a command, we now
Together our axes downed.
The Squire, haughty, with a smile,
Into the center calmly went,
Surveyed his servants with contempt.
The flunkeys, each of them still pale,
Trembled and fussed, from left to right
Shifting their weight, suppressing fright,
Silently thanking the Almighty
That from the serfs they were safe and hale.

And the Lord laughed and mocked away:
"How was it, gentlemen?" he jeered,
"Did the peasants teach you how to pray?
I'm sure your bowing was sincere!
That's very nice, and worry not:
It does no harm. Almighty God
Welcomes a prayer from any place
If said with *love* and with *repentance*
(These words he pointedly pronounced)
When your soul seeks the Lord's embrace."

As though spellbound, kept mum the servants.
And then the Squire turned to us:
"Fools all of you, just plain damned fools!
You are more stupid than determined!
I merely put you to a test,
As a true father tests his sons;
You, by the Evil One possessed,
At that your axes seized at once!
But you, fools; it was just a jest!"

Silent and grim, like a black cloud,
We stood, turned our eyes away.
The Lord said: "You're the ones who crave
Your own destruction. Like a herd,
You blindly rush toward an abyss!
Why? I can tell you now:
You have been told by an evil foe,
Like Holy Writ, some words like this:
That very soon you'll get your freedom,
That they'll abolish tributes, serfdom.
Well, am I lying? Now, pray, tell!"
The men were silent. "Just as well!
I know it all. To a great regret
The vipers' sly tongues did forget
To you one item to reveal:
How liberty's to be deserved?
Now let me tell you, therefore:
He has a life of freedom earned
Who, too, oppression can endure.
I thought I'd put you to a test,
Whether this freedom is for you,
Allow myself a little jest;
And now I see that long you must
Yet wait, and go on with the quest
For brains to tell you what to do."

The men were silent. The head man
Of the guards came, bowed to the Lord.
"Pardon, milord, since the early morn,
We have been running back and forth,
As leaves above the water sway;
We've faced death's peril twice today.
All for a joke, a lordly jest!
Never, milord, are faithful servants
This way by other masters treated,
Nor are they for a jest submitted
To fists and clubs of irate peasants.
Thus we could really be insane
To carry on in your employ.
As of today, we all resign.
Without us, God grant luck and joy."
The Lord just glared—said not a word,
As though the statement of his guard
All of a sudden did display
In a new light the whole affair;
Yet humor didn't disappear
From the Lord's face and mouth and eye.

But then among the peasants' ranks
Somebody groaned and waved his hands.
Men walked right over for to see,
Before the Lord brought presently

The Priest, quite powerless and ill,
Who during the entire upheaval
Lay prone, since falling helplessly.
White as a corpse he was, and shook—
A half-felled tree—beneath his lids
Already shone the dying look;
And hard to hear were these his words:
"The Squire jested, like a father,
His children's faith put to a test;
Did he test also our Creator
And play on him an innocent jest?
Was it a jest that a holy feast
The Lord abolished, our church shut?
Was it a jest that with such zest,
Without due process, I was seized,
Tormented afterward to death?
All as a joke, For this jest, sir,
I place before Almighty God
A charge. My spirit must appear
Today before him. Ere this year
Runs to a close, you shall be called.
Your worldly goods into thieves hands
Shall vanish, and there'll be no trace
Of your existence; your descendants
This jest for ages hence shall curse!"

These threats—or were they malediction—
Like two wings of a darkening curtain,
Over our Lord's world spread a pall.
He started, trembled, clenched his teeth,
Tugged at his whiskers, his lips bit,
Finally spoke: "Blab on, you fool!
All we have here is a senile man.
Well, all get ready to go home!"

He walked away. We left as well.

XIV

The calm after the storm—
The Priest's death—
A complaint to the authorities—
Starosta's investigation—
The Commissioner as an advisor—
The Peasants' delegation—
The delegation as martyrs—
The Lord's lesson—
"God of justice and freedom is not dead"

Like a long, bad, oppressive dream
Appeared to us the day's events.
We had been through a raging storm,
Roaring, explosive sentiments,

A wrong, a threat of coming harm.
Leaving the woods for an open field,
Without a word said, there we found
Everything silent, bare, and dead.
The snowy plain now stretched all round;
The clouds above it, colorless, grey
Covered the sky. The wind was calm;
Only from thatched roofs far away
Rose bluish puffs, from village homes.

In our breasts, after all these
Dreadful events, a tranquility
Settled—and sadness, as though vain
Our hopes were, cut by adversity.
Even the Heaven's augury
Seemed plain: live always on a chain.

Feeling this terrible depression,
Silently, slowly we drove home—
A funeral train. And so in some
Respects it was: our stricken Parson
Was being carried. In a stream,
From his mouth life drained with his blood.
His body now was wholly chill;
His heart beat slowly; he just could
Manage to whisper his farewell.
"Good-bye, my children! Forgive him
And leave all punishment to God.
Submit to gloom, until the gloom
Is led by God upon the road
Toward destruction."

               We're aware,
Without soliciting advice,
That for submission 'twas too late.
As we drove past the Lord's estate,
We noticed that he had secured
His gate with chains—afraid, of course,
That people would regain their sense
And, as a jest, tear him apart.

But we went by quite peacefully
And turned into the rectory,
Took our old Parson off the sled,
Warmed him up some and put to bed.
Then we put down all our complaints,
Elected our delegates,
To go posthaste to the district seat.

Such was our feast of New Year's Day!
There were no services for us,
And there were tears instead of joy.

And by the evening, the whole place
Assembled at the Parson's home,
To say our last good-byes to him
And to kiss for the final time
His frigid hands. For presently
He barely breathed, he closed his eyes.
As the night's gloom intensified,
He died serenely, peacefully.

With his death, though, died not the thing
The Lord had feared; for now began
The opposite, with the first round
Of sparring and maneouvering.
No sooner our complaint was out
Against the Lord, to the county—wait!
Two of his own complaints went out:
One charging that we agitate;
That manor guards we tried to kill
With our axes, and torch the hall.
The second went to the Governor:
The Commissioner stirred the populace,
Spreading abroad all kind of queer
Rumors of rights for serfs; impure
Were his addresses to the village,
In which to crime he did encourage—
That would be proved with witnesses.

Indeed, the Jew had contrived to catch
Some of us wagging our tongues,
With tricks, as he had done for long,
Inducing our drunks to snitch.
And slowly he extracted all
The Commissioner said. Thus for a spell
Abated noise and shouts among
The peasants; and obedient each
We went to work, but couldn't wait
For the results of this commotion.

But once at night—it was quite late—
People woke up in agitation;
Along the quiet village road,
A gentry-style covered sleigh,
With government bells on, raced right by
And turned into the Manor grounds.
We started asking right away:
"Who are they? What are they here for?"
Early next morn we got the message:
The *Starosta* and the Commissioner
Came to investigate the village.

Soon they began to drag us in,
And we discovered in no time

That the *Starosta* not in vain
Came to the Manor with the lean
New Commissioner. Between the two
They shared the labor to be done.
The *Starosta* had all the fun
At the Hall daily: in good cheer,
Dancing and partying and hunting.
The Commissioner, though, turned a deaf ear
To peasant suffering, injustice,
Knew of no legal rights or conscience,
Was never angry, never raged,
But with his imperturbable calm
Pursued his probing in cold blood,
And his unshaken calm drove home
Fear in the peasants who were probed.
Slowly he quizzed, judiciously,
And listened most attentively,
In such a manner asked his questions
That humble people, quite untrained,
Were led to tears and to confessions.
"Lean Devil" he was aptly named.
His inquiry was masterful,
Set down in a German protocol,
But only what incriminated
Among the peasant depositions;
All adverse comments were omitted
About the Lord in these notations.

There is no doubt, our reputations
Were blackened in these protocols:
Swearing our oath was called a whim;
They spoke how we had threatened harm
To the servants, almost killed them all
Out in the woods; and all the rest
Was written down. But that the Lord
Had tried to force his alcohol
On us; had tried to stop our school;
On a feast-day, like an anti-Christ,
Drove us, like heathens, to the wood,
To toil there—there was no mention.
Disgusted left him our people.
"Now we cannot get out of trouble!"
Such were our village conversations.

The *Starosta* sat for three days
Up at the Hall; he'd cast an eye
On the Commissioner on duty,
But never read the protocols.
At last he bid the Lord farewell
And Saturday regained the city.
The Commissioner, like a wet spell,
A week yet hovered overhead

In the village, probing to pursue.
It seemed that very guts he drew
From people, with the firm resolve
To paint each one of us as bad.

It happened once on Sunday evening.
A few of us at the Cantor's home
Were sitting, and it seemed no theme
Could keep our conversation going.
We had lost faith in our cause.
But suddenly: a howling noise—
A storm blew up—an urgent knock
Resounded from the door at once.
The wife went out. Soon in the door
Stood stooping our Commissioner—
The old acquaintance, to us dear.
He bowed. "I greet you all," he spoke.

We sat up in surprise, but he,
Surveying us who sat together,
Smiled, said "pst!" for secrecy,
Sat on a bench, greeted no one,
Then finally said in a soft tone:
"Ugh, we're having blustery weather!"

A word was ventured here and there.
"God help you! Well, how are you, sir?
What business brings you now to us?"
He smiled, said "pst!" in a whisper,
Then bent down low into our cluster:
"You people are in quite a mess!
I know it all. The protocols
I've read. The peasant never will
Lie to escape a certain death!
Why would you say such things? Why talk?
If they put you upon the rack,
Such evil couldn't be drawn out!"

Then we explained: the Commissioner
Put these things down as he saw fit,
Never read back the words he wrote.
"The Emperor's, too, mixed up in there!"
The Commissioner whispered this quite awed.
"I know it all, I've thought this through.
This piece of paper is for you:
Copy it over! Hurry now!
And do you have your delegates?
This very night send them to Lvov!"

To the Cantor he gave this small piece
Of paper with an explanation,
What must be done with it, and how,

To whom the delegates should go.
Then he gave off his final hiss,
Declined a proffered small collation,
Bowed, and went out to meet the snow.
There is no need now to relate
How we all hustled then and ran
Among the houses in great haste.
This very night, our delegates
Departed, as if forced to race
So that they might take their place
At the market on that Monday morn.
However, great was our caution
When we sent deputies to sue,
Someone in our population
At once denounced us to the Squire.
Never before had we been through
Such doing, and thus no one knew
That we were all at play with fire.

How the Lord raved, oh how he stormed,
Right at the coming of daylight,
When by the Jew he was informed
That our empowered deputies
Were off to Lvov to air our plight;
He was so mad he gnashed his teeth.
At once he settled down to write
After the men his warrant letters,
Dispatched them right away with riders
To the estates along the way.
"If you should come across such people,
Stop them, arrest them there, and shackle,
And to this district send at once!"
How can I possibly convey
How anxious after these events
The village a whole week remained!
With what alarm, uncertainty
We waited daily, who would gain
In this war a clear victory!
Would our men fulfill their aim
Or end their trip in captivity?

In a week's time, the message comes:
They have been caught! O God Almighty!
We were all trembling! Even stones
Would have been shaken! Very haughty,
Our squire really raised his head
When he was told that three days' time
Had gone by since a fellow-lord
Had caught them, sent them under guard,
Not to the district, but straight "home."

"A wise and decent chap, this Stas,"
Said our Squire, "he did right.
Call everyone to the estate;
Let before everybody's eyes
The deputies get their treat.
Let them watch, quake in their shoes!"
They summoned us: some came from work,
Some from their homes—the old and kids.
The wives and kids of the unfortunates,
The deputies, on the inner edge
The Squire placed, so they may watch
How they lay open their dads' backs,
So that they their descendants teach:
It doesn't pay the Squire to buck.

Now they lead out each luckless wretch:
Worn out and pale and miserable,
In tatters, bound, and pitiable.
Now as the squire they approach,
He signals bailiffs with his hand
And shouts: "Down in the snow! And stretch
Each of them, beat them till you're told
'Enough!'" And then the Lord began
To whistle calmly. The guards felled
Our men in the snow without delay.
Four henchmen took up their places:
One of them on the head was sitting,
One held the feet; the two remaining
With all their might began to flay.

At first it seemed that those were corpses
The blows rained on, for their faces
Were deep in snow; they couldn't scream;
Each victim's body merely tosses
And wriggles, like a cut up worm.
The Squire whistles, his guard whips,
Blood now through clothes starts to appear,
In rivulets on the snow drips.
From under snow, as though from depths,
A wheeze of pain assails the ear.
The Squire whistles, doesn't hear.
But lo! The wives and little tots
Of the men tortured, all together,
With lamentation, tears, and prayer,
Threw themselves down at the Lord's feet.
The Squire whistles, sees them not.

One wife set out, with trembling lips
On her knees toward the Lord to crawl,
Intending to embrace his feet,

To wash with her blood-laced tear drops
The leather of the lordly boot.
The lord, still whistling, thrust the toe
Against her mouth, so hard, she fell
In the snow backwards, and a rill
Of blood from her mouth, began to flow.

After a spell of dreadful length,
When agony was cutting off
The martyrs' screams, he said: "Enough!"
Raised, washed with snow, they tried to stand,
But couldn't summon enough strength;
They had to lean upon the guards.
To stand alone they were too weak.
"Well, now," the Lord began to speak,
"Have you discovered the Lvov road?
Have you learned well now how it tastes
When the serf against me agitates?
And that's not all you'll get to see,
But a little 'on account' I've paid.
In the district more you may await.
Take them boys to a hideaway!
With a single rope in the granary
Tie them together, give to eat,
And later on they shall report
On their journey. We will come
A little later for a chat.
And after we've been bored with that,
We'll march them to the district town."

We stood there as though we were dead;
In silence. All these happenings had
Taken away the final shred
Of hope from us. Where to go now?
We couldn't hope for the Lord's defeat;
To send a note to the government seat,
Could we employ the wings of a dove?
Our Lord, the *Starosta*—hand in glove.
All we had left was not to speak
Or leave our fields and homes and seek
In far, unknown parts better luck.

The Lord, in order to top off
His victory, abruptly whirled
To face us, and then proudly snarled:
"Did you observe how you get paid
For mutiny? In that case, surely,
In future you shall know exactly
What kind of tickling I provide.
If that's your wish, go on and grumble,

And I'll show you how I can tickle
More powerfully. If your hide
Means little to you—challenge me!
And one more thing: the Commissioner
Has lied to you that the Emperor—
Whoever else—will set you free.
What the Commissioner befalls
For that we'll see in the long haul—

"I wish to make this matter clear:
Don't trust those who such things proclaim;
They bring no liberty, but pain.
No one—be it the Emperor
Or God in Heaven—has the right
To someone what I own to give!
It's not within the royal might!
What God or the Emperor doesn't have
He cannot give away to others.
Now listen to me, listen well:
Of freedom don't you even dream!
It's not concealed in royal coffers.
When I am here, freedom won't come,
Unless I make you free myself."

So blasphemously he proclaimed
And went toward his residence.
The words were probably designed
To crush us; he used them in place
Of heavy rocks; but the reverse
Occurred: we gained new confidence.
We contemplated: "You are blind.
You think you have the entire world
In hand, yet on a zig-zag course
By destiny you're strangely led.
Watch out, lest unexpectedly tears
The flimsy tissue of your pride."

We weren't shocked, we had no fear
Now any more, when in two days,
Our pitiful, half-dead delegation,
In shackles bound, was led away
Along the highway. Like relations,
We saw them off and raised a cry:
"Have courage, brethren! God is kind.
He won't let our foes multiply
And grow in power without end."

Nor was the rumor very scary:
An order had come recently
To the Commissioner; he must hurry

To the Governor in Lvov immediately.
Our Squire certainly did gloat:
"The rebel has been called away!
They'll stick him now in such a spot,
He'll never see the light of day."
Though we were plagued by bleakest
      grievance,
In this conviction we found solace:
"Lives God of Freedom and of truth!"

XV

Holy Saturday, 1848—
An Imperial directive abolishes feudal
servitude—
The peasants do not understand—
"Let's go and see the Squire!"

Behind us was the cursed winter,
The last such wintertime accursed.
Now drawing nigh was Holy Easter.
Ere Maundy Thursday came, commenced
Already labor on the land.
Now Holy Saturday was at hand—
A memorable glorious day,
A holiday special to all.
Every moment I recall
Of that day, as though yesterday
It happened.

                    Since the early morning,
Before the thawing of the rime,
We readied spring wheat seed for sowing
At the estate. It would be time
To go home to an early lunch
As soon as grain work was all done.
"Now you go home, but on the run,
And everyone at once must fetch
A harrow to the common's ground."
The Lord himself gave his command.
And so we ran and had a bite
Of what was cooked of our fare,
Then we rushed back with all our might;
The village was already there.
Some came with harrows, sacks for seed,
Each girl or wife had brought a spade;
They even had contrived to catch
Some boys as drovers; braided ropes
Were used the harrows with to hitch.
The workers stood themselves in rows,
As though some soldiers at a drill.
Our manor boss among us goes,

Counts all those present there and orders
Who is with whom and where to till.

But look! Into the village enters
A buggy drawn by a single nag.
At the driver's side, a flunkey slumbers;
The driver likes his whip to crack.
And in the back? O God in Heaven!
The Commissioner! The very same
Who was supposed to be in prison
In Lvov! Somehow we had a quaint
Sensation: hearts began to beat,
As though expecting something rare,
Some terrible or joyous news
Which soon to hear was our fate.
Even our boss, so hard to scare,
Stopped in his tracks, as though one frozen,
And mumbled softly: "Goodness knows
The meaning of it! Probably
Something nasty."

                    Soon the riders' vision
Included us, and suddenly
The Commissioner gave his man a nudge.
The flunkey started in confusion
And almost headlong—by this much—
Fell off the buggy. Soon awake,
Under the collar scratched his neck,
Bent down at leisure and dug up
Something concealed beneath the straw,
A thing resembling a large loaf
Wrapped in a cloth. Well, what we saw
Surprised us; but the flunkey climbed
Down from his seat, took it in hand,
Like a cask hung it over his shoulder.
He hung it, put the rag inside—
It was a drum! He struck the hide:
Rat-a-tat-boom, he sounded off!
At once the echo bore the clatter
To the village. It soon filled with chatter:
From gardens, fields, from every home,
The old, the small, came on the run.
Agog at the curious occasion,
In a wide ring, the population
Soon mobbed the buggy.

                    "Quiet, there!"
The Commissioner now shouted shrilly.
He stood up on the gig and quickly
Pulled out a paper.

"I have here
A paper I'm obliged to read.
And please, you people, pay good heed:
It is a royal document."
And then he started to emit
Some German words. The populace stands
On tiptoe, some with open mouths:
How can they understand it all!
One here, one there, but heaves a sigh,
Crosses himself, looks at the sky,
And stands there like a wooden pole.

But the Commissioner, with pleasure,
Reads loudly, quickly; for good measure,
For stress, some passages exclaims.
Finished. "All clear, what you have heard?"

"No, siree, not a single word."

"O empty noggins, without brains!
The very liberation's joy
And their own freedom they can't fathom!
Now listen! From the third of May
The Emperor grants you fullest freedom!
From feudal work you are absolved,
All feudal tributes have now ceased.
For your own profit till the soil!
And one more thing I have to tell:
Today the *Starosta's* released
Your delegates from the district jail.
Well, understood?"

                    Still not a word.
"You understand, you peasant fools?
Why do you stand like wooden poles?
It's time the Emperor to cheer!"

Silence again. But through the crowd
Our Elder made his way and bowed
To the Commissioner, and spoke thus:
"Forgive us, sir, that we all show
So little warmth, but we don't know
Whether it's true. Our Lord told us,
The whole thing simply couldn't be;
That you were called to Lvov—a lie?—
To be locked up for eternity;
That the Emperor daren't take away
The servitude, for it's gentry's own."

"O Christian peasants, are you dumb!
It suited him these things to say.

The Emperor doesn't confiscate
Their property; to compensate
He promises from government funds.
I, in his service, never would
Deceive you; I proclaim the truth.
This seal: d'you know for what it stands?"

"Long flourish our Emperor;
And by his side, you too, dear sir,
Long live and prosper. As for us,
We have made many a sacrifice,
And are afraid that this time, too,
We'll find ourselves stuck on the ice.
Now, sir, we would request of you
That you come with us to the Hall,
Read to the Lord this document,
To him, too, please display the seal,
And after this, if he should find
The writ in order, we'll give credence
To it; repay the King with goodness,
Serve the kind King with gratitude,
Offer him love, and even blood—
Sincerely, if he should require."

"You, peasant, give us good advice!
The Lord should also recognize
How things are! Let us see the Squire!"

XVI

"By the Imperial Order!"—
The Commissioner lectures the Squire—
A lordly jest with the Commissioner

The Lord, his spouse on the veranda
Were eating breakfast, when at once,
Like an unruly mob of drunkards,
We occupied the whole courtyard.
The Commissioner—in front of us.
The man beside him, very hard,
Kept rattling on his drum-da-rum-da.
Madame got up and raised her eyes
To see, fell almost in a faint,
Began to wring her hands in pain,
And questioningly, or perhaps
It was a look of sad reproach
She gave her spouse. And clearly much
Of what the Lord saw failed to please
In the weird meeting. Even more
He was nonplussed and clenched his teeth
When he saw who'd whipped up this meet:
The Commissioner was in the fore!

Didn't the devil get him yet?
There would be trouble; that was sure!

Slowly and gravely, so's to quell
His wife's alarm, the Lord climbed down,
And in a drawn out and stern tone,
He asked the peasants: "Very well,
Why are you here?" Meanwhile he stood
Facing the German with his back,
Pretending that throughout this time
He didn't see him. Drummer Jack
Hit with the drumsticks once again;
The Commissioner turned lobster-red.
Just at that moment, the Lord's plan
Was to say more; his ears, alack,
Were jarred by "In the Emperor's name!"
Like a knife screeching on the glass.
The Squire turned: "Commissioner, sir!
A rare guest here! *Nu, nu, wie geht's?*
Long back from Lvov? Are all your trips
Over? What says the Emperor?"

"This a patent royal, from
April the seventeenth, this year,
Which orders in the Emperor's name:
From tomorrow's date, there'll be no more
In this realm of feudal servitude;
No tributes either; the peasants should
Receive the rustic soil they till.
The gentry's loss will reimburse
The Emperor, from his own purse—
Such is the Emperor's literal will."

"*O sapperment! Warum nicht gar!*"*
As though struck by a snake, he cried.
"The Emperor's great! The royal might
Reigns over us! A gift, I'm sure,
To the peasantry! The King is good!
To shower the valiant peasant brood,
As fits their merit, with such gifts,
We have to be deprived of first
Of all that, by the grace of God,
We thought our own, there is no question:
It's wondrous goodness! Thus one should
Win popular appreciation.

"Well, we are dumb, must wisdom seek;
We must obey because we're weak!
But tell me one thing, be so kind:
Is it made clear, too, in this patent,

*Damn it; why not?

If their lord dislike the peasants,
Should they grab scythes and seize and bind?
And does it order conflagrations,
Slaughter, deaths, cruel persecutions,
Looting of manor properties?"

"*Herr Schlachziz,*" spoke the Commissioner,
"*Herr Schlachziz, mässigen Sie sich!*"†
All men means well the Emperor.
Whereas of robbery and slaughter
The royal patent doesn't speak."

"Nor in the Forty-sixth year either?"

"*Herr Schlachziz,* sir, you're very quick
In your suspicions. Learn your lesson
And leave the Forty-sixth alone.
It was your Polish-sent assassins
Who'd started shooting at the peasants,
And on your own heads you had drawn
Much trouble. If you only had
Treated the serfs as human beings,
There would have been no fires, slayings;
The peasants' chests would gentry shield.
If, if—but you have different notions:
For the serf—beatings, servitude;
You plan another insurrection—
Noble times call you—nationhood!
When our King, with legality,
Gives lords and peasants the same deal,
You scream, you've been deprived of liberty.
The King wants the peasants to rebel,
You charge. No, Lord, move over a space.
The peasant sees, he isn't blind,
What things are sound, what causes pain.
Der Bauer, Squire, *ist für uns!*‡
Assassination times are over,
But if some wolves now come around,
Our stable try to overpower,
They shall find here now faithful hounds.
Ear-cuffing then shall be so sound
That many years they shall remember."

"*O sapperment!* A difficult time
When everything has turned canine.
There are many dogs in our dominion,
But, Mister, now, in my opinion,
You are mistaken, if you look
As dogs upon this peasant folk,

†Mr. Nobleman, control yourself!
‡The farmer (peasant) is for us!

92

For faithful dogs know their master;
Defend and shield will trusty dogs
In a dark hour of disaster!
These aren't dogs, but simply pigs!
You don't believe me? Go on, try
Your paper to my dogs to read:
Then you will notice right away
How they will leap at you, to greet."

"*Herr Schlachziz*," The Commissioner
    squeaked.
Offended, he arched high his chest
And raised his hand, but uppermost
Hatred now ruled in the Lord's heart.
He stamped his foot and madly shrieked
And turned red; sparks began to bob
Ill-ominously in his eyes.
"*Der Teufel drein!** Right here to spar
He's come with me! The Swabian slob!
Which one of you are strongest, boys?
Seize him immediately; put
Into the kennel; latch the gate!
Let him read there this writ of his!
You gaping fools (to us he spoke)
Didn't I give you enough strokes?
The devil steers, you never miss
To fall into my hands! The gate
Secure! To all on the estate
I'll serve a breakfast! Switches, rods!"

We froze. Before we our senses
Regained, already the Lord's servants
Seized the Commissioner on the spot.
No matter how he'd buck and yell,
He ran with them against his will.
Behind waved the tails of his frock coat.

XVII

The Lord's kennels—
The Commissioner in the kennels—
The destruction of the kennels—
The Commissioner wants to confront the
    Squire—
"Traditional Polish hospitality"—
The Commissioner as a peacemaker

The Squire had a splendid kennel
Because at hunting he excelled;
To the fun of the chase for long he thrilled.
A pretty penny did he channel

*The devil take it!

For his dogs. Near the stable stalls,
Abutting at the storehouse wall,
There stood his kennels: a tall fence,
The length of it by a roof surmounted.
Within this fence, as though demented
Whimpered and howled the canine race.
A hundred strong, this menagerie;
Breeds, colors, hues—a variety:
Greyhounds, bulldogs, terriers—what all.
Some of the dogs on chains were kept,
Some in dog houses calmly slept,
Others pulled on their chains and leaped
The paling's height, and liked to howl.
But thrice a day the dogs were fed,
And meagerly, lest they get fat:
Lean dogs pursue the game much quicker.
No one could pet or stroke these hounds,
The kennel ground was out of bounds
To all, save Efrem, their keeper.
At times you'd pass the kennels' fringe,
This rabble'd start to yelp and lunge,
Biting the ground on which they walk.
No wonder, when we heard the Lord
Of this unheard of, strange plan speak—
To do this act, insane and cruel,
To shove the Commissioner in the kennel—
The whole assembly there felt sick.

The Lord stands there: a thunderhead.
The kennel rumbles: gravel ground
On querns. But now the canine din
Rises to dreadful yelps and yammer:
They've carried out the wicked order;
The Commissioner is now within.
The lordly flunkeys are still there,
Perhaps the gateway to secure,
Stupidly grinning. But just then
A human scream was heard, so wild
Through the dog noise, from the inside—
Enough the human heart to stun.
"Violence! Help me!" The voice yelled
From the enclosure—then was stilled.
As though touched off by a sudden spark,
"Save him!" together we all roared.
"Hurry and break this fence apart!
God! The Commissioner's been devoured!"
How it all happened knows but God.
All at once, like a thunder rumble,
For the kennels headed the whole crowd.
Beneath our feet the courtyard trembled

From so much thumping. In a tick,
The fence became a pile of sticks.
The kennels, roofs—in splinters all;
The bigger, vicious of the mutts
All, on the spot, were clubbed to death . . .
Noise, violence, and bloody poles,
Blasphemy, screams, repeated blows
Merged in a deafening symphony;
I wish you all—if God allows—
To be spared such cacophony.

Far and wide, later went around
Over the foothills and the plains,
The story, telling how the hounds
By us on freedom's day were slain;
We'd sanctified with blood canine
Our freedom. There's no need to dwell
On how our folk likes funny things;
A schoolboy told of a happening
When the Bastille was France's bane:
If one was put within its walls,
He might well bid the world farewell.
Well, the accursed Bastille was wrecked
By the populace, torn to the ground;
And only then the free sun peeked
Into their homes; a new day dawned.
Our people got the story's gist:
We'll have a fight with the dogs, at least,
Instead of the Bastille. Thus laughs
This battle often did provoke—
But at the time we saw no joke
In it; we only cared to look
For one thing which was on our lips:
"Where is he? Where's the Commissioner?
Where is the writ from the Emperor?"

He was nowhere in evidence!
Anxiety seized everyone:
Did the hounds eat him totally
And didn't leave a single bone?
But look: the dogs had made a home
In straw. A rustle there: let's see—
We got down, raked the straw away:
And there was our Commissioner!
His chest pressed to the ground, he lay;
His trunk inside a kennel hole;
His legs alone were on display.
And he was holding in his hand
The freedom writ from the Emperor.
He shook; it took some strain to pull
The man into the light again,

But soon the poor man groaned with pain
When he stood up; the frenzied mutts
Ripped up to shreds the pants on him.
They tore the flesh, and serious wounds
In many places could be seen,
And blood flowed also; surely, death
The luckless man there would have found
If he had failed beforehand
To hide himself, and if not we
Acted at once to put an end
To such horrific drollery.

"Oh, ah, now lead me to the Lord,"
Moaned the Commissioner, "oh, a-a-h!
*Jetzt wird er sehn!** Each wound's worth
Two witnesses on my behalf.
Now he is going to get his!"

Limping along, he had to lean
Upon the shoulders of our youth;
He had to clench his teeth with pain.
Well, well, the writing on the wall
The Lord could smell, for to excess
He knew he'd pushed his beastliness:
Ours was not a courtesy call.
Pulling his flunkeys in at once,
Pushing the bolts in on the doors,
Himself, a rifle in his hand,
In an open window took a stand.
Such military preparations
Never occurred to the Commissioner,
Who pointed out, as he came near
The wounds on his legs: "Is this, sir,
Old-fashioned Polish hospitality?
Herr Schlachziz, this is your destruction.
As of now, for this playful jest
I place you, sir, under arrest!
What's this? You've joined the troops already?"

The Lord no army planned to join,
At the Commissioner took aim,
And shouted at him: "Do you see?
You'd better run, you son of a Kraut,
Before your life's light is snuffed out
By a quick bullet, instantly!"

He forgot his wounds when he saw the gun,
As though from a snake on the run,
The Commissioner painfully jumped back.

*Now I'll show him!

He looked around him, to make sure
That his new place was quite secure,
And only then he chanced to speak:
"A threat, *Herr Schlachziz*? Very good;
But for this threatening attitude
You shall account! I say again,
Surrender to my custody!
You've been arrested! In Law's name,
Give in; reduce your penalty."

"Come on and take me! I am here!"
Myhucki shouted with derision . . .
At once from every window peered
Barrels of rifles. This was war!
The whole crowd stirred in great confusion.
The Commissioner paled and stood in silence,
Quite at a loss what to say now.
Now, as a spokeman of the peasants,
Our Elder made this utterance:
"Sir, we will act, if you allow!
The day of our liberation
Means service to the Emperor.
The Lord's begun an insurrection,
So we'll bring our force to bear
Upon the Lord, to set him straight!
What say you, people?"

                    "That is right!"
The whole assembly answered shrilly.
"For Horozhana showed us clearly
How from their holes the beasts to scare.
Go get some straw! And strike the flint!
We'll soon see how they shall repent.
We'll lure them out in the open air!"

The poor Commissioner turned paler,
Trembled, and fell upon his knees.
"O peasants!" he implored us. "Please
Just one more time do me this favor,
Do this for me, this final time:
Stop everything now and stay calm!
Don't fire the Hall, but head for home!
Do not destroy me! Let him be!
For if the Hall goes up in flames,
From every side you shall hear screams:
'The Commissioner made them!' Only see
That the Lord doesn't run away,
And I shall bring him down to heel.
Don't make me deal with this as well!
Now you go home and do not tell
A soul what's happened here today."

We thought about it and agreed.
Such was our Squire's destiny
That his foes came to his defence.
"And what of our liberty?"

"Don't you believe it?"

                    "Our God knows
How we are longing to believe.
But so much punishment we've taken,
So often we have been mistaken,
We want to look before we leap."

"Poor peasants! A poor land, indeed!"
The Commissioner raised his eyes and sighed.
"So many woes they've known, and horrors,
Even in goodness they've lost faith!
If that is so, send out your riders
To the *Starosta,* to inquire
If in this matter I have lied!
Your Elder, from this day, besides,
No feudal labor shall require."

"Have it your way! We shall dispatch
Men to the district, so's to judge
The truth of it," was our sentence.
We cleaned his injuries and dressed them,
Took the Commissioner and placed him
Upon his buggy. A whole crowd
Walked with him gaily, noisily
Beyond the town. We gave our word
To act maturely, wisely.
We passed the Lord's estate in silence,
But our watchmen, from the distance,
Observed the Manor and the Lord.

XVIII

Easter 1848—
The Lord is arrested—
The Commissioner and the Lord before the
community

It's Easter Sunday! God Almighty!
We hadn't since the world began
Had us this kind of Resurrection!
Noise, bustle, shouting since daylight;
Like an anthill, the village teems
With people. All without exception,
Head for the church. And when the first
Time came to sing that "Christ is risen,"
We all broke down and wept like children,

So hard, our sobbing shook the joists . . .
It seemed that we had waited eons,
Lived through such suffering and pains;
At last He'd risen in our midst.
And somehow, strangely, in our souls
We felt so light and bright and calm
That everyone, it seemed, was ready
To the whole universe to call,
To shout, and sing: the evil's gone!
Worst enemies were reconciled,
People embraced and kissed and smiled,
And the bells tolled without surcease.
Young people ran around, like drunk,
Shouted in every nook and close:
"No master now; no feudal work!
We all are free now—free, free, free!"
The children see what elders do,
And they begin to shout out, too,
Like some young quail in the greenery.

And when the worship reached its end,
The people filled the cemetery.
Of the one hundred who were there
All fell together on the ground.
The whole community intoned
These worshipful, majestic chords:
The hymn: "We Praise Thee, Our Lord."
Like thunder rolled out in the morning
The noble words, the joyous sounds,
But then the sacred song was drowned
At its conclusion by loud weeping.
Children, in vain would anyone try
At least some fragments to convey
Of what I chanced that famous day
To witness with these very eyes.
For joy, the people lost their senses:
Old people hopped about like youngsters;
Here was one with a pair of horses,
Kissing them as he would his brothers;
He'd talk to them and pet and hug.
A group of village girls, together,
Strip their hair of every ribbon,
Prostrate themselves before an ikon,
And place them there. The men give tongue,
When greeting others, to these words:
"Christ's risen, and the servitude
The devil's taken!" A greybeard,
The oldest local patriarch,
On an ancient, barely visible mound,
Presses his breast against the earth,
Embraces hard the grassy ground,

And shouts: "O daddy, do you hear?
We are free now! O daddy, speak!
For a whole century you bore
The cursed serfdom; you were loath
To die; you pined for freedom; look
We're free. For you it's come too late,
For freedom's ray has pierced our nook
But now. My grandsons fear no more
The Manor'd claim them, just like me!
Ready to join you, father dear;
Your son is certain to die free!"

But lo! Our Priest has barely managed
Over the Easter bread to pray,
When we observe that down the village
Something is moving. Topcoats grey;
The buttons glitter in the sun,
As do the sharp blades overhead.
The heavy mass, in rows, as one,
Thuds as it goes with a heavy tread.
Soldiers! A loud roll of the drum
Sprays, like dried peas, against a wall.
I throw a glance—God bless my soul—
Our Lord's inside of the platoon!
Hands twisted back; despondently
He looked down now, as though he cursed
The day, the sun, and all the earth;
Ashamed of us. An orderly
Held on to the ends of the rope
Entwined around the lordly wrists,
Just as a peasant would who leads
An ox to market. On his gig,
The Commissisoner brought up the rear.
He smiled when they all came near
The church hill and the village throng,
The people who stood there agape
With fear and awe, at the display
They weren't used to. Now at last
The whole procession came abreast
Of us. The Commissioner cried "Hey,
Corporal, hold it!"

       "Halt!" Comes fast
From the noncom.

       "Christ is risen!"
Was the Commissioner's greeting cry.
"Well, do you believe that freedom
Has come to you? Well, now Godspeed!
Here is your Lord. Perhaps you would
Bid him farewell now, and express

Your thanks for his great kindliness?
Come on now, people! Hurry, do,
Becauses no one can say how soon
You will be seeing him again.
He's been asked out to eat the stew
Of which alone he is the cook.
It'll take time before he's back."

We stood there silently; struck dumb.
At once awe, joy, and clemency
Fought in our hearts for supremacy.
The eyes of the whole peasant mob
Were on the Lord. Grim countenanced
And sad he stood, as though he sensed
He had been touched by Divine wrath.
Yet not a single hostile about
Derisive laughter, or a curse
Came from the crowd. Why should we heckle
Or curse a man already shackled,
Already beaten without us?

Silent was not the Commissioner:
His limbs apparently gave pain;
He clenched his teeth; it was severe.
His one desire, it was clear,
Was to find ways in which to rack
The Lord, and clearly with this aim
He forced the Squire now to trek
Across the village; told a lackey
To hold the rope behind his back.

Now to his prisoner he spoke:
"*Herr Schlachziz,* the folk here, you see,
Mere cattle in your estimation,
Have more of human decency
Than you! In your bleak situation,
They all refuse to curse and mock.
They now forgive you your transgressions—
I see it plainly from their mien!
O peasants, peasants, full of kindness!
But I, dear sir, am not like them!
When I am angered, I'm pure malice!
Stupid is he, dear sir, who gives
More than he has, and one who wishes
To appear better than he is!
He who has caused me some distress
Better not fall into my clutches,

By day or night, watch out, beware!
It's likely to cost him dear."
Here the Lord stirred—an animal caged—
And turned around with such dread rage
Toward the Commissioner in the back;
And it was such a hate-filled look
That the man blanched.

        "Headman! Beast!
You evil German spawn accursed!
Hasn't your tongue yet shrivelled up?
Not satisfied with my pain here?
What of my wife's despair and tears?
Wasn't the painful cry enough,
The moment when we had to part,
To make you wholly gratified?
You shoved her, felled her in the mud . . .
You trash! You aren't even worth
One tear of hers! You savage beast!
Now you are urging these brutes on
To claw, to tear us limb from limb!
She's feeble; I'm under arrest.
But no! God's kind, and this affliction,
Like a black cloud, shall also pass!
Lead to the *Starosta* at once!
God's stronger than Kraut persecution."

"Ha, ha," the commissisoner guffawed,
"*Herr Schlachziz,* have you turned to God?
*Sehr schon!** Is this a recent switch?
Because quite recently, I hear,
These very peasants found you'd barred
The door to their holy church!
Of course, we'll go; the time is ample,
To the *Starosta's,* in due course;
Beforehand, though, we'll make you sample
The life in our calaboose!"
He spoke two words to the corporal,
The corporal shouted to his crew:
"*Marsch!*"

        "People, fare you well!"
The Commissioner shouted from his seat.
The whole procession did proceed
Along the road and out of view.

*Very nice.

XIX

The Manor without its master—
The first Sunday after Easter—
"The Lady is innocent"—
The peasants put the Manor in order—
The Lady is ill—
The Lady is host to the community—
The peasants go to liberate the Lord

With feast days over, strange, so strange
We felt. When workday mornings came,
No guard stood in the window frame,
Knocked with his crook, or heaped goddamns,
Driving to work. Now and again
The Manor guards appeared in dreams.
In waking life, there'd been a change.
Out in the fields, the people work
For their own gain, and sing the while;
The blue sky smiles, people smile.
It's noon. The peasant takes a break
Next to his oxen, from toil weak.
He eats his lunch and watches out
Whether the Lord's guard is about;
Then he recalls: he's a serf no more,
And at the firmament azure,
The man directs a joyous tune.
He stops, looks round, and bellows on:
"Hey, perish each and every bother,
And may the devil rip its mother!"

As though accursed, there stood the Manor
In silence at the village edge;
Its trees in bloom. We felt no urge
What went on in it to discover.
Each found so much to occupy
His time: his own concerns and joy;
Therefore we asked not what went on
Inside it. Lolling in the sun,
The servants sat. The ploughs did not
Go out to plow; no cry or shout
Came from the Hall: no hum; no sounds.
The guests, the toasts, the playing bands
Had been, as though by storms quite sudden,
Blasted away. From the estate
No one had come on us to call.
Such are God's own mysterious ways!
A single miniscule word—*Freedom*—
And instantly between the Hall
And us as though a mountain lay!

Then on the Sunday after Easter,
After the Mass we stood outdoors

Around the church. And here once more
We talked of recent tribulations
And of the outlook for the future,
Of freedom and the fear of war,
Of how the Poles had laid a plot
To organize (they said) in Lvov
Councils and guardsmen and what not:
Some cross themselves, while others laugh . . .
Then our Elder cried: "Attention!
Brothers and gentlemen," he said,
"I have a word or two to say."
Talk ceased.

       "Our great Almighty God
Has granted us our holy freedom.
Glory to Him!" He doffed his hat
And crossed himself; we did likewise.
"We have good reasons to rejoice.
However, we cannot abandon
In our gladness such as those
To whom our joy has brought God's wrath.
My sirs and brothers, we know that
Our Lord's in prison." Here he paused
And cleared his throat. "Of course, he often
Allowed himself to jest with us,
And for all that he's getting his.
But, sirs, within the Hall's confines,
His wife remains, with orphaned children,
And it was she who many a time
Helped us; employing words and tears,
She tried her husband's heart to soften . . .
She pled with him . . ."

       "Milady's kind!
You're right!" some voices did concur.
"She's innocent!"

       "Thus, to my mind,
We would be sinning, brothers dear,
If upon her we were inclined
For others' wrongs revenge to wreak.
Has anyone been there this week
To see her? Is she well?"

       "We didn't."
"No one? The Manor House's so quiet;
Some evil may well have transpired . . .
After all that went on before
She fears us, tends now to assume
That the whole village's against her.
Brothers and sirs, here is the sum

98

Of my advice: today let's choose
Some of us to go to the Manor House
And cheer her up. If there's a need
Of any help, we won't refuse.
For this God'll grant us a reward."

"Yes, yes!" the crowd around him cried.
"You must go, Elder, and you, Jake
(The people pointed to my person)
And you, Prokip, and you too, Simon.
Go on! It simply isn't right
To let Milady thus go under
Before our eyes; let the help take
The place apart, and steal and plunder!
What happened is past history.
Now we must come to the lady's aid.
Go tell her, the community
Will work for the estate unpaid
Until the Squire is released!"

"Yes, brothers, thank you for your trust!"
We said then, made a sign of the cross
And for the Manor set our course.

My goodness, what a transformation
We found! As though a lightning bolt
Had struck, or a contagion rolled
Across the place. Throughout the mansion
Doors are agape, and in the byres,
Calling for water, lows the cattle;
The devil knows where the servants dawdle.
One hears but whispers in the corners.
The ploughs and harrows to the harness
Are hitched right there within the barn,
Where a whole week ago, we workers
Abandoned them. Although it's noon,
The lackeys in the kitchen snooze.
The fires aren't lit, and offal
Lies everywhere. A workday noise
Is heard . . . We soundlessly come up:
The coachman and his better half,
In their hands a broken chisel,
An axe; with all their might they whack,
Attempting the Lord's safe to crack.
When they saw us, they turned to stone,
Dropped everything and tried to run,
But couldn't quite imagine where.
"Well, now," the Elder said, "don't bother;
Where would you run to? Run no further!"

"Where is Milady?"

"Lying there,"
The coachman pointed to a chamber.
From there faint cries of sorrow, dolor
Were audible. Our hearts died.
O God, our dear and just Creator!
Yesterday only—glory, splendor,
And so much glitter, so much pride;
Where are they now?

By a side door,
We went into her boudoir,
And thus she couldn't very well
See us at first. She lay upon
Her bed and uttered little moans.
She looked quite blue, she was so pale.

"Orynna, is it you?" (her call
Was for her maid, the only soul
Who with her mistress chose to stay.
Whatever food she could procure
She fed her patient, gave good care.
To the village now she'd gone away:
The Elder she had planned to visit
And some assistance to solicit.)
We came up closer and said, "Nay;
Dear madam, what is troubling you?"

She glanced at us, and her hands flew
To shield her eyes. "O Lord, help me!"
Atremble, said she with a groan.
"This means my final hour's come!
God help me! This is banditry!"

"Milady, don't say this; God keep you!
Don't be afraid, and look around you:
Our sincere hearts we've come to offer.
The village sends us, and we will
Aid you at home and in the field
With all that is in our power!"
Then the poor lady did uncover
Her face and opened her eyes wide.
"Could this be true? Are you all sober?
You're human beings, too, despite
All the repressions, flayings, torment;
Did they not blunt your humanity?
O God! Why didst Thou grant this moment
For me to live through? From today
My whole remaining life must be
But one reproach that I permitted
So many wrongs to be committed
Against you I could have turned away.

After the way you have been treated,
Me worthy of your aid you deem?
God bless! As long as I endure,
Which won't be very long, I fear,
I shall with very high esteem
Regard this present deed of yours.
But I'm so poor, downtrodden now,
And ill! The help will soon remove,
I'm sure, the rafters from the house.
My husband's jailed; where, I don't know . . .
May God repay you. At this time
So hard, at least you've come to call.
May God provide that you all find
Such selfless help in need, as well."

Our lady then dissolved in sobs
And pressed her pale exhausted face
Against the pillows. Well, why tarry?
We didn't chat in there too much,
But to the village sent to fetch
Girls, young men, women, in a hurry.
The Elder rounded up to grill
The servants; if someone did steal,
He brought it back. We sent to summon
A doctor. All the Manor rooms
Were put in order by the women.
Some light the fires, some a broth
Cook for Madame; and each free farmer
With others tries a queue to set,
With whom to pair and in what order,
To plow the fields of the Estate.

Our lady was back on her feet
Within a week. The sole girl kept
Was our Orynna, for the village
Kicked all the other servants out.
For the most part, the vernal tillage
Of Manor lands was now complete.
But our lady, like a mute,
Says not a word, betimes she sighs;
Or she dissolves in floods of tears,
When in her memory reappears
An image of those cursed past days.
But there were other things, as well,
That caused those daily crying spells:
About her husband not a whisper!
How was he? His confinement place?
Was he wiped out without a trace?

Three weeks now have gone by since Easter.
The Lady summons to the Mansion
The village people for discussion.

We come and stand out in the yard,
As in the past, and gaze toward
The porch. The Lady we espy
In a window, beckoning us to come,
Inviting us to the salon.
We enter, look—it's a surprise:
The tables set with plates and glasses,
Liquor and beer in wooden casks
Stands in the corners and recesses.
The Lady entered and spoke thus:

"Take your seats, people! Now's begun
For all of us a time of change:
Your great misfortune is now gone;
Our sins we'll try now to expunge.
I understand now how unjustly
You have been treated by my man,
And you, so selflessly, uprightly
Came to relieve me of my torment—
Moreover, in the darkest moment
When everyone this house would shun.
You, people, now for me remain
My only neighbors and protectors
And brothers. Pardon, if again
Today I also ask for aid.
It's proper, though, ere I begin,
To drink together and break bread.
Gone now for good are slaves and masters;
Peaceful relations we now need!"

And following a peasant custom,
She touched a goblet to her lips
And to the Elder passed it on.
"God grant it that throughout our Kingdom
Shine brightly harmony and peace,
As it does here!" Madame intoned.

"God grant it, too, that by their woes
To live with people gentry learn!
He who treats us as human beings
Will get like treatment in return!"
Thus spoke our people in response.
The goblet went from hand to hand,
In turn, as though it were a dance,
To everyone who sat around.

The Lady also sits among us:
Eats not or drinks—she is so sad,
Fighting the tears—it's obvious.
For us as well, it's very hard
To choke food down. Then our hostess
Bursts into tears. We all begin,

As best we can, to offer cheer.
But she can hardly through her tears
Pronounce: "My husband, my poor man!
Where is he now? Have you, my dearest,
Heard anything? Has anyone?"

"Nobody."

       "Did my husband drown?
O God Almighty! Three weeks' absence!
While I lay bedridden, sick,
Daily I hoped he would come back.
In vain! My friends, for your assistance
I beg! For this is quite outrageous!
The Commissioner may well be furious,
But he holds not the highest post:
He must defer to the *Starost*!
And the *Starosta*'s our friend.
He ate and drank here, came to hunt.
And thus he shouldn't tolerate
That my poor man deteriorate
In jail so long. O the All-Wise,
Thou givest us a heavy cross!"

A spell of sobbing choked her up.
But in a moment she spoke up.
"What is the proper course of action?
To Lvov—Vienna—take a trip?
Or, like the lowest kind, to stoop
To the man who's caused my man's detention,
To fall at the Commissioner's feet
And try for lenience to plead
Or justice? Tell me what to do!"

The present there shook their heads.
The Elder said: "It is not true,
My noble Lady. For the facts
Speak against you. He did offend
The Commissioner, who's now become
The district's boss! When the command
Came for the *Starosta* to move,
I was right there. I recommend:
Too far away is the Emperor's home,
And it is pretty far to Lvov;
And in the offices they shall
Hurry things up in their way;
The Squire, meanwhile, may decay
Before he ever leaves the jail.
No, I would choose another track:
Milady, go and pack your things;
Some of us, too, will make the trip.
We'll plead with words, and you will weep.

Without petitions or anything.
I'm sure the Commissioner'll give him back."

Here our Lady brightened greatly:
"Dear people, thank you most sincerely!
God spare you such extremity!
Your help I never shall forget,
I'll be obliged until my death
For your most selfless charity."

XX

The Lord in prison—
The Lord at exercise—
The Commissioner's revenge—
Liberation and conclusion

Within the walls of his prison cell—
Dirty and damp and dark and small—
The Squire paced and gasped for breath.
He was oppressed by grief and wrath.
A grated window, very high,
As though a cataractic eye,
Surveyed the prison with a squint:
The locked-out beautiful paradise,
The great wide world, the sun's bright rays,
The cerulean firmament—
It showed, tormented, and provoked,
As though a viper's fang, it pricked . . .
Inside the walls, like a caged beast,
Chafing in anguish at the bars,
He prayed to God, and then he swore,
While coughing spasms shook his chest.

My dearest God, how he had changed!
After some twenty or so days,
Less than one half there still remained
Of the old Squire. He'd lost weight,
Scowled grimly; his eyes roamed about
The cell; their spark gone totally.
Life a deep furrow had gouged out
Across his forehead; constantly,
He had to cough and even blood
Brought up. "When he initially
Was brought into this prison building,"
By the jail turnkeys I was told,
"It seemed, he found it very hard
To face his plight. Without a warning,
He leaped up, almost climbed the walls,
And then again he'd shout and scream,
Break everything to smithereens.
Against his cell's door, with his head

He'd pound, and all his prison food
He'd hurl at jailers around him.
Three days he starved, did not sleep either,
For the *Starosta* he kept asking,
But the *Starosta* wouldn't bother
About him; just then he was moving
To Lvov. The Squire then calmed down
A little and began to eat.
But long he couldn't sleep at night
And begged us—for the love of God—
That we bring him some news from home.
But the Commissioner had interdicted
All contact with him. You can guess
What kind of cell he had selected;
He could not find one that was worse.
And in addition he directed
That we but once a day, at dusk
May let him out for exercise."

Today, too, at the fall of night,
The jailer's key grates in the lock.
"Exercise," shouts he. Swift the Lord
Picks up his headgear, "By what right
The damned Kraut holds me here?" he
    whispered
As he went out. "How does he dare,
Without a trial? Will he hold
Me so forever? I don't hear
A word from home. I am exhausted—
That's nothing—but my wife . . . O Heaven!
For all I know, perhaps this villain
Egged the serfs on, and now my home
Is but scorched rubble; and now she
Is perishing in agony . . .
If that's the case, this means your own
Life shall end, too, you Enemy!"

Such heavy ever-present thoughts
Haunted him, seared him, and oppressed;
His hands clenched into fists, he now
Raced round the yard in a frenzied state.
Lo! the Commissioner comes through the gate,
Two pairs of prison guards in tow.
The Commissioner turned now to his person
And smiled at him, full of venom.
This smile hit him with a force,
As though a knife his heart did pierce.
Not waiting for the Commissioner's say,
The Squire suddenly lunged forth,
Grabbed the Commissioner by throat,
And shouted: "You bloodsucker! Knave!
Doesn't all this yet fill the bill?

For my pain do you hunger still?
Dispatch me now if you still crave
For more!"

    "*Gewalt!** Come to my aid!"
Yelled the Commissioner, retreating.
The Lord was seized then by the guards.

He caught his breath and started laughing.
"Ho, ho, *Herr Schlachziz*; jokes aside;
That's how you are! Hey, you inside!
Hey, Mr. Warden, *Bank heraus!*"†
Myhucki paled, "What is all this?
You'd dare? I am a nobleman!"

"I beg you not to worry, please!
We've a constitutional regime.
Before the law, beneath the knout
We're equal. Boys, now *legt ihn platt!*‡
Teach him what this thing's all about!
Twenty-five lashes of the cat!"
In vain, the Lord did struggle, shout—
The constitution made him taste
Of what he oft to us dished out
So generously in the past.

He rose in shock and pale, as though
A corpse. Between his lips pressed tight,
Droplet by droplet, red blood flowed.
And also filling up with blood
Were his eyes' orbs—disturbed, irate.
He neared the German, very slow,
And whispered: "Now you pray to God!
This thing I really won't forget:
This thing, you Kraut, shall be your death!"

"My dear sir, Mister Nobleman,"
The German answered without heat,
And wonderingly shook his head,
"*Gedenken Sie, was Sie da sprechen!***
Don't say it; that is a *Verbrechen;*††
This is a threat! And you alone,
With all your noble haughtiness,
Have been the cause of all your torment.
And I was heading here this moment
To be the bearer of good news.

*Violence.
†Get the bench out.
‡Lay him down flat.
**Consider what you're saying.
‡‡Crime.

Your wife has come here to my place,
With peasants who were subject once
To you; and they have come to plead
On your behalf. Just rustic fools
But good men, Lord. Your wife had thus
A lengthy story here to tell:
How they all had come to her aid
In trouble. I could not refuse,
And came here willing to forgive
My agony and your abuse.
But a commotion of the kind
You've caused here, I can't overlook.
Here *Ordnung's** followed by the book!
For everyone! Now go and leave
All your lost yesterdays behind."

A wonder: the Commissioner's word
Which had announced the Lord's release
Brought to his torment no surcease,
But worsened it. The Squire's head
Hung low now. His eyes' former glow
Was out. So brisk not long ago,
His walk was slowed. Entirely,
He seemed bereft of sense and feeling.
He took a few steps haltingly;
Stopped, looked around; a fit of sobbing
Shook his whole body suddenly.

Why was he crying? But from pain,
Or 'cause his freedom he'd regain?
Or did he sense that death was near?
Was now his hardened conscience
Touched by peasant benevolence,
Ignored by violence before?

My narrative must end right here.
Further events I can relate
In a few words. His conscience stirred
Too late. Imprisonment and worry
Had undermined his constitution,
So that he barely on his feet
Could stand. The medical conclusion

*Order.

Stated, in his case, there was nary
A help, except in Italy's land,
In warmer climes. Well—what to do
But go there if they recommend?
But how if liquid funds are few?
Ho, ho, but there's a helpful Jew!
Our Moshko doesn't miss a clue!
As soon as he'd heard that their lordships
Were short of cash—came like a shot . . .
(But at the time of recent hardships,
He never put in an appearance,
And with the thieves was in connivance
Who manor property stole then,
And which eventually he bought.)
And thus this Judas danced attendance,
Slipped in the money—and a pen;
Despite his total unexpectance,
The Lord signed with the Jew a mortgage.
Before the harvest rolled around,
Their lordships left on their voyage;
For their children homes were found;
They shut the mansion, and the village
The Jew was renting.

A year's passage
Brought back the Lady, now a widow.
In foreign lands the Lord had perished.

She was so sad, and lived alone,
And never talked with anyone.
But Moshko faithfully attended,
And all her properties he rented.
And in this way a few more years
Went by. The lady packed one day,
Spoke to no one, said no good-byes
To anyone, and sped away.
Time has erased her every trace.

And Moshko purchased the whole place.

January and February 1887

Fox Mykyta

Song One

Spring arrived at last: resplendent,
Multifloral, warm, and brilliant—
Like a wreathed, beribboned lass.
Groves and meadows, in renascence,
Filled with talk and sundry noises.
Songs resounded in the bush.

Leo, all the animals' sovereign,
Stamps his writs with seal and ribbon,
Sends then out to one and all:
"Our convention is upon us!
Hie 'self to the Royal Palace,
If you are an animal!"

Pilgrim-like, in mobs and bunches,
Bearing banners of their churches—
All that bray and bark and cackle—
All come; but one seems quite heedless,
Ensconced safely in his fortress:
Fox Mykyta—brigand, rebel.

He hides not without causation.
Conscience calls him to attention:
"You have wronged your fellow beasts!"
In his capital, meanwhile,
Leo, with his Queen, in style,
Sat down justice to dispense.

First appeared one Wolf Unsated:
"Majesty, I have been baited
By Mykyta half to death!
He beats up and bites my babies
And calumniates my Lady;
It is shameful to repeat.

"And myself (where are his scruples?)
Using perfidy and swindle,
The Fox almost killed me once.
It occurred on the occasion
When a royal proclamation
Made me a Justice of the Peace.

"Once Mykyta barged in on me:
'Here's a capital matter, Wolfie!
Four Rams are with me outside.
The estate of their late sire
Leaves his sons a nice half-acre;
By your judgment they'll abide.

" 'See, they all began to squabble,
To divide it quite unable—
A surveyor is called for.
I shall lead them to my lair,
And you act as a surveyor . . .
This job carries its reward.'

"I own up: I was elated;
For the Rams to mediate
I love dearly, above all,
'Cause when I decide the matter,
One or all of them together,
Shall not file an appeal.

"Quickly, I do up my buttons,
Exchange greetings with the Muttons—
They remind of well-filled pods!
'Well, lads, without hesitation,
Seek the parcel in contention!
Do you have the poles and rods?'

" 'Yes, we have all the equipment.'
The Rams go to their allotment,
Start to measure—but no way!
There's too wide, and here's too narrow,
They won't deal across the furrow;
The land's rich there; here it's clay.

"Then Mykyta said: 'I'll tell you:
There is but one certain venue
Whose pursuit the truth shall yield.
You stand in the center, Wolfie;
Each one of them in a jiffy
Seek a corner of the field.

" 'Halt there, and remain there stock-still,
Everyone be doubly careful!
When I holler: one, two, three!
Each one gallop without letup
To where Mr. Wolf is set up,
With your best velocity.

" 'He who can most speedily canter,
Shove the Wolf right off the center,
Shall receive the biggest whack.
Clear?' 'We need no explanation.'
'Places! T'ward your destination!
May God grant you every luck!'

"In the hub I stood meanwhile,
Unsuspecting of his guile;
Th' Fox on the periphery.
Bursting with concealed amusement,
How he growled, and how he whistled:
'Run together! One! Two! Three!'

"Fox Mykyta barely shouted
When at full speed they departed,
The four Rams concurrently.
When they crashed into the center,
It was as though four big mortars
Hit me simultaneously.

"The four Rams, with their blows cruel,
'T seemed had smashed my bones to gruel
During their first foray.
I but gasped in a dizzy whirl,
Took a dive into the soil,
Bloody mist obscured my eyes.

"But the Rams pay no attention
That they're causing my extinction,
That unconscious I repine.
Using his horns, one shoves hither,
Then another pushes thither,
Just to move the borderline.

"Thus for long they litigated,
Once a minute they recoiled,
Just to slam my flanks again.
And Mykyta, that damned monster,
On the ground crawled like a lobster,
Laughing at my mortal pain.

"A pinch of baccy would've been ample
(And an infamous example!)
For the Rams a Wolf to slay.

God sent my dear wife, however,
Who came out to reconnoiter;
Only then they ran away."

Telling Leo what befell him,
Like a very sad news item,
The Wolf spoke in a grave voice.
Yet the Queen could not but giggle,
And his laugh the King must stifle,
To discourage public noise.

On his hind legs stood up Hector,
A poor puppy, and said: "Caesar!
Guardian of legality!
I possessed a piece of sausage,
Which I hid and tried to salvage;
This Mykyta stole from me."

Cat Moorlyk voiced an objection;
"That's your canine law conception!
But the sausage—it was mine!
I doubt not the Fox's thievery,
But I stole it from the pantry
At the blacksmith's at that time."

"Truly spoken; there's no question,"
The Lynx started his oration,
"That Mykyta is a thief.
For a chicken, a shot of liquor,
He'll sell his own soul and honor,
His religious beliefs.

"He's a Judas, he's a heathen,
But a sham is all his civism.
Who'd expect good from his ilk?
I know very well his nature:
To the Jews would sell this creature
Our hides for a pound of pork.

"Here's a blessed soul—the Rabbit,
And his nightly, daily habit
Is to wish harm on no one.
He became Mykyta's pupil,
Hoping that he'd learn the Missal—
Singing of quotidian chants.

"Oh, it was such bitter learning:
From day one the Fox used caning.
When the fifth voice was their theme,
He shook poor Jack like a pear tree;
His soul would have left the body
If I hadn't saved his skin."

Next before the High Tribunal,
In defence, got up his uncle
Badger Borsuk F. Babai.
"Truly quoted our parents:
'From a foe expect no plaudits!'
All this rubbish! My, O my!

"Are you mindful of your honor,
Publicizing your behavior
Warming up old mold again?
Could you reminisce, Unsated,
How you hiked once with Mykyta?
That's a truthful, fresh refrain!

"Fox Mykyta was your partner,
But your own unsated anger
Pays with evil for his good.
Once you walked across a prairie
And both of you were so hungry
You could use your knees for food.

"Then the sound of 'Ha, ha! Gee, gee!'
It's a peasant in a buggy,
Carting fishes to a mart.
'Hey,' says Fox, 'a fine occasion!
Brother, here comes our nutrition,
But look out, now, and be smart!'

"The Fox jumped, in one maneouver,
On the highway and fell over
As if dead; stretched out each paw.
Lo! he lay out there spread-eagle!
Any peasant would be able
To deal him a mortal blow.

"A man drove up: off the wagon
He jumped down, prepared to bludgeon,
With a stone, the Fox to death.
But no breath escaped the varmint.
Softly says the man: 'My profit—
Enough fur for a winter hat.'

"He grabbed Foxie by the brushes,
Flung him up among the fishes,
And drove off in God's good time.
Foxie, with his wits about him,
Flung the fishes off the wagon.
In the tub remained but brine.

"No more fishes. The Fox bolted.
By the roadside he encountered
Wolfie, eating his last pike.

'Hey, you Wolfie, buddy-buddy,
Where's my share of our booty?
Let me now enjoy my bite.'

"The Wolf spoke with condescension:
'Over there's your tasty portion.
Eat, enjoy it, but don't choke!'
Watch ill will at its profoundness:
He gave Foxie only fish bones—
A reward for his great pluck.

"For the Rabbit 'twas no pleasance
To be handled by the short ones.
Did they not tan all our skins?
It's unheard of that the trivium
Without caning fill the cranium—
It's too silly to dwell on.

"And this Hector, short-tailed doggy,
Was caught in his hanky-panky,
For Moorlyk is here to tell
That this sausage, now notorious,
Of which Hector's so censorious,
From Moorlyk he stole himself.

" 'Cause my nephew's man of piety.
Any godless impropriety
Is horseradish to his nose.
It's been a whole year, for instance,
That his mouth has touched no viands,
In a strict fast, self-imposed.

"He caused me betimes a grievance
That this fast would harm his substance . . ."
But at once Babbai broke off.
A crowd of no mean proportion,
Of uncertain derivation,
Marched into the royal grove.

An old Rooster is their leader,
On their shoulders rests a litter,
And the followers come in pairs.
On the litter lies a chicken,
Followed by her kith and kinsmen;
Tears, lament, and sheer despair!

When he reached the seat of power,
Cried out the heroic tenor:
"Majesty, we crave your grace!
Our hope is dead through slaughter;
Fox Mykyta is the killer.
Let your court decide the case.

"We led our mild existence,
Causing no one harm or hindrance,
In a convent. I'd espy
How the Fox would watch our nidus,
Always keeping us in focus
With his predatory eye.

"I know all his crafty flim-flam;
Consequently, tell my children:
Now, be careful; God keep safe!
Do not run out to the forest,
For your toothy foe lurks in it.
He will rob you of your life.

"Once at the gate of the convent,
In the hairshirt of a penitent,
As a monk Mykyta stands.
He invokes the grace of Heaven
And a writ with the royal emblem
He holds open in his hands.

" 'Here,' he says, 'is a safe conduct.
The King says, as of this instant,
Among animals shall be peace.
Wolves and sheep shall live like brothers;
You and I with one another
Shall be as though of one race.

" 'You see, I've become a hermit;
As for meat, I have forsworn it;
Herbs and honey's all I eat.
Peace! May God give you His guidance,'
He said making an obeisance,
And went on into the world.

" 'Freedom, children! We'll be able,'
I tell them, 'out in the stubble,
To pick gleanings, run, and walk!'

Pleasure, joy, and song among us!
We all hurried to the entrance;
Some of us would not come back.

"We came out. Out of his ambush,
Fox Mykyta leapt out at us
And my daughter carried off.
I began to cockadoodle,
But away the Fox skedaddled
And hid in a wooded grove.

"Like church bells, my cries, resounded,
After him our faithful hounds, and . . .
All in vain! O dearest God!
They brought back her lifeless body.
That's how this defiant rowdy
Violates your own command!"

"Well, Babbai," the King said slowly,
"He's been fasting very strictly;
How your nephew saves his soul
You can see yourself. I've had it!
I must finish off this culprit
And his kind, once and for all!"

And the Bear, the Bruin, he summons:
"If you do esteem my kindness,
Brother, gird your scabbard on!
To Mykyta's go, my squire,
And demand that he stand trial,
In the strict, the strictest tone!

"But be wary of this scoundrel!
Brother, he's a tricky animal;
He may throw dust in your eyes!"
"What? He'd dare to try his trickery
On me?" said the Bear, quite angry,
And left for the Fox's place.

Song Two

If you're strange to the forest region,
You can't see, you can't envision
How Mykyta lives in it.
Foxkeep is a famous fortress;
Many's there a walk, a terrace;
Many a hideaway and pit.

In his shack, after exertion,
The Fox relished relaxation,
But at once he heard: knock, knock!

He looks out: O God in Heaven!
Bruin stands out there in person;
In his hands a frightful crook.

"Hey, Mykyta! Where's that varmint?
Come on out! I'm on an errand;
From the King himself I come!
You are guilty of much evil;
Angry's our Father Leo—
It is time now to atone.

"The King calls you to account!
'Show yourself now, and be prompt,
Fox Mykyta, lawless rebel!
And if he decides to shirk,
Let the headsman do his work!
Let him perish like a jackal!' "

All agog with concentration,
The Fox harked with full attention
To the Bruin's dread tirade.
But meanwhile he tried to fathom
How to teach this clown a lesson,
How to mute his foolish pride.

Through a crevice he peeks cautious:
Any danger of an ambush?
But no sign: the Bear's alone.
Boldly then outside he ventures,
His face radiant with pleasure:
"Uncle, welcome, welcome home!

"Uncle, is it you? My goodness!
On the road this lengthy distance,
In this scorching heat outside!
Tired, labored respiration,
Your fur oozes perspiration . . .
Can't His Royal Highness find

"Other envoys altogether . . .
That men in the upper drawer
Are thus in the service pressed?
I am doubly glad, meanwhile,
That for once my domicile
Harbors such an honored guest.

"Piece of cake for me this trial,
For I know that your wise counsel
Will provide the right defense.
One word from you in my favor
And my troubles will be over.
The King's ire shall soon pass.

"We're one clan; I'd follow rather
You through hell and through high water,
But tonight . . . Give us a break!
You'll observe: the skies are gloomy,
You are tired, and my tummy . . .
Well . . . I've got a bellyache."

"My dear nephew, what's the trouble?"
"It's a nuisance, my dear uncle!
I'm a hermit; therefore, meat

Is forbidden. For salvation
Of my soul—a stipulation:
Sickening honey I must eat."

"Honey!" shouted Mr. Bruin.
'Sickening honey?' I'd face ruin!
To get some, I'd sell my soul!
Honey! How do you procure it?
If you add it to my diet,
You'll regret it not at all."

"Uncle, you are being funny!"
"Get me a few quarts now, sonny,
And I'll seal it with an oath!
Honey's like the heavenly manna;
I'll do anything for honey!
Honey is my favorite food!"

"If you're serious, my dear uncle,
Let us go, although I'm feeble,
In this case, there's no way out!
Your wish comes from the Olympus;
For such high guests, it behooves us
To spare neither strength nor health.

"Not far from my domicile—
No more than a quarter mile—
Lives a peasant named Okhrim.
He has mead in obscene oodles,
And apart from being edible,
Truly, in it you can swim."

Bruin's sigh was so desirous,
His heart seemed to skip a synapse.
"Well, Mykyta, let's be gone."
Yonder hills hid the sun's fire,
When they made it to the byre
Of the wealthy man Okhrim.

On the ground there, near the garden,
A huge tree trunk, dry and oaken
Loomed. The carpenter's big sledge
Tried to split the trunk wide open.
At one end, therefore, he'd driven
Into it a giant wedge.

A crack in the log was open
Two palm measures, but the stubborn
Tree trunk failed to split apart.
From the wedge it creaked-croaked loudly,
As though clenching its teeth tightly,
As though saying: "Ouch, that hurt!"

"Uncle," spoke Mykyta softly,
"The log's open now completely—
Feel it gently on its side!
Though the log looks grey and crooked,
It holds honey by the bucket;
It has oft my needs supplied.

"Over the dale the dark is spreading.
A long time, in feather bedding
Peasants are asleep. Don't fear!
For God's sake, go fill your belly,
In the crack there get in boldly,
And meanwhile I'll guard your rear."

Said the Bruin: "Now I thank you.
Wait a moment, though, my nephew,
Lest some devil come perchance . . .
Wow, I smell the honey fragrance!
Place yourself ahead a distance;
Hold this axe here in your hands."

And the Bruin stuck in order
The paws, head, and neck together
In the widely gaping crack.
With a quick tap of his weapon,
The Fox shut the crack, once open.
The Bear was caught by the Oak.

The Oak thought: "I have my power!"
Grabbed the Bruin with full vigor
And began to crunch his skull.
The Fox shouted from the distance:
"Isn't this a splendid crevice?
The churl hid his honey well."

But the Bruin was struck speechless:
Though he groans and grunts and wheezes,
The log holds him firm and tight.
Thrice he tried to yank his body;
His joints creaked; the hold was steady;
And the outlook wasn't bright.

Says the Fox: "From your behavior
I hear clearly that you savor
Honey. But the flies are pests.
Eat it, but don't wallow in it,
For if you exceed the limit,
On your navel you'll eject."

But the honey doesn't grab him.
Back and forth he turns his bottom,
The log holds him like a vise.

He yanks, scratches, twists, poor fellow,
Then from pain lets out a bellow,
So loud, it might reach the skies.

Fox Mykyta keeps on jeering;
"Can you hear my uncle's singing?
Did you hit on the right key?
Now, be quiet, uncle, uncle!
Windows light up! There'll be trouble!
Uncle! Peasants on the way!"

And Okhrim, a well-heeled fellow,
Wakes up thinking: "What's that bellow?"
Peers into the window glass:
"Something black beside the lumber,
Perchance it could be a robber!"
And the peasant grabs his axe.

He came out and looked around him,
And he saw the Bruin struggling,
So at once he raised a yell:
"My dear neighbors, hurry over!
A Bear's captured in my lumber!
Come, be present at the kill!"

The whole village's in an uproar,
Like some wolves in their lair,
Suddenly from sleep aroused.
Seeking weapons, they are ready
To grab anything that's handy;
In nightclothes they leave the house.

From all sides they hit the Bruin—
Flails are flailing, pitchforks pitching—
Women use the oven-rake;
And Okhrim, the big log's owner,
Hit the bear with a heavy hammer:
Bang and bang and wham and whack!

Pain increased the Bruin's power:
One more time, with greater vigor—
And his forehead lost its skin.
One more jerk: he liberated
His front paws, but the log claimed
The skin and the claws off them.

"He is loose, he's free," they holler,
All the people run for cover,
And the Bruin took off fast,
To the woods, into the shrubbery,
Lay down and groaned very heavily,
As though giving up the ghost.

Fox Mykyta then came over:
"Well, well, Uncle, what a supper!
Did it satiate your soul?
If you like to dine on honey,
Say the word, and every Sunday
I'll arrange for such a meal.

"I was really apprehensive
When the man became discoursive;
I thought he'd resort to blows.
In the end, though, you politely
Parted from him, although surely
You had to pay him some dough.

"These Morocco boots you're sporting,
Red, as though you were a-courting—
Or perhaps because you're sad?
Where'd you buy your fancy headgear?
P'raps a present for your daughter?
And the color's also red."

Thus Mykyta made sport of him;
Twitched and twisted our poor Bruin,
Mumbling something as he lay.
On foot, with great difficulty,
He attained the royal party,
Crawling in on the third day.

When His Glorious Majesty saw it
That the Bear was so, so wretched,
He began his hands to wring.
"Hey, dear Bruin, my old buddy,
Who did beat you up so badly?
Who removed some of your skin?"

Said the Bear: "O King, my master!
I have met with a disaster.
It's Mykyta's handiwork.

I have suffered dreadful torment
On account of this bad varmint.
I was lucky not to croak."

The King stamped his foot with fury:
"This whole thing makes me so angry
That I swear upon this crown:
Pain awaits this thief, and torture,
And when we effect his capture,
He won't live to see the dawn."

The King tempered his opinion
And consulted with his minions,
How to string Mykyta up.
His decision was momentous:
He called Moorlyk to his presence
And to him he thus spoke up:

"Here you are, my Moorlyk faithful,
Though of stature not colossal,
But among us you're a brain.
I am sending you in person
And alone to see the villain—
To Mykyta's thievish den.

"Tell him that he must, with promptness,
Show up at the Royal Palace,
Fox Mykyta: brigand, rebel!
Threaten him with torture vile
If he tries to skip this trial,
And the outcome will be lethal."

Moorlyk bowed most courteously
And got ready for the journey,
Although scared out of his wits.
Though he loathed the royal honor,
He could not refuse the order:
The King serves, and you must eat.

Song Three

Cat Moorlyk began his mission,
Set his feet in double motion,
Took for lunch a roasted mouse.
Running through the shady forest,
Just in time for tea and crumpets,
He reached Fox Mykyta's house.

He knocks and awaits an answer,
Undergoes a peephole muster,
To Mykyta doffs his hat.

He bows to the Fox with courtesy,
Greets him very deferentially,
And then speaks to him thus (quote):

"Godfather, don't be offended,
By the King I am commanded,
And my errand's not just wind.
This is now the second instance
That our Emperor summons you
Through an envoy, to be tried.

"I won't stretch it or embroider:
The King's seething now with anger.
Therefore I advise you: come!
On his crown swore our Ruler,
If this summons you don't honor,
Your whole family faces doom."

"Moorlyk? You? How unexpected!"
Shouts Mykyta. "What a visit!
Goodness gracious, what joy!
Well, come here, let me embrace you!
Otherwise, I must forbid you
That we leave here right away.

"Is my Vixen not your auntie?
And she sees you very rarely;
She won't let us go at night.
And the Cubbies, my young children,
Would they part from their kinsman?
No, I tell you, it's not right.

"We shall all sup very nicely,
Sleep, and on the morrow early,
In the coolness—then godspeed!
'Cause this trial doesn't matter;
I will gladly go together
With you; of it rest assured.

"Now, the Bear—a different matter.
Bruin comes—just you consider—
Like a robber to my nest:
He begins to shout and threaten,
In his paws a giant bludgeon—
I am a small and weakly beast!"

"O Godfather," Moorlyk counters,
"Thank you for excessive kindness,
But to go is better still.
The night's clear; the moon's in heaven;
Bid good-bye to your wife and children;
Let's get going, if you will."

"Moorlyk," the Fox says, "see reason!
The night's dangerous. No wagon
Waits for us; nor can we fly.
The woods crawl with things most heinous,
If one of them pounces on us—
Do we fight or run away?"

The words that Mykyta utters
Give Moorlyk a case of jitters.
"You are right!" he gives assent.

"I must stay the night, I reckon.
Is there anything to count on
In the way of nourishment?"

"Don't be miffed, Moorlyk intrepid,
But I am a devout hermit;
To strict fast I must succumb.
But I'll get for your nutrition
The best food in my possession:
A honey-filled sweet honeycomb."

"Honey? Yechk! To me it's poison;
I will leave it for the Bruin!
Nothing better in the house?
Your manorial economy,
In some dark, forgotten cranny,
Harbors not one decent mouse?"

Said Mykyta: "Now you're kidding!
Even to a Turkish heathen
I would never offer mice!
Where'd you get the notion, sonny?
Eating mice?! Not even funny!
Boy, this certainly is news.

"But if mice indeed you fancy,
Moorlyk, we have them aplenty;
With them you can pave a road!
Over in the mayor's building
They are virtually swarming . . .
Right here in the neighborhood."

"O godfather, O my dearest,
Lead me to where mice are nearest;
I'm accustomed to this fare."
"Very well, push on behind us!"
And they crawled through weeds and rushes
To the chicken coup of the mayor.

A hole in the wall, the entrance
The Fox used in an appearance,
When he struck the mayor's roost . . .
Which was just the night preceeding.
He induced a rooster's bleeding,
And the cock gave up the ghost.

Having seen the rooster's plumage,
Left behind the last night's ravage,
The mayor shouted and turned puce:
"Basta, I must catch this outlaw!"
He attached inside the window
A rope made into a noose.

The Fox checked the situation
And called Moorlyk to attention:
"Hear the twittering of the mice?
Like some sparrows without guile!
Here's a hole into the stable,
In the clay; crawl in and chase!"

"How's the safety here, godfather?
We may well be courting danger.
Mayors are a wily folk!"
"Well," the treacherous Fox responded,
"One who is extremely timid
Should avoid this kind of work.

"I've not been inside the stable;
I have seen no wily guile,
And if you, boy, are afraid,
Let's go home and sup together
Of what's inside our larder:
Radishes and lemonade."

Moorlyk blushed with shame quite briefly,
Then he asked Mykyta quickly:
"Do you think that I am scared?
Fear is foreign to my species!"
He jumped boldly through the orifice
And was captured in the snare.

In the air now Moorlyk dangled,
And each movement further strangled
The poor writhing Moorlyk's neck.
He threw himself at the doorjamb;
Through the opening above him,
Peered Mykyta, the treacherous crook.

"Well," he asked, "Moorlyk, my darling,
Are the mousies to your liking?
Don't these creatures taste sublime?
Salt perhaps? I'll ask the mayor
To pass to you his salt cellar . . .
Or you'll skip the salt this time?

"Well, you've even started singing.
What a tenor, fulsome, ringing,
You possess. It's a delight!
And the melody—so mournful—
I swear, makes me want to snivel.
Thanks for a *bel canto* night!"

The door opened, creaky, rusty,
And the mayor, dishevelled, sweaty,
Burst in, wielding a long cane.

And behind him—sons and menials,
Swinging leather belts and ferules.
Here poor Moorlyk will taste pain.

The mayor shouted: "Beat the robber!
Yesterday he snatched a rooster!
Beat him till he's dead and stiff!"
The blows rain whack, thump aplenty;
Moorlyk takes the licking mutely,
Like one struck both blind and deaf.

"Beat him!" the mayor shouts and thrashes,
But Moorlyk swings 'round and catches
Mr. Mayor by his conk.
Crunch, crunch, like a giant rodent;
The claws give his face a treatment,
Like the devil's very rake.

The Cat's nature contains courage:
He regained his breath; the cordage
He began to gnaw and bite.
Then he jerked upon it mightily,
The rope broke, and momentarily
He was free to think of flight.

He forsook the murine genus,
Failed to look back 'round the locus
Of the henhouse. To the wood,
Through the opening he absconded,
To the Royal Court he legged it;
Was the devil in pursuit?

When the King beheld his menial,
Battered like a pickled apple,
From sheer anger he turned green.
"What?" the animal Ruler bellowed,
"That escapee from the gallows
Dare laugh at my words again?!

"This is more than I can stomach!
I'm a dog, and not a monarch,
If I pass this by the board!
Let the army catch the culprit;
Once he's caught, up on the gibbet!
I'll smash up the whole damned brood."

Fiercely roared and stamped King Leo,
Would devour the Fox *in toto*,
Bones and all, if he'd been there.
When the fury'd ebbed a little,
Then spoke up Babbai, the humble,
Which the courtiers could hear:

"Sire, it is known in common
That Mykyta is a freeman,
And in our law is writ:
Thrice subpoena every suspect,
And if thrice he is in contempt,
In absentia convict.

"Truth or lies? I cannot fathom
What is always blabbed about him,
But the law supposed to treat

All alike! Please send me, Sire,
To Mykyta's, to inquire
If he'll fall down at your feet."

The King merely nodded assent,
With his scepter signaled consent,
But he didn't say a word.
And Babbai departed promptly,
Made good time throughout the journey,
At night at Foxkeep arrived.

Song Four

Of an evening, home at leisure,
Savoring domestic pleasures,
The Fox chatted with his young.
"I have made it to you, finally,"
From the grove a voice called suddenly,
"Are you feeling well and strong?"

"It's Babbai! It is *you*, nunky?
It's momentous news, I fancy,
You conceal beneath your hat.
Sad? Or weary? In our purlieu
A night's sleep will help restore you;
There'll be time to chew the fat."

Polite greetings, salutations,
Exchange of health information,
Cherry cordials drinks Babbai.
On the stoop he sits, relaxes,
The Fox asks about the Palace:
"Come, speak up, and do not sigh!"

"Sonny boy, come to your senses!"
Thus Babbai the Fox addresses.
"Why of messengers make sport?
What's the point of this tomfoolery?
Could you truly be too leery
To attend this royal court?

"My dear boy, I estimate it
That within a single minute
You could shut your enemies mouths.
As compared with your brain power,
Theirs is like a wooden sliver—
And that goes for the whole crowd."

"My dear uncle, you speak truly,"
Said Mykyta, "and you've greatly
Raised in me my willingness.

I'll go! Let them come and witness!
Their laugh shall change to sadness.
Royal rage shall turn to grace.

"Well, right now the King feels anger,
But he knows, in times of danger,
In the bleakest days of woe,
They advise at sixes and sevens,
But the Fox gives wisest guidance;
He alone has the know-how."

They go in the house in tandem;
In the parlor waits the Vixen;
Each at table takes a place.
The two cubbies, Mick and Minah,
Their laps began to climb on.
Conversation went apace.

"Does the King breathe fire and fury?
I know why he feels so angry:
The Bear's pain makes him upset.
We had an old score to settle,
And I waited quite a while
To catch him into my net.

"A few years ago, I reckon,
Leo, our Dad, made Bruin
Royal Governor of the Woods:
To control our Piedmont forests,
Settle animal things and conflicts,
Justly, for the common good.

"At that period, the Unsated,
So that I'd be castigated,
With the Bear had hatched a plot.
For my concept brain-creational,
To the court gubernatorial
He against me filed a suit.

"And the concept? My friend, listen!
With the Wolf once, hunger driven,
We went foraging for food.
Daytime, we hear church bells' clangor,
The fierce winter, though, and hunger
Force us both to leave the woods.

"We came warily to the village,
Sniffing 'round, how we could manage
To get decent breakfast fare.
We smelled suddenly meat and bacon,
With our noses—nay, paws even—
Strong; we could collapse right there.

"This delightful, pretty odor
Led us to the parson's larder,
Which we followed, like a thread.
We began to scan the building,
Checking safety with our hearing,
And we found a tiny vent.

"We were struck by the window's smallness.
'Wolfie, going in?' 'But doubtless,'
The Wolf says. 'You lead the way!
Look around for traps of iron!
I'll be coming right behind you';
(Said the Wolf.) 'Go in; be brave!'

"I squeezed in without discomfort,
Looked around, 'Move steadily forward,'
I said to the Wolf; he came.
Even though the Wolf was svelte
'Cause his belly was quite empty,
His trunk barely cleared the frame.

"And the larder—may God bless us—
Put the world for us in darkness
By the plenitude of choice:
Meat and lard and well-smoked gammon
And four sides of fatty bacon,
Sausages on a long horse.

"I began to think and perpend
How this nourishment to husband—
But my Wolfie went berserk:
Sank his teeth in the bacon carcass,
Ripped, bit, chewed in self-hypnosis;
Stood and chewed and gasped for air.

"Well, I figured, good luck fellow!
But to me this has no value,
And the sausages I attack.

Gently they come off the horse-pole,
I eject them through the porthole,
Till they all are off their rack.

"Through the window, right behind them,
I jumped out and went to get them—
All according to my plan.
Round my neck, just like a necklace,
Each one landed; in the distance,
In the woods I hid my gain.

"Having secreted my treasure,
Having breakfasted at leisure,
To the larder I return.
And I see: The Wolf's still at it;
Sick of bacon, he's just dropped it,
Started on a lard-filled bin.

" 'Wolfie, we must go,' I whisper.
'The church services are over;
People will be coming back!'
Shocked, the Wolf became quite lucid,
Ran toward the narrow exit:
Barely, he squeezed in his neck.

"He was round now, like a barrel;
At the window much too little,
He stood frozen, goggle-eyed.
Fear had rendered him quite speechless . . .
'What has halted now your progress?
What's the matter now?' I cried.

"Mindlessly, in desperation,
He shoves, shedding perspiration,
His trunk, in a futile try,
Through the window; mad and helpless,
He began to wring his forelegs.
'Foxie,' says he, 'here I die!'

" 'Wolfie,' say I, 'are you crazy
Or from lard completely tipsy?
Come on out! It's time to scram!'
'Foxie,' says he, 'I can't do it
'Cause my belly won't pass through it.
Give me all the help you can!'

"If you were in my position,
What would be your course of action?
How would you relieve the bum?
If I left him, he might perish;
I thought, rather than relinquish,
I would see the priest within . . .

"To beg that a saw he lend us,
That he his permission grant us
The small window to enlarge.
Driven by this clever brainstorm,
'I'll be back,' I told the glutton,
And ran to the parsonage.

"The priest was then in his parlor,
In post-prandial good humor,
Standing, puffing on a pipe.
I looked in and tap-tapped lightly
With my paw, to ask politely:
'Please come here and open up.'

"The priest looked up in amazement:
'A Fox's peering in the casement
Window. After him! Go catch!' "
In a jiffy—god knows where from—
Servants swarmed after my person . . .
In one jump I cleared the hedge.

"The run after me and holler . . .
I run straight toward the larder
And hide 'neath the wooden floor.
Soon arrives the flying posse:
'Where is he? Where are you, Foxie?
Showed his tail and disappeared!'

"They look up, and from the transom
The Unsated's looking at them;
In the sun they see his head.
'Oh, you poor, unfortunate noggin',
You will take a lot of thrashing!
Beat on him, and kill him dead!'

"The Wolf, in this dire predicament,
In the larder sought concealment,
Standing at the very door.
As soon as the door was opened,
The Wolf leaped out, at the moment
When the door was pushed ajar.

"He got from the startled minions
Blows across his lumbar region;
With great effort reached the wood.
For this incident unpleasant,
To the Bear, that very instant,
He against me filed a suit.

"Although guilty as a glutton,
The Wolf faked a charge of treason,
Malice, and a breach of faith.

Do you fancy that the Bruin
Would all evidence examine,
Legally adjudicate?

"When it came to the Bear's knowledge
That the case involved some sausage
I'd obtained with work and zeal,
He jumped on me very roughly:
'Give it back, you thieving bully!
I will teach you not to steal!' "

Babbai asked: "Did you abide by
His decision?" "I must, Babbai;
He said he'd cut off my tail.
As regards the total number,
Four I gave him, thin as a finger,
But I left six for myself.

"Well, this was the Bear's decision:
'For the beating, defamation,
T' Wolf—one sausage, as amends.
For me—three. Mykyta, darling,
Be glad you've escaped a whipping.
Beat it, or I'll break your bones.'

"Thus the Bear mistried us foully!
At the time it stung me deeply,
And I swore on the King's tail,
For his tricks, lowdown, dishonest,
I'll invoke *Lex talionis*,
When I lay him by the heels."

Roast grouse, served in natural feathers,
Soon arrived for their supper,
And for nothing did it lack.
Having eaten thus in style,
They conversed for a short while,
Then all of them hit the sack.

In the morning, fresh and rested,
They were served a lovely breakfast:
Garlic bacon—the first dish;
Goose ragout, the next selection,
And to top this preparation,
Came a platter of smoked perch.

Then Mykyta dressed for travel
And took leave before removal
From his children and his spouse:
"Fare thee well, my wife, my pretty;
I must go to the capital city.
Take the keys to our house.

"Keep an eye on our pantry,
For the Mice are quick to thievery,
And about me do not fret.
Though the King's now in high dudgeon,
But it easily can happen
That he'll smile at me yet.

"And you, children, don't be rowdy,
Cause no trouble for your Mommy,
Don't roam far from the household!"

Just look at my Mickey, uncle;
Would you trust that this young animal,
That he's only one year old?"

Then he kissed both Mick and Minah,
In her ear spoke with *aphonia*
What he had to tell his wife.
As though going to a party,
To face wrath in Lion City,
He departed with Babbai.

Song Five

"Ho-ho-ho," the Court was booming.
Here was an unheard-of happening:
Fox Mykyta has arrived!
And Mykyta seems oblivious
To his enemies massed phalanx,
Radiating spunk and pride.

He went to the seat of power,
Bowed profoundly to his Ruler,
And proceeded to report:
He said: "O magnanimous Caesar,
Harking to your personal order,
I appear at your just Court.

"I trust in your spirit's greatness;
To whomever bear false witness,
You would never lend an ear.
They spread lies, exaggerations,
Would among us sow dissention;
It is bound to cost us dear."

The King's grim expression boded
Nothing good. "You vile toady,"
Shouted he. "Don't twist your tail!
Dare you still for justice clamor,
Dare you curry our favor?
You don't flatter us at all!

"The Cock, in sackcloth and ashes,
Moorlyk nursing bumps and scratches,
And the Bruin, my *Baron*!
Recollect their shame and dolor?
Guards, go grab him by the collar;
Take him to the Court! Now scram!"

"King," the Fox—all meek, obedient—
"Is my guilt all that transparent?
Is my case now open? Shut?

'Cause the Bruin was insistent
To get honey from a peasant,
Could you judge it as my fault?

And Moorlyk . . . O God Almighty!
How can he complain about it?
Which of us, while we hunt,
Bears not beating, deprivations?
As for our Constitution . . .
The poor Mice—are they exempt?

"They say, I'm a thief, a nasty,
But Moorlyk, your envoy trusty,
Is no lesser criminal.
Was his purpose not plain stealing,
Bloody carnage, ruthless killing,
When he crawled into the hole?

"King, I am your faithful subject.
If your temper is so incensed,
Let them try me and condemn.
Send small criminals to the gibbet,
So that big ones thereby profit!
If so, life ain't worth a damn!"

But the Lion turned his back to
Fox Mykyta. The guards pronto
Tied him up and led away,
To appear at the Assizes,
Where old Billy Goats and Asses
On the court Bench there held sway.

Here the Fox presents his argument,
But the senior Jackass president
Has been deaf five years almost.
They ruled: "The Fox is to dangle
On a rope until he's strangled,
Or till he gives up the ghost."

117

Bruin, Moorlyk, the Unsated
At the verdict were elated;
Happiness their minds suffused.
They offered themselves as hangmen,
And they menaced their victim:
Before death there'd be abuse.

When they led Mykyta outdoors,
The Bear punched him in the choppers:
"It's for the Morocco shoes!"
To exacerbate his megrim,
The Fox's hands were tied behind him.
"Now you won't escape the noose!"

Moorlyk climbed a branch that likely
Would hold up, and tied securely
Thereto one of stronger ropes.
Purposely he called the Raven,
'S soon as he was up in Heaven,
To pick out Mykyta's orbs.

The whole world came round to ogle,
To watch how the Fox would dangle;
The guard round them—like a wall.
The Fox walks like a wet chicken,
The Unsated right behind him,
And the others have a ball.

"Fear not instant strangulation,
'Cause we have no such intention!"
The Unsated emphasized.
"For a spell you'll jerk and tremble,
Until Mr. Gopher's able
To dig out a grave your size."

To the Wolf Mykyta bantered:
"Couldn't you get a rope that's stronger,
To make up a decent noose?
Moorlyk would not be much troubled
To obtain the one he dangled
And jerked on at the mayor's house."

"Shut your mouth," the Bruin bellowed.
"May your tongue be frozen solid!
Quit the jokes before it's late!
The time's nigh; think of repentance;
Cleanse your soul of sinful weakness!
The grim gallows is your fate."

They came to the tree they'd chosen,
Placed a noose upon the victim,
The Fox climbed up a few rungs.

He turned so's to face the public.
Bowed sincerely to his Monarch,
And then uttered these remarks:

"Oh, the hour is approaching,
Unique for each living being:
The time of eternal rest.
Our Monarch, I implore Thee
That Thou condescend to grant me
A traditional request.

"Here, while facing death and burial,
I wish to expose the evil
And confess my sins and shame.
I shall bare all my offences,
Lest someone *post mortem* chances
For my sins to get the blame."

The Fox bowed to the population
And shed tears in great profusion,
And thus moved all predators souls.
The King pondered this a minute
And then said: "Agreed, so be it!"
He sank his scepter, a badge of rule.

The Fox beat his breast a little:
"I confess now, my good people;
I've committed many sins.
Is among you just one person
In whom of my words or actions
A good memory remains?

"From childhood, on my own instance,
I trained in the ways of violence,
Though my father did reproach.
The poor Chickens, Ducks, and Geese!
My heart's breaking now to pieces,
How I ripped and gnawed your flesh!

"Though I'm hardly a big bruiser,
One theft led to yet another,
Ever deeper yet; to wit:
Tiny lambkins now and kiddies,
Who had strayed from their daddies,
Landed up in my own pit.

"I ran on the road well-trodden:
I became the Wolf's companion;
He instructed me in crime.
If today you see me standing
Underneath the tree of hanging,
For all this he bears the blame.

"Once at a pre-harvest difficult,
We were bound in a thieving compact:
My department—petty theft.
The Wolf's province was grand larceny.
Any profit—fifty-fifty;
I alone now get the shaft.

"When time came to split the spoils,
It was never down the middle;
The right thing was never done.
The Wolf growls—you daren't ask it;
If it means to burst a gasket,
He'll devour every crumb.

"If at times a larger payoff
We had managed to get hold of,
Then the Wolf let out a howl.
As though answering a whistle,
Soon his wife, sons thither hustled;
Even bones, they wolfed down all.

"Oh, how well do I remember,
In the household of a farmer,
I climbed to the loft one night.
In the chimney there was hanging
A real pretty side of bacon,
And to get it seemed just right.

" 'Wolfie,' " I said to the varmint,
'Rip the thatch! For fun and profit,
I'll get it with no ado!'
I climbed up on the roof transom,
With much pain unhooked the bacon,
Dropped it straight in the Wolf's craw.

"The Wolf grabbed the meat and beat it,
But I thought I'd use the pretext
For my meal a hen to heist.
In the loft of the said farmer,
On the most proximate rafter,
Was the Chickens' lengthy roost.

"Crawling slowly down the rafter,
On the beam like a rope walker,
Finally I reached the roost.
My heart's beating . . . Silence
        . . . Darkness . . .
At such times, the Devil doubtless
Most prefers to play and jest.

"Sure enough, ahead lay feces!
I expected Chicken species,
Not a vigorous Turkey Tom.

I aimed at his throat and sinews,
But I hit a turkey pinion,
And the bird let out a scream.

"I aimed at the Turkey's jugular;
The whack of his wing was stronger;
My experience did no good.
For a mo' I lost my sentience,
Wobbled on the beam, lost balance,
And went flying with the Bird.

"Here I found me in hot water!
Down the shaft I took a flyer,
And not on the attic's floor.
I slammed down; the total impact
Left, I thought, no large bones intact.
I was shattered to the core.

"I was not out of my steambath:
The small room was like a casemate,
With no door toward egress.
The near nook I crawled into, and
Turned myself completely rotund:
'Wait now! Let this evil pass.'

"But vain hopes can easily fool you:
A voice called: 'Hey, wake up Andrew!
Take a look-see in the hall.
Something cried out, very frantic;
Something fell down from the attic . . .
Andrew! Getting up at all?!'

"Now the hired man is mumbling,
Rising, thumping, scratching something,
Set, I thought, to light a lamp.
Slowly the big door swings open,
In his hands he holds a lantern:
'What the hell made such a thump?'

"On the floor he spots the culprit:
'Are you making all this racket?
'T' Turkey fell down from his roost!'
Then he saw me accidentally:
'Ah! Hey, mistress! Get up quickly!
I see that we have a guest!'

" 'Well, who is it?' 'Fox Mykyta.'
'Beat him, Andrew!' Beat him? What with?
Hurry up, get up from bed!
Two of us, without much bother,
Will catch this no-good intruder
In a sack, in two shakes cold.'

"While waiting for the woman,
Coming close up with his lantern,
Musters me the curious groom.
And I hear it all and tremble,
My mind with the thought aboggle:
How alive to leave the room.

"Finally the woman creeps in.
I awaited her to open
The door to the proper house.
Zoom! Between her legs I darted
Through the doorway, then departed,
Crashing through the window glass.

"My momentum broke the glass pane,
Left upon it streaks of crimson.
On my body—streaks of blood.
I was free, though, and I scurried
Through the orchard, through the furrows,
Like a madman, to the wood.

"For a long time I ran quickly—
Out of breath, fagged out completely—
Till I reached our Wolfie's lair.
'Wolfie,' said I, 'I have had it.
Let me have a meaty tidbit,
Which you've salvaged as my share.'

" 'Yes, I did,' the Wolf did smile.
'This will hold you for a while.
Please accept my generous gift!'
Can you gauge his low down trickery:
'Twas a piece of oaken hookery!
On it they hang up the meat.

"It's my duty to admit it:
The one sin I have committed
Is this partnership in crime.
But all that brought me no profit,
And expenses out of pocket
Gave me means to stay alive.

"This disturbed me in no measure;
Over King Horoch's famed treasure,
After all, I still held sway.
It was so immense in volume:
Seven wagons in a column
Could just cart the wealth away."

Of the riches very mention
Quickly got the King's attention.
"Fox, now what's this all about?

Now, what kind of treasure is it?
At this time, do you still have it?"
The Fox said: "Without a doubt!"

"Caesar," says he, "dearest Sire,
Ere to my grave I retire,
I wish to relieve my soul!
And what for no love or money
I would tell to my own family
To you I disclose it all.

"This great wealth accumulation
Would have meant your own destruction
And the source of every woe.
Had Mykyta not been larcenous,
Your own end would be sanguineous—
A horrendous overthrow!"

As though stung, the mighty Lion
Jumped up, bellowed, like a madman.
"What you're saying? What? What? What?
What's the meaning of this rubbish?
Revolution? Woe? Who'd perish?
Tell me, so I know the facts!"

The Fox says: "The King's desire
I shall satisfy, but Sire,
The tale's for your ears alone.
With your gracious Queen together,
You'll hear of this weighty matter,
And Horoch's wealth you shall own."

"Hey, take off Mykyta's shackles!
Bring him over here, before us!"
To his henchmen the King yelled.
They untied him with reluctance,
Wondering, what kind of nonsense
To the Lion would be told.

And Mykyta, smelling freedom,
Sighed, relieved of his great problem;
Whispered: "Glory be to God!
You must learn to lie with relish
If you do not wish to perish."
He faced Leo with this thought.

"Well, Mykyta," spoke the Ruler.
"Tell us now, in a fortright manner,
The whole truth unerringly.
If the truth you twist, or bend it,
By a leg you'll be suspended;
You will dangle from the tree."

Song Six

Listen now, how Fox Mykyta
Took off like a charging racer,
Took up lies and flattery!
And he didn't even scruple
His dad's honor to defile,
To besmirch his memory.

"Caesar, and you worthy people!
Great, enormous, vicious trouble
Beats on me, as well it ought.
I shall die here for my thievery,
But I'll tell the horror story
Of a crooked secret plot.

"A score years ago, my father
Somehow managed to discover—
Who knows now the exact spot?—
King Horoch's illustrious treasure;
But this treasure in no measure
Profited my dad a whit.

"My dad was all pride and arrogance,
And the science of high finance
Was his favorite discipline.
He fawned on the King, changed color,
Hoped to head the King's Exchequer,
On which he was very keen.

"Sir, you saw through his ulterior
Aims, and sacked Mykyta Senior;
Mr. Lynx came in exchange.
To the wilds went off my parent,
Full of ill will and resentment
And ideas of revenge.

"There he found the cursed treasure;
In his mind began to figure
How to raise revolt and war,
To depose our present Ruler
From the throne, and to hand over
His crown glorious to the Bear.

"He got quite a few supporters.
He sent Moorlyk out with letters
To the Bruin: so and so.
'We want to depose the Lion.
If you wish to bear the burden
Of the crown, just let us know.'

"At such tidings, our Bruin

Did not write, but came in person,
As though stung, in greatest haste.
'Brothers,' says he, 'I am with you!
Either we shall bag King Leo
Or the very death will taste!'

"Bruin, Moorlyk, and my parent,
The Wolf, their relatives distant
Families arranged a meet.
For revolt, for black betrayal,
Internecine vicious struggle,
Solemnly they swore an oath.

"From all kinds of foreign countries,
They recruited mercenaries;
Horoch wealth to pay the tab.
I eavesdropped on their discussions,
Analyzed their machinations,
Searching for its dreadful hub.

"I knew Bruin's cunning malice,
His *persona,* quite renownless,
Ludicrous from any view.
I compared him with you, Sire:
Can this eyesore, I inquired,
Be our King? I beg of *you!*

"You could find a wealth of piasters.
It's a shame, a better master
You have never come across!
If the Bruin ruled our Kingdom,
We'd lose our honor, freedom,
Silent would be truth and troth.

"And, as though a voice from Heaven,
Spoke to me: 'To stifle treason,
There's a need, a need, a need . . .
Though the traitor is your father,
You be steadfast to your Caesar!
You must be a patriot!'

"Thus all things I did consider;
Then I waited for my father—
As decided beforehand
By the traitors' evil coterie—
To recruit the mercenaries,
To go to a neighboring land.

"Earlier, before the harvest,
Looking for my father's secret,

His adytum I did find.
Now I didn't dilly-dally,
Dragged the wealth out daily, nightly,
Till I cleaned out every dime.

"And within a short time period,
From abroad returns my parent:
Armies now await his call.
Now you pay for the recruitment,
Secure generals' appointment,
And the soldiers will storm hell.

"He forgot his home and family,
To the cache he went directly,
Looked—and fell into a swoon.
For the cave was wholly empty
That had been so full of booty.
The whole cache had been swept clean!

"So he scratches, sniffs, and paces—
Of the wealth he smells no traces.
The old man here lost his mind!
Toothache-like, gave off a whimper,
Made a noose out of a halter,
On a bough he found his end.

"And the Wolf and his friend Bruin,
Fathoming my father's ruin,
Backed away, as from the pox:
They became extremely loyal,
Servants at your Palace Royal,
And the enemy is—the Fox.

"Now they're main props of the system!
And I—saviour of our Kingdom,
Who caused my own father's doom,
At the hanging tree stand humbly,
And I see my death above me.
Go on! Hang me! I am done!"

Thus he stunned the whole assembly
By the boldness of his flummery.
And the Lion shook a bit.
"That's the core of the whole matter!
Thank you very much, Mykyta!
And the treasure . . . Where's the loot?"

"In the Chornohora's ridges,
Where the Cheremosh so rushes
Its clear waters to the glen.
At Hoverla's heart, its center,

Near the third rib you must enter:
There's a lair—a rocky den.

"Therein lies the precious metal,
Quite untouched for your disposal.
King! I hid it for your use!
It's a shame I told nobody
How to reach the hidden booty,
So that after my decease . . ."

The King wouldn't let him finish.
"Who would dare to talk such rubbish?
Who would mention death at all?
It's a royal right to pardon.
Takes these ropes right off his person!
The whole trial I annul.

"You have earned yourself more merit
Then the Rooster or the Rabbit;
And for what you were to hang,
Frankly speaking, as contrasted
With the service you've invested,
Isn't worth a tinker's damn.

"In good time we'll start tomorrow,
Both of us, for Chornohora,
We'll leave at the crack of dawn.
Thus the passage to the cavern
Where the King Horoch's wealth is hidden
To me only will be known."

"Majesty," the Fox said sadly,
"With a cheerful heart, I'd gladly
Tread with you the mentioned path.
When I stood under death sentence,
I pledged that I would do penance
For my sins if I survived.

"First to the Peloponnesus
And thence to the Khersonesus
I have pledged to go on foot.
When I'm back, Illustrious Sire,
The whole treasure you'll acquire
You shall be the richest yet!"

"Well," the King said, "Very pious!
You can't balk and break your promise.
May you travel in good health!"
Then he tells the royal criers
To proclaim these royal orders
To the total commonwealth:

"Hear ye all to whom it matters,
Be concerned about these presents:
To His powers pursuant,
The King's gracious to vacate the
Judgement on one Fox Mykyta,
Whom he grace and favor grants.

"He who'd dare to vilify him
Or to lay one paw upon him,
In absentia to debunk,
For such crimes the King will order
To such patriots whomsoever
Quickly to excise their tongues."

When the verdict was negated,
Moorlyk, Bruin, the Unsated
Thought of it as infamy.
First, they all began to grumble,
Then to shout and start a rumble—
They and their progeny.

But it was too late already.
From his throne, the King snarled grimly:
"Who dare now to squawk and moan?
Ha, it's you, you cursed enemies,
Who swore to assassinate me
Right inside my very home!

"Holier than thou! Behold them!
While venom fills their bosoms!
The Fox—a bone in your craw?
Long enough you've honed your weapons,
Now it's time to make acquaintance
With the justice of our law!

"Hey, you guards, grab hold of Bruin
And confine him in good irons!
Screw the Wolf in the pillory.
Catch the Cat now and imprison
Him directly in the dungeon's
Sunless, grim obscurity."

Song Seven

There's a dungeon in the castle,
Cold and damp, dark as a tunnel—
In't three convicts under lock.
The Cat's silent; the Bear dozes;
The Unsated only cusses:
"Oh, Mykyta, may he croak!"

Since it wasn't their custom
To eat gruel cooked in prison,
The three wretches wouldn't eat.
When they saw the three big dishes,
They sniffed at them and pulled faces;
They began to sneeze and spit.

After cogitation lengthy,
The Wolf shed tears of self-pity;
He did certainly howl and wail!
To his partners in misfortune,
Of his sorrows and adventures,
He narrated this long tale:

"Heavens, Earth, and all the Oceans,
From the depth of my dejection,
You I tearfully implore
That my tears and lamentations—
Of my misery a reflection—
Shake you to the very core!

"They all call me the Unsated.
By God I have been provided
With an appetite. A shame?
Can I help it if eternally
I stuff things into my belly,
Which for 'more and more' exclaims?

"The Unsated, the Wolf Vicious,
Doubtlessly deserves to perish;
Beat him anywhere you find!
That the same Wolf suffers hunger,
Is his wife and kids' provider,
Never enters people's minds.

"The Wolf's greedy and a bandit!
But my soul is oft in conflict;
Troubled is my conscience.
For my heart is free of perfidy,
Sensitive, and full of pity.
The world, though, I can't convince.

"I am pious, I am decent;
If the world were wholly vacant,
If I had no appetite,
I'd be good and I'd be faithful,
I'd be gentle, I'd be humble—
In the world's eyes I'd be right.

"Even now—and why deny it?—
When my stomach starts to cry, it
Tends my conscience to blunt.
Yet how many times I follow
It's lead, always to my sorrow?
Honestly, I've lost the count.

"Going hunting, fit and able,
I met Geese once, a whole gaggle.
'Geese, O Geese, your number's up!'
'Very well, eat us,' they comment,
'Will you, please just wait a moment
Till we pray all as a group.'

" 'Go on, pray! You have one moment!'
Their wings toward the firmament,
Piously, they raised aloft.
Raised them, cackled, in a hurry
Took off flying, like a fury,
And I stood there like an oaf.

"Well, I thought then, feeling stupid,
What am I, and what's this method?
Am I a sexton or a priest,
To observe the Geese at prayer?
Then I went to reconnoiter
For a different type of beast.

"Lo! a Sow lies in the puddle,
And pink-brown around her huddle
Piglets—seven in the bunch.
'Hey, you Sow, my heart's desire,
Will you come out of the mire,
I will eat your kids for lunch.'

" 'All right, eat, if that's your penchant,'
From the mud spoke up their parent,
'But therein's contained one sin
(In the Writ it isn't covered)
But these Pigs have not been scoured.
Eat them in the state they're in?'

" 'Ah, indeed, that is a problem!'
'But, Unsated, will you listen?
There's a mill beside the stream.
Now come with us, like a good boy,
Place yourself down in the spillway;
There I'll wash my children clean.

" 'I shall christen them and wash them,
One by one, to you I'll toss them,
In your mouth, for you to bite.'

Well, I thought, I'm in agreement.
This Sow's pious, and she's decent.
After all, Pigs don't take flight.

"I stand low down in the spillway,
The Sow up, upon the gangway;
Mumbles, splashes, grunts to boot.
Well, I think, a pious moment
I cannot intrude upon it:
She is christening her brood.

"She stood high above the sluice work,
Grabbed the handle with her bridgework,
Raised the sluice gate bit by bit.
Wow! The wet and chilly ocean
Crashed in force upon my person.
Honestly, I lost my wits.

"I was captured by the water—
Ten men couldn't have done much better—
Carried downstream, like a straw!
I was headed for my *karma*
Ere I gained the *terra firma*!
I looked round: there was no Sow.

"I stand there, all wet and gaga:
Look at that false-saint virago,
How she pushed me in the stream!
I must be quite idiotic,
Either Orthodox or Catholic,
That baptized pigs I consume!

"Having made a firm decision
To be fooled by no deception,
I'm so hungry, I could cry . . .
When a Ram I soon encounter,
Head toward him, doesn't scamper,
So I shout from far away:

" 'Stop, you Ram! You horny creature!
I have news of latest nature.'
The Ram halted: nay, he asked:
'Well, speak up! What is the latest?'
'Ha, I'll eat you for my breakfast!
Is the latest to your taste?'

"And the Ram? Who would have thought it?
Wasn't scared, tried not to beat it,
But bowed deeply at my feet:
'Sir,' he says, 'The Lord has sent you;
Three days I've been searching for you,
Looking forward to this meet.

" 'Do not laugh, and try to fathom,
I'm a suicidal Mutton;
This world's life is not for me!
My whole people die in bondage,
We live strictly for your usage.
Death is no ignominy.'

"Hearing such a wild oration,
My jaw dropped in cogitation:
I stood there, like a dumb twit.
'What's this blether, you comedian,
Without any rhyme or reason,
I don't get the gist of it.'

" 'Sir, give me a moment's attention,
Learn the cause of my destruction,
Why I do not mind to die.
Why from now the hornéd order,
As their savior, as their father,
Shall know you and glorify.

" 'Know, O Sir, my secret agony:
I'm no Mutton ordinary;
I'm an ovine patriot!
My ideal: to awaken,
From their chains to liberate them—
Our entire sheepish lot.

" 'Long I've thought the best of causes
Is to be an ovine Moses,
And to lead my people out,
From the stall to outright freedom.
Of much effort, pain, the burden
I took on—but all for nought.

" 'In the stuffy sheepish cranium
There's no room for e'en a modicum
Of fresh thought. And their hearts
Are so timid. What is freedom?
Wolves shall eat us in the open.
It is sin to have such thoughts!

" 'O kind sir, now give attention
To my grave spiritual tension
And the irony of it all:
In my soul—prophetic theses,
And around me—ovine faces,
Hay, the cud, a cozy stall.

" 'To relieve myself a little,
I consulted an oracle,

And she gave me this advice:
To obtain the sheep's salvation,
Give your life of own volition:
Yourself you must sacrifice.

" 'Roam three days out in the prairie
(Your act must be voluntary)
There you'll meet the Superwolf.
All my indices pursuant,
Your star'll be in the ascendant,
If he eats you in one gulp.

" 'For all sheep the Star of Freedom!'
Yearning tears my pericardium;
I must ask; I cannot help:
Have you this prophetic order?
Can you, O my dearest Savior,
Swallow me in a single gulp?'

"Go ahead with your dumb twaddle,
Thought I, but I must be able
T'sink my teeth into you, Ram!
You should see how I can swallow!
But I thus address the fellow:
'My dear sonny, keep your calm!

" 'I saw a prophetic presence
And I expected your appearance.
I shall swallow you at once.'
'Glory be to the Almighty,'
Said the Ram, 'and my fate's charity!
From now on, my soul's at peace.'

" 'Sir, stand in the same position,
And I'll seek that elevation,
Run, and jump into your mouth.
And you'll swallow me directly;
As you do, though, please think kindly:
This was a real patriot's death!'

"I had to be a real idiot
That I did agree to do it.
The Ram's horns hit me quite rough:
Wham! At once my body folded,
I fell on the ground and fainted,
While I saw the Ram take off.

"As I rose after this torture,
I cried, blaming my misfortune,
And my dumbness I did cuss.
What am I? An ovine father?

I should, in my quick, smooth manner
Grab the Ram and eat at once!

"It's because of my darn softness!
Why did I possess the patience
To hear all that silly talk?
Well, no more of such dumb dealings!
From now on, I'll steel my feelings.
I am hungry! It's no joke!

"I set my jaw in a square line,
Pursuing my policy outline;
Firmly now I hit the road.
Walking on, and crawling, limping,
I met with a human being:
Just a Tailor, and no threat.

"Soon as he came in my vision,
I assumed a tough position:
'Tailor, Tailor, you're my meal!
Don't run, and no controversy;
Don't you start to beg for mercy!
I'm so hungry, I am ill!'

" 'Running? I'm not fast enough.
I'm too weak to fight you off.
Who'll trust my veracity?
Can you eat me up at all?
It would seem, you are too small.
Let me measure your capacity.'

"Ere I fully comprehend,
He already had extended
'Long my back his measuring stick.
Grabbed my tail all of a sudden,

Whacked me quickly half a dozen
With the stick; it made me sick.

" 'What's this you are doing, Tailor?'
'Now, remember without failure
Never humans to attack!'
'Never, never, I swear off it!'
But the Tailor—nasty, irate,
Flays away; I thought I'd croak.

"Though I howl and wail profusely,
Though I swear and beg for mercy,
He still holds me by the tail
And he thrashes, full of venom,
Soon will come off from my skeleton,
Seemingly all flesh and fell.

"Feeling that that this could be fatal,
My strength I did finally marshal:
I tore off some of my tail.
I ran nineteen to the dozen;
When I reached my den, well-hidden,
For three days I wasn't well.

Such pain wolves have to contend with.
Tell me, how I can keep quiet,
When I pine in such distress?
And to top it all, that traitor
Fox Mykyta got the Emperor
To heed slander against us."

"No, I'm beyond consolation,"
Droned the Wolf on. "My solution
Is a noose made out of rope."
The Bear, the Cat slept already;
The Wolf—from despair and pity—
Ate three portions of jail slop.

Song Eight

After breakfast, the next morning,
All attired for a journey,
To the King the Fox kowtowed.
"I am ready for my pilgrimage;
King, be now a father image:
Blessings, please, on me bestow."

The King said: "It's a shame, really,
That you're leaving us directly."
"O King," cried the Fox, "please don't!
My heart's breaking, too, asunder,
But what's God's to God I render;
With God settle my account."

The King said: "Quite, quite, dear fellow.
I feel gratified and mellow
That you have become devout.
May I give you something personal
From me to help ease the travel—
Anything to help you out."

"Royal . . . tee," the Fox lamented,
"You are so . . so kindly minded . . .
I don't have a *nécessaire*. . . .*
And there's Bruin, who has plenty

*Small traveling bag.

126

Of good pelt; I'm sure he'll spare me
For a bag, a piece of fur. . . ."

"His concurrence doesn't matter;
We shall rip it off by order!"
Said the Lion. "What else, sir?"
"O my King, you are so kindly,
If a pair of boots you'd find me,
For, you see, my feet are bare.

"I must tramp on all this distance,
Stumping, cutting in the process
My bare feet. I'll wreck my health!
The Wolf has two pair of footwear,
And I'm sure he would surrender
For my use a pair of boots."

"What he wants is immaterial,"
Said the Lion, sore and spleenful;
"Go inside the calaboose!
From the Bear take off some bag pelt,
And remove from the Unsated
For the Fox a pair of boots.

"You, my retinue illustrious,
To make generally obvious
For Mykyta our grace,
Give him honorary escort
To the mound before the forest,
And I'll go and rest a space."

And the Fox went, treading gently,
Lamb-like, quietly and humbly,
With a bag; a crook in hand.
And the barons and boyarins,
Like crows, from all sides surround him:
The whole court the Fox attends!

Billy Goat—the secretary,
Jack the Rabbit—an honorary
Guardsman, walk beside the Fox.
What a pleasant conversation!
But here's their destination:
The mound, their parting place.

The Fox speaks and shows great sorrow;
Wipes the tear drops on his elbow:
"My dear Jack, let us embrace!
At the thought of parting from you,
Sadness shakes me, like the ague.
This is something I can't face!

"O, my friend, my dearest Billy,
Oh, I love you so, so dearly!
Sans you life holds no appeal!
Don't refuse this one entreaty,
Walk along with me, my buddy,
On this road another spell."

He shed tears after this sentence,
Then he made a deep obeisance:
"You two from among all beasts
Are so just and without blemish;
You eat grass and juicy foliage
All the time—as I did once.

"Violence, attack, and killing
Are outside your sphere of thinking,
For you have no use for meat.
Your souls righteous and straightforward
I chose, when I was a hermit,
As the types to emulate."

With such flattering conversation,
He lured them to the location
Where the Fox's compound was.
The Fox said: "Now, listen, Billy,
Wait for us; just dilly-dally,
Nibble on some blades of grass.

"And you, Bunny, my dear kinsman,
Come with me inside my warren,
For, you see, when my dear wife
Hears from me about the latest,
How I am a pilgrim-pietist,
Tears will come, and on my life,

"I hate most to weep with women;
I don't know how to console them,
Or with talk to set things right.
In this you're an expert crafty,
So come with me, my old buddy.
She'll take heart at your mere sight."

Bunny Rabbit, so soft hearted,
Weepy's soon as he had heard it,
Piped up softly: "The poor dear!
I would love her, like my mother!"
With the Fox, they slid together
Through a hole, to the Fox's lair.

They came in. Inside the cavern,
Mrs. Vixen with her children
Weeps; the tears pour out in streams.

When she saw Mykyta enter,
She jumped up: "Mykyta! Father!
Children, our father lives."

And she covered him with kisses,
Smothered him in her embraces:
"Darling, has the trouble passed?
Tell us all about it, daddy,
I thought you were dead already . . .
Oh, a sea of tears has oozed . . ."

"Let's rejoice!" Mykyta parried.
"Our King—and may great glory
Cover his entire domain!
He's forgiven my transgressions;
With immediate inception,
I bask in his grace again.

"And my foes most unrelenting
Must today be barely breathing:
They are facing royal wrath!
Moorlyk, the Unsated, Bruin
Got themselves into the dungeon,
And they had to shut their mouths.

"And this Rabbit, two-faced dummy,
Who once testified against me,
From now on remains my slave.
Should I let him live at present?
Should I strangle him this instant,
If a ransom he can't pay?"

When Jack heard this, the poor patsy,
Weakness spread throughout his body,
As though hearing the hounds' yelp.
"Help," he shouted, "dearest father,
I'm to be the Fox's dinner;
Billy, hurry up and help!"

"Will you shut your mouth, you hoodlum!"
Screamed Mykyta, grabbed his victim,
And bit quickly through his throat.
"That's a bit of legerdemain
And for all mad dogs a lesson
For Mykyta to look out!"

Sucking blood from the Rabbit's body,
The Fox spoke up, fresh and jaunty:
"He's quite tasty, the darned creep!
Listen children, now, and mother,
We'll have rabbit roast for supper.
It induces splendid sleep.

"And now, my beloved, listen,
How I faced complete extinction,
And how lies have set me free."
And he sat in total coziness;
Step by step about his progress
He told them a history.

And the Vixen and her kitties
Settled down around their daddy,
Laughing, shivering by turns.
"What a story! Goodness gracious!"
Here the wife became loquacious.
"You knew how to grab their ears."

"But there's one fly in the ointment.
That you'll take off on this junket
And leave us alone to fend . . ."
"Woman!" the Fox shouted. "Really!
Do you think I've gone completely,
Totally around the bend?

"When one is in deathly peril,
One is liable to prattle
What with spit may cross one's tongue.
Well, do I look like a pilgrim?
For a pilgrimage, for the Lion
I don't give a cannon's bang.

"If your mouth draws, salt's the remedy;
I'll stay with you in our shanty.
Of the pilgrimage keep mum!"
From outside a voice was calling:
"Jack, how long shall I be waiting?
Where are you? Why don't you come?"

T'Fox popped out. "My dearest Billy,
I apologize sincerely:
I have failed to entertain.
Inside, Jack and my small family
Are just chatting amiably,
Unaware of passing time."

"You are saying: 'Friendly chatter,'
But I clearly heard Jack holler
'Help me!'" said the Billy Goat.
"Right," the Fox said, "when the Vixen
Heard that I've become a pilgrim,
She passed out, she's so distraught.

"But here Jack—O may he prosper—
Drenched her with a jug of water

And began to call for help:
'Come and help us, my dear Billy,
'Cause my aunt is failing quickly!'
But at present all is well."

"Glory be to the Almighty!
I had fear that Jack, my buddy,
Was just being skinned alive."
"How can you suspect such rubbish?
In a minute, bearing baksheesh,
He'll come out—maybe in five.

"O my bearded *Rebbe* Billy,
May I ask you most sincerely . . .
The King told me at the Court
'Ere I started on my voyage,
Of a thing we both have knowledge
I should write him a report.

"While Jack had his entertainment
With my folks, I was efficient:
Two epistles of great size
I composed. To you, my buddy,
I present my great entreaty:
Take them to the King, O please!

"Very well," to this said Billy,
"Only tie them up securely,
Lest I damage their seal."
"That's a thought. You wait a moment:
From the Bear's bag, a neat packet
I'll make up now; if you will!"

He ran back inside his warren,
Smiling in his heart with venom:
"Quite a letter! Wait and see!"
The gory head of the Rabbit
He shoved in the bag and wrapped it,
Gave it to the Goat with glee.

"Dearest Billy, here's the package:
It contains one bulky message
And two of the smaller kind.
Carry them with great care, Billy,
And the seal will fracture, surely,
If the twine you should unwind.

"Have no care about the Rabbit!
Inside he's become so gabby
That he offers his regrets.
You just run ahead a distance,

And Jack will in a few instants
Catch up, with his speedy feet.

"One more thing: you know, dear fellow,
How our dearest Father Leo
Loves slick style—smooth and chaste.
Therein—modesty forbids me—
The King's eye will find the acme
Of my wit, to please and sate.

"And wherever it behooved me,
I slipped in a complimentary
Word about you—fear you not!
Surely, our paternal Ruler
Will bestow on you more favor
Then at present you have got.

"Only be awake and nimble;
Do not play extremely humble!
In all wars the bold win most.
'With these letters,' tell the Emperor,
'I served as Mykyta's mentor.
He wrote them at my behest.' "

And when Billy heard the statement,
All his nerves shook with excitement.
He jumped up; he was so thrilled.
He began to kiss Mykyta:
"From now on, I shall know better
Who has really wished me well!

"Brother, friend! I am elated!
With your wit I'm well acquainted;
This will raise the Lion's tail!
I'll be lionized and fêted,
Nationwide I'll be chit-chatted:
'What a stylist our Goat Bill!'

"With aplomb I'll make my entrance,
For no one knows in this instance
How the matter really went.
Farewell now. May God allow it
That I may repay this benefit
In a way you won't resent.'

"Farewell now!" The Fox responded,
And when Billy went, a torrent
Of pent up abuse he spoke:
"This moronic silly-billy
Is the Honorable Secretary!
I feel faint; I'll get a stroke!

"What a system! What a country!
Fools are given honors, glory,
And the poor and the weak cannot
Save themselves. On this tribunal
Which condemned me to a funeral
Sat not this dumb Billy-Goat?!

"Whether he is dead or living,
I have had my vengeance on him:
He won't get rid of the blot
Now adhesive to his dial—
The expletive gone proverbial—
'As dumb as a Billy Goat!' "

And meanwhile, our Billy
At the Court arrived quite happily,
Before Leo took a stand:
"Fox Mykyta, from his journey,
To the King bows most profoundly
And conveys this box by hand.

"The three writs therein are lengthy;
Their language is noteworthy.
And no wonder: in each line,
I advised him on construction,
Syntax, and stylistic scansion.
Therefore, sir, the credit's mine."

Here the King accepts the package,
Bit by bit unwinds the cordage,
Looks inside—and is amazed!
"What is this? Ears on a letter?
You have brought a gory letter!
Billy Goat, be you accursed!"

He looked at Jack's head with sorrow,
He gave off a frightful bellow;
The Goat fell down in surprise.
"Thus the Fox is laughing at us!
And to send this package hideous,
The Goat served him with advice!

"By my mane, I swear assurance
That I'll nevermore give credence
To Mykyta's curséd lies.
On the double, to the prison!
Get the Cat, the Wolf, the Bruin!
Free them from their heavy chains.

"O you conscienceless liar!
My good servants suffered dire
Pain that they do not deserve.
They'll get paid for their damages:
Billy and his fuzzy species
May be stripped of their fur!

"Since the Fox, the tacky varmint,
Through deceit escaped the gibbet,
He's outside legality.
Whosoever meets this phony,
Without legal ceremony,
Kill him with impunity!"

And thus Billy and Jack Rabbit
Laid their lives, were liquidated,
Somehow guilty without guilt.
Felled by power and sheer savagery,
Left not even a good memory
As their legacy to the world.

Take poor Billy in particular!
What thanks and what royal favor
Did he garner, did he win?
Though he fawned on the high and mighty,
Built his nest next to the royalty;
His godmother was the Queen . . .

Though a decorated courtier,
Though he was a privy councillor,
Though a judgeship he could boast,
For a joke, a trivial matter,
Because of the Fox's "letter,"
That his silly life was lost.

If today they hear this fable,
Who among the Christian people
Ever spares a kindly thought?
If one dies who has been evil
For a cause completely trivial
He has perished like a goat.

Who puffs himself up, and parties,
Curries favors and deals dirty,
Banking on dishonest bribes.
'Always glad to chatter with you!'
Will his death fail to remind you
Of a billy goat's demise?

Song Nine

Fox Mykyta, in his tower,
Drained a tankard after dinner
Of good mead, with utmost calm.
Puffing on his pipe with pleasure,
He let's nothing mar his leisure—
Of one innocent of harm.

"Knock, knock!" at the gate; quite sudden;
The Fox runs out with his children.
"Babbai, is it really you?
Babbai, greetings! Tell me: surely
You come from the King directly.
Do you bring us some good news?"

"Nothing good among the latest,"
Said Babbai, "But a rich harvest—
A rich crop of dreadful news.
The King's sworn to your extinction,
Consultations, mobilization; They should be
          here in three days."

"Is that all?" Mykyta parried.
"If it is, then don't you worry,
My old friend, my dear Babbai!
Give no credence to this threat!
You and I to the royal Court
Will proceed this very day.

"I shall lie me out of trouble!
May I ask you now, dear uncle,
To step inside our home?
Time for supper! The aroma
Of the roast made by our Mama
I can taste within my bones."

They went in and sat down to supper;
The fox cubbies played together,
And their dad said to Borsuk:
"Minnie has been catching chickies;
See this resolute beastie Mickey?
Yesterday he bagged a duck!"

Said Babbai: "Be a proud parent,
But they couldn't turn out different;
They take after their dad."
"Nature? Certainly: it takes talent,

But here nurture is more valent,"
To Babbai the Fox replied.

"Time for us now to get going!"
"What?" the Vixen started screaming.
"You are off again to roam?
To the Royal Court? My goodness!
You will make us into orphans!
You wise up and stay at home!"

And the tears poured out in earnest
And her hands grabbed him the tightest,
Trying to make him stay put.
Though he covered her with kisses,
He slipped out of her embraces,
Saying: "Quiet! You must quit!

"I'm sure Leo won't devour
Me alive. I will not cower,
Waiting for the bolt to strike.
Hide not from the coming evil,
But go out and meet the peril,
As per maxims in my book:

"Our life is constant warfare.
In it, we use our best hardware:
Some use wings, and some use teeth.
Others fight with mighty talons,
Others still outrun the lions . . .
What saves our kind from death?

"Our strength is not terrific,
Unlike Carps, we're not prolific,
And at night we are not Owls.
We can't match the Rabbit's swiftness,
But one thing keeps us in business:
Our brains, both sharp and cool.

"We must be alert and nimble,
Razor-sharp hone our noodle,
Think things over in a flash.
We set snares for our quarry,
But we also must be wary
That we don't become a catch.

"On the warpath is the Lion,

And although all his battalions
Do not frighten me a bit,
It makes sense that it is better
To prevent this altogether
Than, by God, to fear and wait.

"For such action, my dear woman,
I feel strength within me burgeon,
For I practice what I preach!
When I think ahead, my darling,
Of the lies I shall be telling,
My whole tongue begins to itch."

Once more farewell oscultations.
The wife felt much consolation.
But the gates were to be locked,
Said Mykyta; with the Badger,
On trails sinister and dexter,
They departed double quick.

A breeze makes the foliage rustle,
In the sunshine the green trembles,
Not a cloudlet in the sky.
The Fox basks in Nature's splendors.
Sadly next to him meanders,
Worry-worn, Borsuk Babbai.

"What is eating you, dear uncle?"
Spoke Mykyta full of sparkle.
"Darn it! Throw your cares away!
See this beauty in abundance:
Brightness, freedom, warmth, and fragrance?
If you live, you're king today!"

"My dear fellow," said Babbai,
"You are flying much too high!
This one penalty you can't duck!
You chewed off Jack's head and sent it
To the Lion as a present,
Using Billy's travelling bag.

"Ha-ha-ha! (Mykyta's laughter);
A cheap vicious maneouver!
It makes me swell up with pride!
The King must have run a distance
Ere he bumped into real evidence . . .
As for punishment . . . never mind!

"He who wants to live, not wither,
Cannot be a holy roller
Or a desert anchorite.
If you're too slack in your habits,

You may well get what you merit:
Wind up in somebody's teeth.

"Jack was jumping up before me,
Vulnerable as a baby,
As though teasing: 'Catch me, Bud!'
I grew queasy, hot all over,
And I really don't remember
How he suddenly lost his head.

"And the Goat! Now be impartial!
How he smeared me at the trial:
'Guilty, Guilty! Let him die!'
After lying myself 'Not guilty,'
Suddenly I'm his kissing buddy!
May the devil get his hide!

"It's his loss and my transgression!
Killing, vengeance are the fashion
Which among the beasts prevails.
Often plunders, too, the Lion,
And if he's averse in person,
He sends in the Bears and Wolves."

Here Mykyta smiled softly,
Took a pinch of snuff discreetly,
Sneezed, and thus addressed his mate:
"Poppycock! All stuff and nonsense!
But consider this one instance
Which my story illustrates.

"They say punishment for plunder . . .
Here's a case for you to ponder:
When one wanted to go straight.
Goods and money in abundance,
There's no customer resistance,
But the goods cannot be bought.

"Once the Wolf and your narrator,
Tiring of our haunts familiar,
Foreign lands began to trek.
But beyond strange woods and waters
We found no hotels or shelters—
Just steppes, meadowlands outback.

"The sun's rays get ever warmer,
Not to mention gnawing hunger.
But look here: a grazing Foal!
It's so fat and sympathetic,
And my Wolf turns quite frenetic,
Foaming, trembling overall.

"The Wolf's into heavy breathing,
But his Dam is with the offspring;
She'd prevent a try to steal.
The Wolf says: 'Go on, Mykyta,
And inquire of the mother
If the Foal there is for sale!'

"I went and bowed low before her:
'Madam, pretty decent pasture
You have here; it's really nice.
And your youngster! What a laddie.
For adoption, are you ready
To sell him at a good price?'

" 'Buy it, if your heart desires!
As for me, I won't require
From you, folks, a lot of dough . . .
Just read what the price amounts to
From the list on my hind horseshoe;
There you'll find your *quid pro quo.*'

"I'm not crazy as a March hare
To come near a horse's footwear!
I made a respectful bow:
'Sorry, Ma'am,' I said retreating,
'I don't know the art of reading.'
And went where the Wolf lay low.

" 'Friend, our Mare is good and gentle,
And her Foal is marketable
At a price we can afford.
Current prices, so she stated,
On her hind shoe are detailed there.
Pity that I couldn't read.'

"Said the Wolf: 'You worthless bungler!
A few words you can't decipher
From the equine alphabet?
Of this I possess full knowledge:
First in high school, then in college,
Five whole years I had to swot.'

"So the Wolf went out in person
Over to the Mare to bargain,
And the Mare responded: 'Right!
Just read what the cost amounts to
From the list on this hind horseshoe.
There the prices are inscribed.'

"The Unsated bent down low-low,
Focusing upon the horseshoe,
When the Mare unleashed a kick!

Right between his eyes she placed it.
Her steel horseshoe did its meanest.
He went out like a candlestick.

"The Mare roared her hearty laughter,
Cantered off fast with her youngster,
Vanishing without a trace.
The Wolf meanwhile lay prostrated,
Helpless, incapacitated.
Wholly like unto a corpse.

"Then he forces his eyes open
And surveys his near environs,
But cannot rise to his feet.
I said to him: 'Hey, Unsated,
You ate the whole Foal, and failed to
Leave for me a single bite?

" 'There you are, you monstrous glutton!
Not enough to fill your gut on?
You insatiable beast!
After all, ungrateful Billy,
I first bargained with the Philly.
I rate a *pourboire** at least.

" 'Tell me now the truth, quite frankly
Did you purchase the Foal cheaply?
The price—was not out of sight?
And there wasn't too much haggling,
Parted on a friendly footing?
She seemed happy as she left.

" 'And my friend, you napped so sweetly—
So salubrious for the belly
After such a hearty meal.
Wolfie, you are the world champion
In your knowledge of horse idiom—
The world must know of your skill.'

"I jeered at him till the evening,
But he lay there, his eyes bulging,
Groaning only: 'What an ache!'
Then he said: 'Now give me justice!
In this deal, we made good progress,
Then the savage starts to kick.' "

Babbai said: "Alas, however,
In your joke there is no humor,
For it harbors bitter truth.
The worst part of your dilemma

*Drink at the conclusion of a bargaining session.

133

Is: the Wolf is your sworn enemy,
Fondly hoping for your death."

"Well," Mykyta said, "spit on him!
The Wolf's always full of venom,

But such malice blinds the brain.
He would swallow the whole planet,
But it won't pass through his gullet.
The wise treat it with disdain."

Song Ten

Deep in talk, along the highway,
Fox Mykyta, his friend Babbai
Marched ahead with measured stride.
By Mykyta suddenly nudged,
Babbai heard: "There's a camouflaged
Hole; come on and quickly hide."

Babbai, in a state of terror,
In the culvert ran for cover.
Could a hunter be abroad?
Hush! Mykyta, all atremble,
Sought a place where he was able
From his hole to watch the road.

From Lvov-City, on this artery,
A mob in the centenary,
Walked back from a day in court.
An old Cock leads the precession,
Behind him all his relations,
But the litter's not aboard.

In their hearts they hid their dolor,
Drowned their woes in a quart of liquor,
And began to sing "The Gnat":
"What a racket in the forest,
From a tree the Gnat fell head first!
Summon, summon—get the vet!

"He smashed up his great big noodle
On an oak root that protroodled,"
Rings the Rooster's solo lead.
"The Fly flew out of her mansion
To give medical attention,"
Lends support his whole fowl brood.

"O Gnat, you my favorite beetle,
I care for you not a little . . ."
(The Cock's lead maintains the tone.)
"How to find the right specific?
'Cause to me you are terrific . . ."
(Roars the choir in unison.)

"I'll sell the house and all possessions
But I'll summon a physician;

The right drugs I'll get.
I'll sell farm tools in a hurry,
I'll pay the apothecary,
And restore the Gnat.

"The Ticks jumped from their oak perches
When they heard the Fly's loud message,
Stemmed the flow of blood.
To the scene the Ants are rushing,
Bearing their little cushions;
Sleep would do him good."

This whole family gallinaceous
Gave full vent to its shrill voices,
Till the Cock to the bridge came up,
Now Mykyta—a flash of lightning—
Left his hideout without warning,
Grabbed the Cock in a flying swoop.

"Now I got you, you brute villain,"
The Fox shouted, seized the victim,
And bit off his head at once.
The Cock flapped his wings a little,
His legs twitched some for a while,
In the pit then went the corpse.

"For God's sake, my dearest nephew!
A new mess you got us into!
Have you totally lost your mind?
This Cock here was a great power,
He enjoyed the Bruin's favor,
And the Queen to him was kind."

But the Fox paid no attention
To the Badger's admonitions.
Happily he plucked his prey.
"Sneeze upon it all, my dearest,
And observe this sumptuous breakfast.
May I serve you? Won't you stay?

"As regards this present Rooster,
For long he had caused to fester
In my innards a great hate.
Not because of a court summons,

But because of one occurrence,
Which is shameful to relate.

"Once in tears from violent hunger,
Past an orchard fence I wander:
A Cock crowing in a tree.
How could I entice this fowl
To descend to my own level,
To grab hold of him for me?

"Presto, to suit the occasion,
I staged a monk imitation,
Mumbling softly: 'Praise the Lord!'
Then I came up to the willow,
Raised my eyes, so meek and mellow,
Priestlike, I spoke to the bird:

'O thou, one of my own children!
O thou wondrous bird of Eden!
With this day I welcome thee!
Fervently I care and suffer
For thy own spiritual welfare.
Let's begin a colloquy!'

"The Cock shouted in derision:
'Why, I'm sure, Mykyta, cousin,
It's been long since you last ate!
You lean more toward the carnal
In love for me, than spiritual!
Hunger breeds religious thought.'

" 'Sin no more, O honest creature!
I've abandoned meat as nurture;
Roots and honey's all I eat.
A strict fast observing daily,
In the desert I dwell solely,
At the darkest end of it.'

"The Cock shouted in derision:
'O Mykyta, my dear cousin,
Your words are quite oily-smooth.
Your tongue constantly drips honey,
But your teeth grab with great villainy.
Your head harbors evil thought.'

"I said: 'O thou Bird of Beauty,
What thou sayest are sins weighty!
For thy sake I come today
From the desert, all this distance,
Purposely to thy own residence.
Here is what I have to say:

" 'In my sleep, a voice from Heaven
Called: Mykyta, you've been chosen:
To the village you must walk.
Do not tarry, do not worry,
Go there in the greatest hurry—
In a tree you'll find a Cock.

" 'For this Rooster is a cynic,
A polygamous agnostic,
And a sinner. So proceed:
Move his conscience to repentance,
Wash away his sinful hardness,
And to heartfelt penance lead.

" 'Thus, my cockscomb-sporting squire,
You may easily expire,
And your soul shall go to hell.
Come on down, make your confession,
And repent all your transgressions,
And your soul shall be left whole.'

"And the Cock spoke with derision:
'Now, Mykyta, my dear cousin,
Tell me: wherein lies my sin?
Do I steal, or do I plunder?
Do I kill, or do I murder?
Or of you do I make fun?'

" 'You poor creature!' I said sternly.
'Repent while it's still timely!
From your heart cast out all pride.
Living in your sins abundance,
Unaware of their presence—
That's one really ugly side.

" 'Don't you always have aplenty
Of young chicks—fifteen or twenty—
Each cohabiting with you?
By what law or common usage
D'you maintain this sinful outrage?
In hot pitch, in hell, you'll stew!'

"Here my sharp and grave expression
Robbed the Cock of self-possession:
Seems, I finally got to him.
'O Mykyta, my true parent,
Now it's clear and quite apparent
That I bear a stain of sin.

" 'But forgive me this last instance!
My soul's moved not to repentance.
No fast, and no time to pray.

This may mean a bad confession,
And I stand with trepidation
That once more I'd go astray.'

"Here I bellowed: 'You speak evil!
Sinner! Through you speaks the devil:
Of confession he's in fear.
Repent! Chase him from your presence
And do not delay your penance!
Instantly report down here!'

"That's the kind of line I fed him,
Until even in this ruffian
A soft spot at last I found.
Branch to branch, in a slow movement,
He climbed down, and in a moment
He stood with me on the ground.

"Here I grab the Cock and bluster:
'If it isn't the young master!
The confessing's up to you.
But your final, greatest penance
Will come now—and no avoidance.
To your life now bid adieu!

" 'I shall be a monkey's uncle
If I don't make your blood trickle;
And your coat, your great panache,
I shall pluck, and I shall scatter,
And I shall stuff your cadaver
In a coffin—my own paunch.'

"Fathoming his depth of trouble,
The Cock did not try to struggle.
He let sadly hang his head.
And he spoke up very sadly:
'Very well, Mykyta, daddy,
What to do? Go on and eat!

" 'If it's God preordination
That the path to my salvation
Must begin between your teeth.
Go ahead! Begin to gobble,
Let my body crunch and crackle.
Good-bye now! Commence to eat!

" 'And my coat, so rich and crimson,
Which I often, with abandon,
Flaunted so among the hens . . .
Rip it, shred—I don't regret it,
But the hope in me inspirit
That from tar I'll be exempt.

" 'One more bitter disappointment
To eternity intransient
I shall carry off with me.
On my heart—a heavy burden,
'Cause my killing will result in
A loss to your dignity.

" 'See, our priest was so enchanted
By my gorgeous *bel canto*—
Which became of such renown—
I was to become a cantor
At the choir capitular
At the near cathedral town.

" 'While I'm about to perish,
There are, toward your desert refuge,
Three monsignors on the way,
To wind up your mendicancy,
Offering you a sextoncy,
Bringing an advance in pay.'

"I'm an artist, my dear uncle;
To me every word is able
To raise strongest imagery.
When such words came to my hearing,
All my fancies started dancing:
My soul wanted to leap free.

"My mouth opens, quite unmindful;
Lively, my hands clap approval,
'The Lord Fox here!' I exclaim.
Instantly, this Cock repugnant,
Leaps and flies up, like a serpent,
On a branch—a lightning flame.

" 'O Mykyta, my dear parent,'
From up there he spoke defiant,
'Aiming at the upper class?
For the office of the sexton
You'd give up the Heavenly Kingdom.
You had me and lost me, Fox!'

"Fie! Today I'm still resentful
Of the jeering of that criminal.
He showed off, like a martinet!
I am quiet and submissive,
For wounds, beatings I'm remissive,
But a scandal calls for death."

Thus absorbed in their palaver,
Both ate up the Cock together,
Rested up a bit to boot.

Our honorable travelers,
Like some saintly Holy Rollers,
Resumed their trip on foot. .

"You say this Cock was a power,
He enjoyed the Bruin's favor,
To the Queen he worked his way.
That's exactly our system:
Not a step without a patron.
May God's bolt destroy its sway!

"A professional or a teacher,
Into business if you venture,
If you're a poet or a clerk,
Be you first in skill and dilligence,
Without pull and unfair preference,
You'll get nothing for your work.

"Lordly favor, female suasion
Supersede all education:
Whispered words from a baronet;
From a princess a short letter;
Now your efforts do not matter:
Shattered into useless dust.

"Knowing the political odium,
I know where's the power fulcrum.
After all, I'm not a fool.
I fear not what is familiar,
So I glued somehow together
For myself a tiny pull.

"At the Court there serves at present,
The Queen's medical assistant,
Frusya—a widowed chimpanzee.
She's something of a doctor,
Sorceress, and fortune teller—
Owl-like, a hideosity.

"Although hardly a teenager,
And a dreadful women's libber—
For, like poison, she hates men—
For me, in a quiet fashion,
Her heart feels distinct attraction—
Justly, if the truth be known.

"But to be completely honest,
Her employment as assistant
At the Queen's for her I found.
Now I'll tell you, my dear fellow,
At the Court she's a wheeler-dealer;
She turns things her way around.

"If I were a total stranger,
She would still be in my corner,
For she hates the Wolf the most.
Why this hate extraordinary?
I know, and I'll tell the story,
To make travel time the least.

"In those days when still in tandem
With the Wolf I worked, an alien
Primate land we strayed into.
Hungry both, completely feeble,
To catch our food unable,
Wait for death—what else to do?

"Here among the crags hostile,
Frusya had her domicile.
The Unsated thus opines:
'Go, Mykyta, to that hovel,
P'raps it'll have us as a hostel,
'Cause we're hungry as church mice.'

"I go. Inside, in the middle
Stands a monkey, like a devil,
The kids round her in a ring.
All of them are so disgusting—
Verily, the Devil's offspring—
They are scary, the poor things.

"All of them are looking daggers.
I am seized with icy jitters
Down my back. O vanish! Fie!
All the eyes are staring fiercely,
All the teeth are bared completely:
Will they soon eat me alive?

"And their hideous Chimp-Mother,
Like a black cloud, full of thunder,
Comes up, asking: 'Who are you?'
Instantly I started lying:
'I am bringing you my greeting
And regards long overdue.

" 'From the distant land of Piedmont,
I'm an animal pious, decent,
Possibly your family.
I am a returning pilgrim
Who's heard of your beauty, wisdom.
Please accept my fealty.'

"At this the Chimp mellowed posthaste
When my words she licked and tasted.
'Sir, you wish to indicate

That abroad I am no stranger?'
'Madam, hardly, ever stronger
Fama shouts your accolades.

" 'And these cherubkins: such sweeties,
Are your children? And their daddy's
Momentarily away?'
'No, dear sir, I am in mourning
For him. But you must be starving . . .
Let me fix you a nice tray!'

" 'Thank you, no, my dearest lady!
(A march hears my starving body,
Drummed by empty intestines.)
I could not impose upon you.
My desire is to imbue
With your word my heart and mind.'

" 'I see, friend, that you are gallant,
Clever, too, and wholly pleasant;
You're a rare and welcome guest!
We have plenty to talk over,
But before all that palaver,
You must eat and quench your thirst.'

"She rushed over to the larder,
Brought out platter after platter
Sausage, *Schnitzel,* meat galore.
She put all of it before me
And then—honestly!—implored me:
'Eat! Why don't you eat some more!' "

"I eat till the rafters rattle;
The She-Chimp keeps up her twaddle,
Prattling nonsense endlessly:
T' female tender nervous system;
How men tend to lov'em-an'-leav'em;
Women—slaves of the family.

"When she mentioned her late husband,
She did so with the profoundest
Sigh: 'Alas, he knew me not!'
Then she touched upon our culture,
Palmistry and literature,
Fashion, politics, and gout.

"I nod, munching *Wiener Schnitzel,*
But *pro forma,* to seem normal,
I provoke an argument.
Flushed, she heatedly takes umbrage.
Seeing no end to this deluge,
I present my compliments.

" 'Madam, I am overpowered
Such a gem to have discovered—
What a happy sudden turn!
With a stronger body 'n spirit,
I must rush, though I regret it,
Hoping for a quick return.'

"And the Monkey kept on prattling,
But I took off like greased lightning,
Stopping at where the Wolf hid.
'O Mykyta, here I perish;
A whole hour—you just vanish!
Have you got it? Did you eat?'

" 'Brother, I have stilled my hunger.
As for dragging the provender
With me—that's downright uncouth.
Just go to the house, my buddy,
Guests are welcome at the Lady
Chimp's. She'll feed your hungry mouth.'

"He goes in. I watch the creature;
I know well his lupine nature,
So I stay close to the wall.
I hear him. He says good morning,
And the Monkey asks him something.
On the bench I hear him sprawl.

" 'You dumb monkey, where is dinner?
What's this? Devlets? Wouldn't wonder!
God protect! Are they unclean?
And yourself! Without an effort,
At your sight milk turns to yogurt.
Where is Satan, your old man?'

"Thus the Wolf kept blabbing crazily,
The She-Chimp grabbed a brick nimbly
From the wall. And could she hurl!
His mouth suffered the most damage:
Four teeth missing from his frontage.
Goodness gracious! Did he howl!

"The Unsated would have killed her,
But the Monkeys were much faster.
Here the Children joined the fray,
Peppering the Wolf with gravel.
For his eyes goes one daredevil;
Two great clubs begin to sway.

"Without mercy, they beat on him,
But I managed to pry open
The front door a tiny crack.

'Run!' The Wolf obeyed my summons,
Else he, like the Jewish Haman,
Would have got it in the neck.

"Frusya counted me from then on
As a proven favorite person.
T' Wolf was worse than wormwood tea.
I trust in my luck's puissance:
When hell or high water threatens,
Others drown, and I float free."

Thus amid such constant banter,
They continued to canter
Till they reached the capital town.
During the post-prandial silence,
On the common near the Palace,
The Fox stood where he'd be arraigned.

Song Eleven

As wise people often banter:
"To be happier, get smarter!"
To this fact the Fox subscribed.
Although jitters chill the body,
His mien's always bold and steady,
His head's always high with pride.

The Fox sold his public image:
All the others searched his visage;
All felt worry and chagrin,
Fearing thunder and turmoil . . .
The Fox faced this rank and file
As the merriest of men.

"Ha, the killer! Ha, you heinous!
How dare you appear among us?"
The King bellowed angrily.
"Observe, how he seems oblivious
Of the present, gross and hideous,
He sent us; he walks so free!

"Ha, you bag of lies and treason!
No; do not expect a pardon!
You have cut Jack Rabbit's throat!
For this, Billy, your accomplice,
's been already torn to pieces,
And the same shall be your lot!"

This news—sudden, grim in nature—
Shook the Fox's cool composure:
All atremble, he turned pale.
Then came furious hand wringing
And effusive tear outpouring,
Then the Fox began to bawl:

"Woe is me! My darkest moment!
Jack is dead—the lively spirit;
Billy's rotting somewhere, too.

And Mykyta, you poor victim,
Your great treasure has been hidden!
What to do now? Boo-hoo-hoo!"

"What's this babble, now? You phony!"
Leo, without ceremony,
Jumped on him. "Yes, kill me, sir!"
Said the Fox. "My treasure's missing.
I don't see much point in living.
Instant death I now prefer.

"What an error, I was certain
Jack and Bill could be relied on.
I entrusted to their care,
In a safely sealed up package,
Great gems meant as personal homage;
It's unequaled anywhere.

"In't a diamond of great excellence,
Like a full moon in its brilliance,
As it illumines the gloom.
There was, too, a ring of rubies,
Which aroused adoring sympathies
To the one who had it on.

"These I gladly gave the Emperor.
For the Queen I sent a mirror,
Fashioned out of emerald.
Under sunny sky conditions,
Health and physical attraction
It gives; it could raise the dead.

"Such rich jewels I entrusted,
Thinking not of a disaster
To Jack, to the Court *en route*,
Could I in a wild nightmare
Fancy Billy as a killer,
Eager to possess the loot.

"And what now, O my dear mother?
Jack's one dead, the Goat's the other;
And what of my treasury?
Evil tongues here, in my absence,
Placed a great sin on my conscience,
To assure my misery.

"Majesty and Noble Lady,
Throw away distrust unworthy,
Sweep away the rumors' raft!
So that yet unborn descendants
Judge not: the most faithful servant
For his goodness got the shaft."

The Fox quit. The King frowned adverse,
A loud sob gave off his Empress;
She was in her sentient flux,
Since when at a tea refection
She peeled off a hairy section,
Ate a quarter of an ox.

"No," the Fox resumed, "I see it,
How my enemies have blinded
Once again your royal sight!
I feel now my *vitae tedium*,
For love royal and *encomium*
Are you subjects' strength and light.

"Good-bye, World, and you sworn enemies
Who have whispered lies against me;
Come on out, you cursed foes!
If you have an accusation,
Come on out! Life or perdition,
We shall fight, and bar no holds!

"How come I don't see you, cowards?
All you know is spreading canards,
In my absence filing torts;
To stand boldly, giving evidence,
Risking life for simple justice—
No, you haven't got the guts!"

"That's a lie, you stupid braggart!"
The Wolf shouted, pushing forward,
Boldly, from the animal mass.
"I will fight against you gladly,
And I'll shorten your tongue, mainly
To end your contempt for us.

"As the King here is my witness,
Before God, I do mean business;
Without mercy, to the death!

To prove that you are a villain
And a liar and a con man,
Trampling goodness underfoot.

"In this fight you shall be facing
The sum total of your doings,
To all beasts, not me alone.
In the suffering of my Missus
Of my vengeance lies the onus,
Not the injuries of my own.

"Listen now to the dishonor
He caused her, so that forever,
Of it she shall bear the mark.
My wife passed along the pond's edge,
When she saw Mykyta's visage,
Eating, choking on hot carp.

" 'What's that that you're eating, Myki?'
'Fish, of course,' he answers quickly.
Says my wife: 'Then give me some!'
Says the Fox: 'Now, Auntie, listen,
You want fish? There, on the bottom,
There is of them a real swarm.'

" 'In the pond? Ah, don't I know it?
From this knowledge I don't profit.'
'I'll teach you the fishing art.
Any day you care to mention,
I just haul them by the dozen,
Every time I spread my net.'

" 'What net, then?' my wife inquired.
'That's the knowledge you'll acquire
If you follow me around.'
Winter, snow, the cold wind's awful;
In the ice, a single ice hole
Someone cut upon the pond.

"Thus he led her to this ice hole
And advised my wife as follows:
'Auntie, look, there's fish galore!
Stick your tail into the opening,
In a moment they'll be biting;
You shall catch fish by the score.'

"So sweet was the Fox's manner
That my wife was quite bowled over,
And she took him at his word.
On the ice she quickly squatted,
Dipped her tail into the water,
Holding, waiting . . . what a nerd!

" 'Foxie," says she. 'Something's pinching!'
'Quiet now! The fish are biting!'
Frost was gripping at her tail.
'Time to haul them out now, Myki?'
'You'll get few if you're lucky.
Keep it down if all goes well!'

" 'Foxie, I feel pulls and twinges!'
'This must be the giant sturgeon,
Like a sheep, so big in size!'
Now the ice got a grip on her.
'I'll get them out of the water!'
'See, you're feeling the Carp bite!'

"Finally she lost her patience,
Tugged it with but small insistence:
It was stuck; 'It's time to land,'
The Fox says, 'So many of them!
Land them quickly, land them, woman!
Else they'll scatter in the pond!'

" 'Here the She-Wolf pulled much harder,
But the ice grip was much firmer:
It holds tight; pull all you will.
"Thank God, auntie, here to aid you,'
Says the Fox, 'toward your rescue,
Coming twenty men in all.'

"When she got this information,
She forgot her situation.
And let out a dreadful howl.
Peasants came, all vicious, evil.
They began to swing their ferules,
When they saw her in the hole.

"Blows are raining, like a hailstorm;
The poor woman twists her bottom:
Twist or turn—the blows keep on.
Finally, leaving her tail's portion
In the ice, from desperation,
She broke loose and ran safe home."

Here Mykyta said politely:
"You have stated it correctly,
Save for one untruthful point:
It is really quite uncalled for
To charge gluttonous behavior
Of your wife's to my account.

"If she had been moral, decent,
She'd have chosen the right moment
To get fish and keep her tail.

But she seemed to have gone batty:
The whole pond she wished to empty.
Now tell *me*: where did I fail?"

Laughter shook the whole assembly,
And the Wolf became so angry,
He began to chew the sand.
"Ha, the scum!" he howled in anger.
"How he twists things in his favor!
The Fox's always innocent!

"You won't see the day, you devil,
To make fun of every animal.
Of your base tricks there's a swarm.
What about the well-head incident:
Was it the She-Wolf's misjudgement
Or your malice all alone?"

"At a well, as it occurred once,
On a chain around a windlass
Hung two buckets made of steel.
Thirsty for a drink of water,
The Fox rode a bucket under,
While its mate came up the well.

"Well, as accidents will happen,
My wife walked in the environ,
And she heard his whimpering noise.
She peered down into the water,
Asking him: 'Fox, what is down there?'
In her kindly, tender voice.

"Hasty, eager was his answer:
'Auntie, what of fishes, lobsters
Down this well you'll find a lot.
Half an hour I've been at it,
Filled with fishes half a bucket;
Like a pea pod is my gut.

" 'There is more than I can handle.
See the bucket up there dangle?
Jump in and ride down to me.
Eat as long as you desire,
For your Old Man take a pile,'
Thus the Fox lied cunningly.

"It's the usual situation:
My wife was close to starvation—
It's a secret too well known . . .
When she heard 'bout fish and lobsters,
Zoom! The She-Wolf jumped in head first,
In the bucket, and went down.

"In her bucket plummeting downward,
She saw the Fox flying upward,
In the other bucket seat.
'Farewell now, my dearest auntie,
I am off to Ypsilanti!'
Cried Mykyta as they met.

" 'You have made a famous ladder:
I come up and you go under;
That's the way life operates.
Down there you will find no fishes.
How to gain the upper reaches
You'll have time to contemplate.'

"Listening to his barbaric
Talk, my wife was in a panic,
Victim of a violent stitch.
The pail hit the water level;
To the top rose up the bubbles;
Her howls did the village reach.

"People heard her jeremiad
And assembled at the well-head.
Do you think that one would try
To be merciful and aid her,
As a woman and a mother?
Once they grab you, you must die.

" 'A wolf down the well; let's pay him
For the foals and sheep he's taken',
The men holler as they come.
'Exercise your personal safety,
But beat till he's dead and ready;
Now's the time to kill the bane.'

"Now consider, worthy Sires,
What within her heart transpired
As the bucket rode up, up!
Down below—Dave Jones' locker,
Upstairs—men, a score in number,
Staves in hand, prepared to rap.

"Soon as she rose in the open,
Noise and blows rose up to heaven—
Thrash her, like a sheaf of wheat!
She crouched in the pail, poor darling;
The sun of her life was setting,
Desperation in her heart.

"Her strength by sheer fear augmented,
From the bucket she alighted—
In the thicket of the staves.

It's beyond my narrative power
To count all the blows dealt to her,
She had to live through that day.

"Finally, how she did manage
To flee and her life to salvage,
I can't tell you. I know not.
This deed wicked and malicious,
O you liar base and hideous,
Was another of your plots!"

"Wolfie, pal, if you knew only
How I thanked her most sincerely
For that merciful great act:
For the blows that she accepted
Which, by rights, would have been meted
Out to my own scrawny back.

"Noble She-Wolf! Quite an honor!
You take pride in her endeavor!
I take credit for this, too . . .
When it comes to flagellation,
Knotty cudgels, without question,
She stands better than I do."

The Wolf fumed; the crowd laughed merrily,
As the She-Wolf was mocked cruelly.
The Wolf shouted: "Lying fake!
May your tongue be drilled by weevils!
In broad daylight, with your guile,
You have changed white into black!

"Never mind your lying prattle:
Teeth and arms shall win the battle,
Even if my life's the price.
I will make you, liar, killer—
O you treacherous bloodsucker—
Stop your filthy insolence."

The Fox called: "You foulmouth peasant!
Think not that your tongue malignant
On my honor leaves a stain!
You are strong on curses, yokel,
But you come and fight a duel,
And I'll teach you what is pain!"

"Enough squabbling! I have had it!
Hell knows: righteous or bandit?"
Getting up, the King pronounced.
"Let's tomorrow's final duel
Show who's righteous, who's evil.
That shall be your acid test!"

Song Twelve

The sun woke up very early,
Washed his face in dew so pearly,
And now smiled, didn't burn.
Fox Mykyta, with great pleasure,
Stretched his frame the bed's full measure,
But a nudge gave him a turn.

"Rise and shine, you sleeping beauty;
Daylight's calling you to duty!
Do you know what day has dawned?
It decides if you'll be victor
Or achieve misfortune, horror
In this battle—death alone."

It was Frusya who had spoken,
Trying thus the Fox to waken,
And his hand she gently shook.
Last night she'd not slept a moment,
Told all that the Fox was innocent;
To all she could find she spoke.

The Fox muttered something angrily,
Then he rubbed his eyelids quickly,
And saw Frusya at his bed.
"Frusya, is it you?" he shouted.
From his bed he nimbly bounded.
"What good news you bring, by God?"

Frusya said: "Mykyta, darling,
Memories of our joint living
Will not let go off my mind.
For the female hearts will cherish
Always those from whom they perish,
Even if men *are* unkind.

"So I always worry for you,
I try always to protect you,
Though no one's aware of that.
The impending struggle mortal
Today brings me to your portals,
Tortured by a dreadful thought.

"The Wolf is so strong and vigorous;
Canny, though, you are, impetuous,
And your tongue can twist and mock,
Yet quite easily, dear brother,
In this fight you may go under;
The Wolf's not inclined to joke.

"Thus, obsessed by this great worry,
My friend, to your side I hurried,
With one thought: to offer help.
Where there's conflict or contention,
Old wives may have a solution.
So—accept my words yourself."

The Fox smiled: "Frusya, darling,
Not a single tooth is missing
In your face. So, why betimes
You pretend to be senescent,
When you could be a contestant
Both in beauty and in brains?

"Frusya, you are truly selfless.
I'm prepared to take your guidance.
I am listening—advise!"
Frusya clapped her hands and presto
All the chimps, who had been resting
On the green, came in a thrice.

"Well, well, tell me: what significance
Has here all your family's presence,
Though they are among the best?"
Frusya: "Have no apprehension;
Sit down, stretch your corporation,
And forget about the rest."

Here three chimps of mien malevolent
Give Mykyta their treatment:
Lather him and shave and wash.
Soon his body was clean-shaven,
They fetched oil and made sodden
His most sumptuous fuzzy brush.

Frusya said: "Mykyta, buddy,
All clean-shaven is your body,
But the tail retains its fuzz.
That is so there's no location,
On the chest or the lumbar region
Or the skull for the Wolf to seize.

"When the Wolf's attack commences,
Show you're scared out of your senses.
Full retreat! But do not race!
When quite close you hear his canter,
Drag your tail through sand and cinders,
And then whack him in the face.

"He will not enjoy the flavor;
It will surely cool his fervor.
Ere he rubs his blinkers clean,
You shall stoutly mount his *cervix*
And perform the greatest service.
Let the deuce take the spalpeen.

"On your knees now, very humbly;
I'll recite a spell that surely
Will put everything aright:
'No isiv seye krad—cigamtsrifeht;
No saer raelka—cigamn iat rec;
Thgi msgn ilee fruo yhg ouhttset, aerg.'

"On your feet, now, friend, don't tarry;
We add wishes salutary,
And return victorious.
Now you kids provide an escort
For the Fox, where animal cohorts
Stand before the grove of trees."

The peculiar unit's marching.
Proudly Fox Mykyta's heading
Straight before the royal throne.
The King's belly rocked with merriment
When he saw Mykyta's raiment:
"O you beastie, you sly one!"

The Fox to the Royal Presence
Made the deepest bow of reverence,
Half as deep to his Consort.
And so, on the field of battle,
All encircled by the rabble,
He stood calm and undistraught.

Lo, the Wolf is there already—
A cloud threatening and nasty;
He's emerging from the ranks.
His teeth gnashing with excitement,
His two eyes seem fluorescent.
He'd eat the Fox, both skin and bones.

The King gave his *imprimatur*,
Nodded, signaled with his scepter,
For the struggle to begin.
Trumpets sounded, shrill and strident,
Thereupon the mob fell silent.
Who is destined here to win?

The Wolf, with his big paws, lunges
To get the Fox in his clutches,
To give him eternal rest.

The Fox howls, for the Wolf is scary,
Beats full retreat in great hurry.
The Wolf's catching him—almost.

The Wolf was so near his quarry,
When the Fox, with moderate hurry,
Dragged his fuzzy tail through sand.
The tail whipped all of a sudden
Put in Wolf's eyes its whole burden,
Made the day a foggy night.

"Why, you bitchy crooked vermin!"
Cried the Wolf, but could not chase him;
He stopped dead and rubbed his eyes.
"Wolfie, do you want to battle,"
Said the Fox, "or would you settle?
Come on, let me hear your voice!"

Here Mykyta's quick maneouver
Aimed to sever the Wolf's jugular;
He was ready for the kill.
The Wolf darted, though, toward him,
Grabbed Mykyta by the hindlimb,
Whereupon Mykyta fell.

"You are a dog, and you are bogus;
Well, the harvest time's upon us:
You shall reap what you have sown.
Since I have you in my clutches,
You shall get your proper wages
For your wrongs and pranks and scorn!"

"Oh," Fox thought, "This is ugly;
I can perish very quickly.
Let us sing a different tune."
To gain time, the Fox began to
Turn his act to a plaintive venue,
And thus he began to moan.:

"My dear uncle, *Deus tecum*!
Aren't we kin, from the same *phyllum*?
Uncle, why this sudden wrath?
Just how seemly is a *bellum*
When the Fox fights his *amicum*
Lupum, like some scum, to death?

"If you let slide this one instance,
I'll swear my life-long allegiance.
Uncle, listen to my say!
Without hindrance, and compliant,
We'll work loyally as your clients:
I and folk under my sway.

"For your benefit I'll toil;
I'll assume all hard travail,
I won't eat or sleep my fill.
And for you of geese and duckies,
Of fish, lobsters, and fat chickies
I will fill a kitchen full.

"Do you think I was intent on
Fighting your specific person?
How long did I hesitate?
Even in today's exchanges,
I did always pull my punches,
For my strength to moderate.

"Name your tasks! Be they heroic
I shall do them, and in public
I'll own up to lies. For shame!
Oh, it hurts! O uncle, prithee!
Show great quality of mercy!
Do not let me pray in vain!"

"No," the Wolf growled. "I have had it!
I know that you are a bandit
And a liar and a cheat!
You will promise a gold ducat,
In the end, though, from a doughnut
A large hole is all I get!

"I would know that you were foolin',
If you swore here that gold bullion
You'd give us would make us bright!
Is this how you pull your punches
When a sandstorm your tail launches
And deprives me of my sight?

"Twist and turn all you desire,
But your life must now expire;
I won't buy your fairy tales!
Pray now with contrite repentance;
Time to travel that last distance,
To meet your ancestral shades."

The Wolf growled now, in proud language,
Holding his foe's hind appendage,
Wishing that it were his throat.
While in his weepy doldrums,
The Fox cooked up a stratagem,
When he mastered his first fright.

While he faked to pray sincerely,
His hind foot sought the Wolf's belly,
Looking for the touchy part.

The Wolf's world changed coloration
When the Fox found the location
Of the Wolf's spleen, and ripped hard.

The Unsated screamed in agony;
In a flash, his wily enemy
Freed his leg from the Wolf's mouth.
Pressing hard on the Wolf's belly
Made the Wolf faint; the Fox quickly
Grabbed his enemy by the throat.

"Well, come now and beg my pardon!
For all instances of treason
You'll get paid!" the Fox did shriek.
Foaming at the mouth, but stubborn,
The Wolf twitched with mad abandon,
Growling, gurgling, growing weak.

But Mykyta is no half-wit;
He puts all his vigor in it;
Holds the throat tight as a vise.
He pulls, yanks, and tugs with gusto
Till the Lion hollers: "*Basta*!
The Fox gets the victor's prize."

The Fox, when the word resounded,
Let the Wolf loose and responded:
"Sire, I obey your call.
I wished to erase the blemish;
I don't want the Wolf to perish;
I kick not the ones who fall."

What a pleasure! Noise and babble!
Frusya squeezed through through the rabble,
Even brought a laurel wreath.
All the friends now came together,
Praised and greeted Fox Mykyta,
Hero—now a man of grit.

Many who in recent memory
Wished him dead now shouted "Glory!"
"Live Mykyta many years!"
But Mykyta turned, knelt forthwith
At the throne, to hear the verdict.
He thanked friends for their cheers.

"Rise, Mykyta!" said the Emperor.
"You have cleared your name and honor;
You have shown your stuff with zest.
Let the bygones now be bygones,
For the King forgives and pardons
If there was crime in the past.

"This ends all the feuds and quarrels.
From now in the royal council
You care for the common weal.
From me please accept this honor:
I name you to be our Chancellor.
I am handing you the Seal.

"And how smartly you were able
To fend off all kinds of trouble—
Thus defend the ship of State!
And the King will heed your counsel,
What you'll write he'll never cancel;
Do what conscience dictates!"

The Fox said: "My King and Father,
For your rich and generous honor,
How can I repay in kind?
Though my energy is paltry,
To yourself and our country
I'll devote my heart and mind.

"Grant me, Sire, this indulgence:
My poor family, in my absence
Must be pining without help.
Today would be most opportune
If about this turn of fortune
I could tell them all myself."

"T'Queen and I," spoke up the Lion,
"This sincere wish hold in common:
That their sadness disappear.
You have leave for three days' absence,
But return here with your loved ones,
So we welcome them right here."

At this point ends our story.
The Almighty in His glory
Long life to our audience grant!
May all our sadness vanish;
Those who lie for us in ambush
May all have a sticky end.

About the Translator

Adam Hnidj is a polyglot writer, translator, and teacher, born in Ukraine and educated at European and American schools. His ambition is to translate *all* of Franko's poems.

With his wife, Pamela, Mr. Hnidj lives in New Jersey. They have one son, a recent Rutgers graduate.

IVAN FRANKO:
MOSES AND OTHER POEMS

Translated from the Ukrainian
by Adam Hnidj

Ivan Franko (1856–1916) was born into the family of a village blacksmith in the Ukrainian Carpathians. Both his parents were dead before Ivan graduated from high school. A brilliant scholar, Franko received his Ph.D. in Slavic philology from the University of Vienna, under the famous scholar V. Jagić. The local establishment prevented Franko from teaching Ukrainian literature at the University of Lvov, misunderstanding Franko's enlightened humanism for militant socialism; Franko was jailed for it twice.

Franko lived by his pen, producing one hundred short stories and dozens of novels, all with social significance. He wrote a dozen dramatic works. Franko's poetry was the most outstanding and innovative of the post-Shevchenko period; he produced four major poetry collections, three major poems on philosophical themes, and half a dozen long poems for children and translated poetic masterpieces from fourteen languages, from Homer to Heine. In turn, many of Franko's major poems have been rendered into most European languages, even in his lifetime.

The present centennial edition of Franko's works runs to fifty volumes. Franko was nominated for the Nobel Prize for Literature in 1916, which went to a Swede, Verner von Heidenstam.